# COSTA RICA
# THE UNARMED DEMOCRACY

DEDICATED TO DON JOSÉ FIGUERES FERRER

who had the courage and foresight, when Leader of the Military Junta in 1948, to announce the dissolution of the Army.

*Her ways are ways of pleasantness*
*and all her paths are peace*
                    *– Proverbs III 17*

# COSTA RICA

## THE UNARMED DEMOCRACY

by LEONARD BIRD

LONDON: SHEPPARD PRESS

First published September 1984 by
SHEPPARD PRESS LIMITED
RUSSELL CHAMBERS, COVENT GARDEN
LONDON WC1E 8AX

MADE IN ENGLAND
Printed for the publishers by Nene Litho and
bound by Woolnough Bookbinding, Wellingborough, Northants.

# CONTENTS

# ACKNOWLEDGEMENTS

My thanks are due

to many people with whom I conferred in Costa Rica, especially Professors Señora Rosemary Karbinski and Señor Urcuyo and the Staff of the Congress Library. Also to my Friends Kenneth Clay, Marigold Best and others who made translations from Costa Rican newspapers and reports.

to John Whitehead, Rowland Dale and my daughter-in-law, Elizabeth, for reading the manuscript and making most helpful suggestions and comments.

to my publishers, and particularly to my friend Trefor Rendall Davies for considerable help in a field of which I know little.

to the Trustees of the Alfred Speight Bequest for providing funds towards the costs of one of my visits to Costa Rica to seek out information.

most especially to the Northern Friends Peace Board for encouragement to amass the material and write the book and, not least, for providing funds to enable it to be published.

L.A.B.

# FOREWORD

Nearly fifty years ago the prolific American travel writer, John Gunther, in his book *Inside Latin America* described how he stumbled on Costa Rica in ignorance. "If anyone had told me," he wrote, "that Costa Rica was one of the most delightful countries in the world and one of the purest democracies on earth, I would have gaped. Now that I have been there I know it to be true."

It was 1940 when Gunther wrote those words. Europe was at war and largely in the grip of Fascism. Central America was at peace, but slumbering in a long night of backwardness and dictatorship, though the dictatorships were relatively mild by the European standards of those days. Today the situation has changed. While Europe lives through a fragile peace, most of Central America is at war or in the grip of murderous élites. Yet through it all Costa Rican democracy has survived, and the traveller of today would also gape to see how this small country can remain so calm and sane in a sea of chaos and death.

Of course Costa Rica never was, and still is not, quite such a perfect democracy as Gunther made out. Nor is it as isolated as it used to be. Its neighbour Nicaragua has overthrown the Somoza dictatorship and replaced it with an experiment in mass democracy, which is different from Costa Rica's, but also a valiant attempt at social justice.

Yet Costa Rica was the pioneer. It introduced free and mandatory primary education in 1869, and abolished the death penalty in 1882. And in one vital element Costa Rica is unique, not just in Central America, but the world. In 1948 it became the first country to do away with a national army.

That fact alone makes Costa Rica a country whose importance far outstrips its size. For this reason, this book is of particular value and importance. If Costa Rica provides a crucial lesson in political harmony to the rest of Central America at a time of crisis, it also offers a beacon of hope for Europe at a time of maximum East-West tension and creeping nuclear madness. Costa Rica shows that social peace is not just a matter of reducing armaments but of finding new and imaginative political arrangements for dealing with the conflicts that underlie the arms race.

Non-alignment and de-militarisation are not just slogans or daydreams, but solutions which can be made to work. If this book can puncture the cynicism and despair which afflict so many people in the fact of the military build-up of the last two decades, it will have done its job.

JONATHAN STEELE
Chief Foreign Correspondent
*The Guardian* newspaper, London

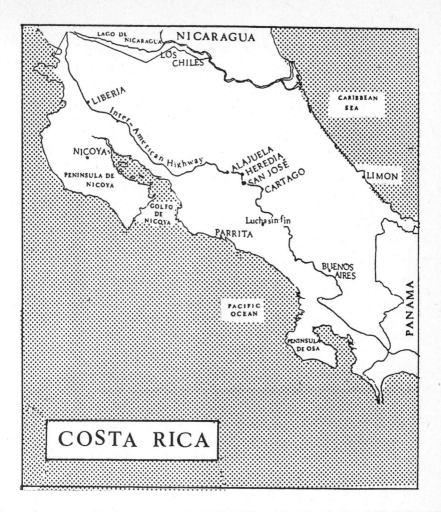

COSTA RICA

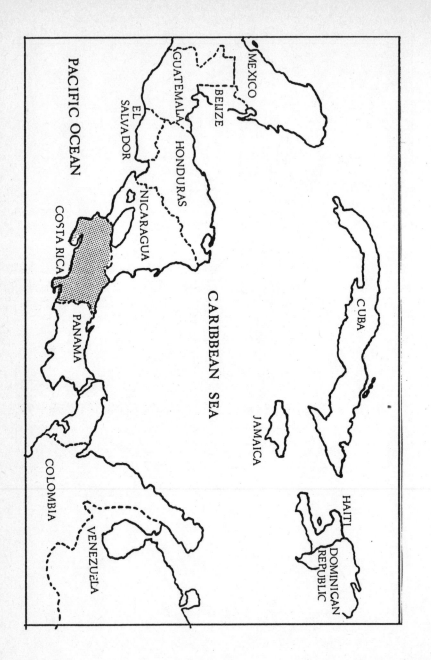

PACIFIC OCEAN

MEXICO

GUATEMALA

BELIZE

EL SALVADOR

HONDURAS

NICARAGUA

COSTA RICA

PANAMA

COLOMBIA

VENEZUELA

CARIBBEAN SEA

JAMAICA

CUBA

HAITI

DOMINICAN REPUBLIC

10

# INTRODUCTION

In December 1948 the President of the ruling Junta of Costa Rica, Don José Figueres Ferrer, announced peremptorily and without any previous intimation of any kind, that the army was to be dissolved. There was no public outcry; no-one exclaimed 'We shall all be murdered in our beds', no-one appears to have expected the country to be suddenly invaded. Indeed it was only a week later, by an ex-President who had been planning the invasion for some time. What led to this unique decision to be apparently defenceless and how has the country fared in succeeding years?

In February 1948 the governing party was defeated at the polls but claimed the election result was a fraud and declared it invalid. Civil war broke out, in which the Governing party, with its army support, was defeated and the leaders fled into neighbouring Nicaragua. At the end of April 1948 a great parade was held through the streets of the capital, San José, when José Figueres Ferrer, leader of the victorious revolutionaries, was given a tumultuous reception.

How could he then, only seven months later, announce that the army was to be dissolved? What had happened to cause a military leader, with the powers of government in his hands, to take a step unprecedented in world history. There is no single answer; a web of contributory factors lay behind the decision.

Costa Rica, not the 'rich coast' Columbus thought he saw, was, in fact, one of the poorest of the Central American Republics. The Conquistadors exterminated or drove out most of the native inhabitants, leaving only a few to work for them, as distinct from other Latin American countries they conquered and exploited. Accordingly, Spaniards who settled in Costa Rica were not so much conquerors but farmers and smallholders. Even the Governors had to work and one at least complained to his overlords in Spain that he had to work his land himself or he would have starved. The degree of identification with Costa Rica by the settlers was such that, when the Spanish Empire came to an

11

end, there was no fighting and it is said Costa Rica was 'handed its independence on a plate'.

Only three Presidents of Costa Rica, of a total of over 60, have been military men; and only six Presidents, whose regimes total no more than forty of her one hundred and sixty three years of independent political existence, could be said to be of the severe dictatorial type.

The country has much forest and mountainous terrain and the arable land is divided amongst many small farmers so, again in great contradistinction to its neighbours, economic problems caused by large landowners and a landless labouring class have not been experienced.

In December 1948 the party of Figueres was politically weak but he was still the leader of the ruling Junta and there was some suspicion his 'Caribbean Legion' still survived. The largest political party of Ulate Blanco, which had won the election with Figueres in February that year and fought with him in the succeeding revolution, was uncertain of his motives. Ulate's party won a resounding victory in the election held on 8th December 1948 for the Assembly to revise the Constitution. Although a draft Constitution submitted by Figueres was not accepted by Ulate's party, they accepted and adopted the clauses to proscribe the army and make a standing army illegal. That has ensured Costa Rica shall have no armed defence. Could it have been deliberately arranged that these clauses should be proposed and passed by the Constituent Assembly on the commemoration of the United States Independence Day: 4th July 1949?

But, a few days later, the forces of Calderón Guardia, defeated in the civil war earlier that year, invaded from Nicaragua with tacit support from Somoza, dictator of that country. Fighting broke out and Costa Ricans of all political parties volunteered their services to repel the invaders. What is more important, however, not only for Costa Rica, but also for world history, is that a year earlier at Rio de Janeiro a Treaty of Friendship and Mutual Assistance had been signed by seventeen American nations forming the Organisation of American States. This Treaty had been ratified and brought into force only a few days before the invasion. The Costa Rican Government appealed to the Organisation of American States (the very first such appeal under the Rio Treaty) which, fortunately, acted very promptly and condemned Nicaragua for its support of the rebels. On that support being withdrawn, the invasion collapsed and Guardia and his forces left the country. An important step forward for the settling of international disputes by diplomatic methods instead of military hostilities.

Again in 1955 a similar invasion was mounted; this time with the bombing of San José and other Costa Rican cities. Once more, an appeal was made to the Organisation of American States – with the same result. It is noteworthy that, only three years later, Calderón Guardia, leader of the invading group, was permitted to return to Costa Rica without any allegation of treason or trial for his part in the civil war or the two invasions. Indeed, he not only took part in the 1958 election but, in 1962, once more stood as a candidate in the Presidential election, defeating Ulate Blanco and finishing in second place. In San José one of the larger hospitals is the Calderón Guardia Hospital. Could such forgiveness have occurred anywhere but in Costa Rica, with its strong independent and democratic tradition? In 1982, Guardia's son was a candidate for the Presidency.

In recent years Costa Ricans became closely embroiled in Nicaragua's violent struggle to free itself from the Somoza dictatorship. Allegations of arms being ferried through Costa Rica to the Sandinista rebels and of training camps being established in Costa Rica were repeatedly made by Somoza and Costa Rica complained its frontiers were constantly violated and its citizens attacked. Appeals from both countries were submitted to the Organisation of American States. The Costa Rican Minister of Public Security was attacked by planes of the Nicaraguan Air Force when he was making an inspection of a frontier incident in October 1977. At one time Somoza threatened to invade Costa Rican territory in order to destroy the suspected Sandinista training camps. Planes from Venezuela and Panama were quickly brought into Costa Rica with the threat of bombing Nicaragua in retaliation if there were any such invasion. This reinforces the assertion, despite doubts being expressed in some quarters, that Costa Rica does not have an army with which to defend its territory. Whilst it is clear that Costa Ricans are not pacifists, it is equally clear they have learned how to live without having an army – and have prospered accordingly. One has only to compare their standard of living with that of their neighbours to appreciate the difference. It is important to notice the presence of the planes from Venezuela and Panama aroused considerable opposition from prominent Costa Ricans and after a week they were withdrawn.

In June 1978 a splendid contribution was made by the Costa Rican delegate to the United Nations Special Session on Disarmament. He emphasised his country had dissolved its army over 30 years earlier and proposed that nations which disarmed should be rewarded for doing so and given funds with which to improve health, education, housing and other services to benefit their citizens.

In September of that year a proposal to set up a University for Peace in Costa Rica was accepted by the United Nations – provided it did not call for any funding by the UN. A site has been made available on the mountainside south-west of San José, commanding a magnificent view over the central upland plain. Buildings providing a Council chamber and administrative offices were erected in 1982 and an International Council of the United Nations constituted to prepare a suitable curriculum. Can this imaginative proposal be encouraged and supported in order to enhance Costa Rica's claim to be a truly democratic, peaceful nation, which does not have an army to 'defend' it?

From time to time there are reports of endeavours to embroil Costa Rica in the struggles taking place in Central America. Attempts by the USA to oust the Sandinista Government in Nicaragua and to strengthen the repressive Government in El Salvador led to pressures upon the Costa Rican Government. On November 18th 1983 Costa Rican President, Luis Alberto Monge, issued a Neutrality Proclamation which reaffirmed the Costa Rican Government's commitment to keep out of a regional military intervention. Events in Guatemala and Honduras could result in similar pressures in the future.

The colossal increase in the price of oil and other imports, together with the decrease in the prices realised for Costa Rica's primary products and exports of coffee, bananas and sugar, have combined to undermine very seriously the economic stability of the country. With the USA as its most accessible market it is bound to come under pressure from time to time to identify with the aims and objectivities of that great Power. Costa Rica will indeed require all the skill and adroitness of its politicians with the full support and backing of its people to ensure it continues to be 'an oasis of unarmed democracy in a region of heavily armed dictatorships'.

# Chapter One

# THE EARLY YEARS
## Before the Spanish Conquest

Costa Rica, one of the smallest of the Central American Republics, is situated to the north west of Panama and south of Nicaragua. A coastline of about 130 miles forms its north-easterly 'frontier' to the Caribbean Sea and to the south-west a coastline of about 600 miles looks out over the Pacific Ocean. Its land area of a little less than 20,000 square miles is about two-fifths that of England, but its population, now exceeding two millions, is barely one-twentieth.

Europeans are apt to think history commenced when adventurers from our Continent 'discovered' remote lands. As the late Jawaharlal Nehru points out in his *Glimpses of World History,* advanced civilisations existed in China and India even before the epic periods of Greece and Rome. It was so in the Americas; the empires of the Aztecs, the Incas and the Mayas all flourished prior to the coming of the Spaniards to the Western Hemisphere. It is thought early settlers came from the Old World by way of the Bering Straits between 20,000 and 40,000 years ago and in Costa Rica, as well as other Republics of Central America, remains of its inhabitants 13,000 years ago have been found. At first the tribes were nomadic and lived by hunting but later, as with other civilisations, they began to cultivate the terrain and establish settlements.

Some advanced cultivation of the soil began as early as two thousand years B.C. Pumpkins, primitive forms of maize, beans and chile made their appearance. So too from tiny hamlets with rudimentary political structures, towns and states were later constituted. The examination of pottery and ceramics by archaeologists has been of great importance in discovering and developing knowledge of these early inhabitants. Archaeological studies have faced considerable difficulties because of the persistence of the rainy seasons which have not helped the preservation of the remains left by man.

When examining the culture of the country prior to the Spanish conquest, Carlos Melendez in his *Historia de Costa Rica,* upon which this chapter is based, indicates three main areas: the dry tropical forest of the North Pacific, the humid tropical forest of the South Pacific and the humid tropical forest of the Atlantic. The first of these, the dry tropical forest, comprises the area from the mountain range of Guanacaste to the Pacific Ocean including the Gulf of Nicoya, being roughly the north-west of the country. About the 8th century of the present era the Olmecas, a warlike people, came from the region south of Mexico and subdued the area as far as the Gulf of Nicoya. This was a well cultivated land, the economic base being the maize of which three crops at least were obtained each year; also beans, cotton, cacao and a good deal of fruit were harvested. It seems to have had a sophisticated social pattern, including such niceties as that the length of the women's petticoat depended upon the social level of the wearer. Those of the higher standing wore it as far as the ankles; the poorer, as far as the knees! Ceramics were painted with various colours, and decorations of a symbolic religious character were supplemented by others representing animals such as the jaguar, monkey and lizard. Stone was also worked, especially the curved stone used to grind the maize. Fine jades have been found, used generally as necklaces or ear-rings, and coloured cotton was known. It does not appear that metal work was carried on and the few pieces of gold and copper that have been found are thought to have been brought in as a result of commerce carried on with other peoples of the isthmus.

There were three main classes of the society. The priesthood and warlords; the common people and the slaves or prisoners of war. Government rested in a Council of Elders but, for affairs of defence, a chief was appointed. There were religious celebrations to honour their gods and at harvest time, human sacrifice took place at these celebrations, usually of a prisoner or a 'volunteer'. Virgins were sacrificed in the volcanos to placate the powerful spirits residing there. The common people were limited to monogamic marriage but not so the wealthy, who had two or more wives according to their economic resources. Wars generally originated in territorial disputes or to obtain slaves for ritual sacrifices. Land belonged to the community and not the individual, in a form similar to that of the Aztecs. The communal crops provided for the needs of the population, but the distribution of the harvest was related to the needs of families and not to the individual work contributed. By this means the old and the widows with children received what they needed and the bachelor, although doing the same work as a married man, received only a portion corresponding to his needs.

It is probable these Indians had books made of parchment from

16

deerskin, but these have not been preserved. Only on some of the ceramic objects is it possible to find symbolic representations, similar to, if not the same as, those contained in the old manuscrips. In art, there existed an emphasised realism in the form and model usual in ceramics, which seemed clearly to be based on the vegetable form of the chocolate cup. As a decorative element one can observe the frequent representation of certain animals and of geometrical figures which seem to be derived from the pattern of basket work.

As Carlos Melendez points out, we need to comprehend that the people of this North Pacific area of Costa Rica had an elaborate and developed culture of which we can now only trace the most salient features.

The second area is that of the humid tropical forest of the South Pacific; this extended from the mountain range of Talamanca to the Pacific coast, being roughly the south-east of the country. Data is lacking to follow precisely the migration which brought people to the area where they were found by the Spaniards. It is, however, evident there were strong ties with the culture of Chiriquí (now in Panama) so that, even if in Costa Rica reference is made to Cultura Brunca, it would be more correct to deem it as that of the Gran Chiriquí.

Although they also grew maize, this did not have the importance it had with the people of the northern area. In addition, they cultivated yucca (tapioca), beans, squash, cotton and various fruits. Game and fish had for them some importance; deer was one of the preferences of the hunter; the tapir and some other animals were domesticated. Their dwellings rested upon a base relatively high, within which lived several families with ties of kinship. They began to form real settlements, some of them strategically placed at the confluence of two rivers and with the protection of double palisades with intermediate ditches; others formed clusters of huts. In both cases it seems to have been considerations of defence which determined the form of the establishment, since the gold they possessed was always coveted by their neighbours, even those of the same culture.

The men wore a loincloth of cotton; the women wore a type of short skirt which was arranged round the waist as far as half way down the leg. The most characteristic ceramics were of a natural tone and of a cream colour, very highly polished, some decorated with representations of animals. They were distinguished most especially for their working of gold, first in a simple form, then, through the method of beating into sheets or hammering to make discs or large medals, to a more complete technique. On these latter are frequently seen animal and human figures, including frequently those called 'eagles', perhaps better referred to as 'turkey buzzards'. Other representations are of turtles, armadillos,

17

sharks and tigers, those possibly being deified as live species. In stone, perhaps the most excellent in the area, being of the best quality, the significance is not very clear but it is possible symbols of power or social prestige are represented.

The social organisation was of individual chiefs and, even when for reasons of security a number of them grouped together, this did not begin to constitute a centralised organisation. It is possible the chiefs co-ordinated the co-operative efforts, for example, to construct the strongholds in which they lived. No details have survived of a priest caste or of witch-doctors, but it is probable these existed. It is known they had human sacrifice on low hills near the villages, not even of a ritual type.

They believed the souls of the dead gained for them the benefits of an agreeable life in the other world. Accordingly there were animals which had the duty to plunder the flesh of the dead; to carry them to the heavenly world. It was believed these creatures, when the cry of war was heard, raised themselves so as to obscure the sun. There were, for that reason, sacred birds which were not to be destroyed, and representations of these creatures were made in gold. War was one of their most frequent activities and women intervened in it in a very active manner. Their fame was spread amongst the neighbouring peoples and they were called the 'biritecas', a term equivalent to the amazons. The women reasoned: today in Boruca the work of spinning is, above all, feminine; men worship war above everything else – and there are the old ones who can prepare yarn for weaving! As a result, the younger women took part in warlike activities.

Land belonged to the clan and in the plantations it was the custom on occasions to make a simple camp to guard the crop prior to taking it to the stronghold, which served as a safe refuge at night. In decorative art the lineal and decorative tendency predominated. In sculpture the mobility of the figure is limited and their representation of the human activity is not realistic.

The third area designated by Carlos Melendez is the humid tropical forest of the Atlantic. In addition to the Atlantic watershed it included the Cordillera Central, the Central Valley (now the most heavily populated part of Costa Rica with the capital, San José, and most of the other large towns) and a small section towards the Pacific Ocean as far as the region of Parrita. This area continued the South American Amazon tradition and its influence on Costa Rica was quite considerable.

The inhabitants were not really an agricultural people because of the inferior land they occupied; they could more accurately be termed cultivators. They based their food on the cultivation of tubers, in particular the yucca and the fruit of the palm. Maize, when they knew it, they used in a modest form as with the cacao. Edible fruits were less abundant in tropical forests and it was realised food from animal sources was greater, so that in the life of the native, hunting and fishing, especially in the rivers, played a more important part. Even today descendants of these early settlers live much the same sort of life. For a cultivated area they cleared part of the forest, usually by fire, and in a valley made the first sowings of the yucca and other food crops. The limitations of their economic life prevented their beginning to build real towns. Their dwellings were farmhouses in a conical form, within which lived several families bound by ties of relationship. Generally two or three such farms were grouped in the vicinity of a watercourse and, in this way, a 'town' was constituted. Generally the natives went about entirely nude, or they wore only a girdle of a variable width fastened at the waist. Sometimes however the men wore a type of loin cloth made from the bark of a tree and the women wore a kind of small apron.

Even when they worked ceramics these were of a utilitarian type made by using simple techniques and, although sometimes they added animal or human figures, generally they preferred just to make incised patterns. The crockery was monochrome and predominantly for the community. In their art, they excelled most in working stone, for they were real lapidaries. The most representative stones are of human figures, some in a squatting position and in a posture as though smoking; others on foot, some female, and some with trophies of war about which they boasted; an axe in one hand and in the other, a head. Later there were curved stone altars a meter or more high, with mythological images, animal and human figures, generally a dish with a border and three large feet; others had a circular form with cat-like figures on the borders. Later came rectangular plates with ornaments of animals which must have been superstitious symbols.

From the point of view of social organisation their structure must have been quite simple. The government was in the hands of a chief; hereditary and with ample powers. In the religious world the power descended upon priests, although doctors, wizards and witches had also great prestige. While they worshipped the bones of their ancestors they also practised human sacrifice and head hunting. They worshipped the sun and the moon, believed in a celestial power and a civilising hero. In some cases it seems clear there existed centres of a ceremonial charcter in which were brought together the different groups dispersed throughout an area. They used to get themselves drunk, with due ceremony, with a fermented beverage made from yucca. War was very frequent amongst them and served to enable the men to acquire social prestige. It is probable that in their cemeteries the dead were placed according to the clan to which they had belonged. The land belonged to the clan and, in a given territory, they became gradually displaced, due to their method of rustic farming, so that it can be maintained they were in fact nomadic.

In art and sculpture these natives appear to have followed the natural tendency, i.e. representations of people and life as it is in reality. This came to be the characteristic of the South-American traditional culture.

By way of general conclusion it can be said that the natives who populated Costa Rican territory, did not represent a single influence nor a single culture but three different traditions, each one of which can be sited in a very characteristic atmosphere. Besides their degrees of distinct evolution and level of culture, it is possible to observe that, in the case of Costa Rica, they have been able to survive in defined zones. Those who belonged to the more advanced northern tradition have sustained an intense process of cross breeding. Despite the degree of the disappearance of their language and other unique characteristics of their culture, in Guanacaste above all, a part of this ancestral ethnic heritage is still living. The Costa Rica of today, from the point of view of its social form, conforms to the cultural tradition of its primitive peoples. The subsequent process, will have to be, in consequence, the result of a political process established first by the Spanish conquerors and later by the strength of the national political action, tending to give it unity in the practice of politics, inside the territorial boundaries of Costa Rica.

# Chapter Two

# THE SPANISH DISCOVERY AND CONQUEST

It was not until ten years after his first voyage of discovery to the Western Hemisphere that Christopher Columbus ventured as far as the mainland of Central America. This was his fourth voyage and, after sighting Guanaja, one of the Bay Islands of Honduras in July 1502, he sailed east along what is now the coast of Honduras. This proved to be difficult with high and contrary winds so that when he reached the point where he could turn southwards, along what is now the coast of Nicaragua, he aptly named the Cape, Cabo Gracias a Dios (Thanks to God).[1] From the 25th September to the 5th October he stopped at a place the Indians called Cariay, believed to be the present Puerto Limón on the Caribbean coast of Costa Rica.[2] He saw Indians wearing ornaments of gold and was inspired to write that he had seen more signs of gold there in two days than in four years in Spain. The Spaniards' lust for gold, however, was not met in Costa Rica. The name, meaning 'Rich Coast' was not used in documents for almost forty years. Columbus, convinced by the difficulties he had encountered in reaching these shores, decided nobody except himself should find the way there. The name Costa de Veragua was applied to all the territory discovered by Columbus on his fourth voyage.[3]

In 1509 the first settlement was founded and four years later Vasco Núñez de Balboa crossed the mountains and looked upon the Pacific Ocean. In 1514 the King of Spain established the province of Castilla del Oro and appointed Pedrarias Dávila as Governor.[4]

Pedrarias contributed a great deal to the establishment of the Spanish domination but at a cost of many lives, both Spanish and Indian. In 1519, with the establishment of the 'city' of Panama, ships were built and exploration began of the Pacific coast, seen some six years earlier from land. Punta Burica was rounded and, with the discovery of Golfo Dulce and, further north, the Golfo de Nicoya, the outline of present day Costa Rica was drawn.[5]

21

Between 1511 and 1517 natives were seized and shipped to work in Cuba, and this slave trade, together with smallpox, seriously decimated some of the Indian tribes. In 1522 and 1523 the west coast of Costa Rica was explored by Gil González de Avila who, with only a hundred men marched from Panama as far as the great lakes in Nicaragua, from which he retreated because of the hostility of the natives.[6]

In the 1540s there were four quite important developments for Central America. Firstly, owing to the depletion of labour through warfare, kidnapping and smallpox, slaves were brought from Africa. This affected mainly the countries to the north of Costa Rica, which appears to have been barely concerned. Secondly, new laws were promulgated in 1542, declaring the Indians were to be treated as vassals of the King of Spain. Principally this meant they could no longer be treated as slaves nor forced to labour. Thirdly, the area from South Mexico to Panama became unified politically with the establishment of the Audience of the Boundaries. At first the seat of the Audience was in Honduras but shortly afterwards was moved further north to Guatemala, once again emphasising that Costa Rica was of less consequence than its more populous northern neighbours. Fourthly, under the guidance of the new Audience, many Indians were concentrated into larger settlements, of which Nicoya, now in Costa Rica, was one.[7] There followed a period of about seventeen years comparative peace with but minor attempts at further exploration. Despite being included legally between the Castilla of Panama and the office of government in Nicaragua, it has been said that, at this first stage, Costa Rica had proved to be, in practical terms, unconquerable.[8]

In 1561 Juan de Cavallón penetrated to the Central Valley. Some two years later he was followed by Juan Vásquez de Coronado, whose treatment of the natives was better than that of Cavallón. With their help he undertook further expeditions towards the Pacific Ocean in the region of Parrita, the plains of Bueños Aires (not to be confused with the City in South America), the mountain range of Talamanca and the valley of Estrella which are near the border with Panama. In his journeys his aim was to pacify the areas, to win the confidence of the inhabitants and make them his friends. He then went to Spain, where he had friends at Court, gained benefits for himself and the province and was invested Governor and given a title which he could pass on to his heirs. Sadly in 1565 he was lost in a shipwreck leaving the province without one of its most devoted servants.[9] He has been described as the founder of Costa Rica. His successor, Perafán de Rivera, had had a long experience in Honduras, but faced rebellion and many difficulties. With his rule, however, the conquest of Costa Rica may be said to have been achieved, although this was chiefly the subjection of the Indians of the Central Valley.[10]

In the middle of the sixteenth century, the Audience of the Boundaries, having lost Panama and other parts of Central America, was terminated but in 1570 was replaced by a new Audience of Guatemala. For two and a half centuries this was the governing body of the isthmus from Costa Rica to Chiapas in Southern Mexico.[11] This was a period of consolidation and quiescence when every inhabitant was virtually a farmer. The main crops were maize, kidney beans, wheat, cane sugar, rice, other grains and vegetables. European fruits had been added to earlier varieties; sheep and poultry were introduced. Cotton was an important crop, the demand having increased as the Indian peoples adopted styles of European dress. The economy, however, remained almost static except for two other crops; cacao and indigo. Although these brought fortunes to those, invariably Spaniards, who owned the farms, their Negro slaves and the masses of Indians were less fortunate. The rulers in Spain, being more attracted by other areas which were producing mineral wealth, neglected the isthmus and at the end of the eighteenth century it was said 'the roads are impassable, the great rivers are crossed with danger, and in the uninhabited places travellers are exposed to destruction by outlaws and wild beasts'. Matías de Córdova, the friar responsible for those words, also said the real trouble lay in the unwillingness of the controlling class to share its prosperity with the mass of the population; 'give this vast majority of the population a chance to respect itself and its requirements would make the whole regime prosperous', he argued.[12] That was two hundred years ago.

In 1570 there were five episcopal provinces, one of which, Nicaragua, included Costa Rica. Four towns had cathedrals and bishops, but none was in Costa Rica. Similarly books and studies about the Indians were largely concerned with the tribes living in the countries to the north; and even a recent work about the cultures of the isthmus, from Guatemala to Panama, omits Costa Rica.

In order to govern more effectively, the Spaniards established settlements or towns in places most convenient for their security. It can be said that the towns were the base of the conquest. Until the end of the seventeenth century Cartago, in the Central Valley, was the only such Spanish town in Costa Rica. Around the church were a cluster of huts in which the Indians who had submitted to the conquerors were required to live.[13] Other native peoples lived in the mountains and in regions away from the Spanish domination, surviving with many difficulties, but at least free from total servitude. Early in the eighteenth century the town of Heredia was founded, followed by San José in 1736 and Allajuela in 1782; all being in the Central Valley. When Artieda Chirinos, was the Governor of the province of Costa Rica in 1573, the boundaries were defined more precisely. A large area in the north-east, being the territory north of the River San Juan (now part of Nicaragua) was removed from his jurisdiction.[14] Costa Rica was still part of the Capitania General, or Kingdom, of Guatemala where the Audience was located with its functions of government and justice.[15] Governors of provinces were required by law to make regular visits in their territories to deliberate upon and prescribe remedies for problems presented to them and deal with matters of justice. Because of the considerable distance from the province to Guatemala, the governor here was given an authority more than was usual throughout the administrative system. However, governors, being required to live in Cartago and thus far away from the main centres, and often being veterans of wars in Europe, were generally mediocre, if not worse.[16]

Although very much in a minority, the Spaniards exercised not only the control of such central government as there was, but also municipal decisions were substantially under their aegis. The President of the Audience was the personal representative of the King. The Indians who became Europeanized were referred to as *ladinos* (derived from Latin) and they did not return to be Indians.[17] Where their civilisation was strongest in the isthmus the Indians have increased in numbers, but in Costa Rica the white man pushed the Indians into the remoter areas. There are different views as to the number of Indians presently living in the country; mainly in the south-east on the border with Panama. One wonders how far they trouble themselves with, for them, an academic question as to whether they are living in Panama or Costa Rica; they are having to exercise all their endeavours to wrest a living from the land as their forefathers have done for many generations. Most of the *ladinos* were held in *encomienda* – bound to the land in a system comparable with the feudalism of Europe and when, after the first century of conquest, they were freed, they still had to pay tribute[18] or render services when compelled to do so.

As the 'rich coast' did not have the wealth, especially of gold, which the early conquerors had anticipated, the Spanish colonists did not become a privileged class. It was necessary for them to resolve by their own efforts, and those of their families, the satisfaction of immediate necessities without thinking of better economic or social provisions. The last decades of the 16th century and the first half of the 17th were most difficult for the establishment of colonial life. It seems evident that, in the case of Costa Rica, the province was not, during the whole of the Colonial regime, capable of meeting the costs of the Spanish governmental administration. Ownership of the land was a not unimportant contribution to the economic system as, despite not being highly productive, it usually passed by inheritance.

24

In the year 1601 occurred an important development for the extension of commerce beyond Costa Rica's boundaries. A mule train appeared from Panama, crossed the river Grande de Terraba and followed a ridge of mountains as far as the region of Chiriquí. Subsequently mules were brought from Honduras and Nicaragua and many inhabitants of Costa Rica became muleteers – but only during the dry season![19] One of the first productive activities was cattle raising which contributed to the development of the ranch especially in the dry tropical forest of the North Pacific region, where it became the most characteristic form and was most prominent in the second half of the 18th century. Subsequently the price for cattle fell and this, with the increasing demands of the Government in the north and the growth of the indigo trade, led to the elimination of cattle raising.

Another activity of much importance was the cultivation of cacao, to which reference has already been made. This continued until the second half of the 17th century chiefly in the region near the central Caribbean coast.[20] The appearance of the English, who had taken possession of Jamaica in 1655, led to attacks on the commerce being established between Central America and European countries. The activities of these pirates in the late 17th and into the 18th century did not affect Costa Rica as much as its neighbours, especially Honduras and Nicaragua, to which also Negro slaves were escaping from the West Indian islands.

The cultivation of tobacco also flourished despite the establishment by Bourbon monarchs in 1766 of a monopoly. In the plantations around San José was produced the tobacco for the greater part of the 'Kingdom' of Guatemala as well as for the New Spain and other places.[21] For the first time a plan was adopted from Guatemala which favoured the economic development of Costa Rica. The building of a tobacco factory in San José, later occupied by the Bank of Costa Rica, changed the neighbourhood into a centre of unusual activity and played a not unimportant part in that city becoming the capital of Costa Rica.

Costa Rica, being generally ignored by the Spanish empire builders, attracted the hardy, small farmers of Spain, who being allowed to bring wives, preserved the European race and culture. This was undoubtedly a major factor in the very strong independent spirit which led to the establishment and preservation of the basic democracy and freedom from dictatorship for the greater part of the country's history since becoming independent in 1821. Costa Rica has been described as 'an oasis of democracy in a region of dictatorship'. It must not be overlooked that it was, throughout the era of the Spanish occupation of Central America – and for many years afterwards – the poorest of the countries there. Whilst Spanish governors in other regions lived in comparative splendour, the

25

governors of Costa Rica were obliged to work their own land to survive. One at least complained bitterly to his peers in Spain but without any success. The population was tied to the land; a patriarchical society sustained by the work of the family and without the means to hire paid hands. Through the lack of roads and bridges the inhabitants of the Central Valley were isolated, especially when the heavy rains came. This was a disadvantage not only from the point of view of social relationships but also in regard to more fundamental elements such as religion and culture. At the beginning of the 18th century civil and ecclesiastical powers joined to compel people living on their tiny plots, and barely subsisting, to become concentrated into settlements.[22] External pressures were applied; the Bishop threatened with the penalty of excommunication those who would not form groups. Later the authorities even went to the extreme of burning the dwellings of the more obstinate in order to compel them to reside in the settlements being formed. Throughout the 18th century settlements, which became towns, were being constituted in the Central Valley and it is noteworthy they are about ten kilometres distant from each other.[23] It is thought the reason is that this is the length of a morning's journey which could be made in the winter when it rained a great deal. Journeys were usually made in the mornings when there was less likelihood of getting drenched. Other small settlements were established on the Pacific Coast and on the way to Nicaragua.

The poverty of the Spanish colonial period, coupled with the rural isolation, limited cultural development. The church influence, being strong, helped preserve some religious art with images of Saints and simple representations of the crib and the infant God.[24] Literature was largely limited to books of prayers. When a local council decided to open a school and pay the teacher the pupils were chosen from the children of influential citizens. Teaching was limited to learning to read, add, multiply and subtract, and memorising the catechism and the principal religious prayers. Those who learned to write were required to fulfil the duties of scrivener in the settlement. Very occasionally, for some notable event, such as the marriage of a chief, part of the festival would be the presentation of a short piece of a play or ballet. On the death of the King (of Spain) mourning was obligatory for all. Those who showed some intellectual capacity were encouraged to study for the priesthood, and some funds were even available to enable recipients to go and study at the Seminary at León in Nicaragua. Those who could not obtain clerical office in Costa Rica often took parishes elsewhere in other parts of Central America.[25] Two such men who became particularly prominent were José Antonio de Liendo y Goicoechea (1735-1814) and Florencio del Castillo (1784-1834). The former was a proponent of Cartesian rationalism and experimental science; the latter, at one time a professor at León, was distinguished for his endeavours in the defence of the Indians and to secure benefits for his province of Costa Rica, where he was vice-president and later president.

In 1814 the principal inhabitants of San José interested themselves in inaugurating the 'House of Education of St. Thomas', the first education centre established under their own inspiration.[26]. At the end of 1660 the Kingdom of Guatemala had its first printing press.

For over 300 years Costa Rica was part of the Spanish empire, during which period it became gradually transformed into a country. In the absence of any large economic resources the people lived by subsistence farming. Because of this, the introvert character of the settler was one of the notable features inherited from the austerity of colonial life. The pattern of possession of the land is the direct consequence of the colonial model: the 'ranch' was modelled by the cattle raising in the dry tropical forest;[27] the 'plantation' appeared within the inhospitable area of the wet Caribbean forest region, which kept most white men away and secured support for slave labour; the 'small isolated farm' was established in regions of a more temperate climate with abundant water and fertile soil – predominantly in the volcanic Central Valley, preferred by the immigrant colonist, who lived a life devoted to hard work, in which 'he who did not sow did not eat'. Preference for the Central Valley remains one of the most important features of Costa Rican life. At the beginning of the 19th century, of sixty thousand inhabitants, practically 90% lived there, but that did not include the region of Nicoya which at that time was not part of Costa Rica.[28]

In addition to the Spaniards there were brown skinned people, descendants of those of African origin. In time cross-breeding led to a mixture of races and by the end of the colonial period established the fusion of the races which is the ethnic basis of the Costa Ricans today. The social inheritance of the Colonial period stamped indelibly upon a large part of the 19th Century every kind of social discrimination. Resorting to a popular phrase, the Colonial conception with regard to ethnic groups was based on the idea 'United but not easily changed'. It is said that the group which founded Cartago constituted a Colonial aristocracy often strengthened by means of marriage with immigrant Spaniards which added prestige to that of birthplace, though frequently few resources were contributed.[29]

The conquest, and subsequent process of securing Spanish domination in the Central Valley is certainly the foundation of Costa Rica's history. The difficulties and struggles required to survive created a man of strife, perhaps not very developed mentally or culturally but potentially capable. Without wealth, closely tied to the earth, he learned that his future rested upon his own efforts and determination. Dreams of gold were easily ignored and he was urged in consequence towards benefits, perhaps less ambitious but more realistic, with the conviction that the future would be that which he himself wished it to be.[30]

## NOTES TO CHAPTER 2

1. Melendez, p. 40
2. Parker, pp. 43/4
3. Melendez, p. 41
4. ibid, p. 41
5. ibid, p. 41
6. Parker, p. 45
7. ibid, pp. 47/8
8. Melendez, p. 45
9. ibid, pp. 45/7
10. ibid, p. 48

11. Parker, p. 48
12. Parker, p. 66
13. Melendez, p. 62
14. ibid, p. 63
15. ibid, p. 64
16. ibid, p. 65
17. Parker, p. 50 referring to Richard N. Adams 'Cultural components of Central America'.
18. Parker, p. 47
19. Melendez, p. 68

20. ibid, p. 69
21. ibid, p. 71
22. ibid, p. 73
23. ibid, p. 74
24. ibid, p. 75
25. ibid, p. 76
26. ibid, p. 76
27. ibid, p. 77
28. ibid, p. 78
29. ibid, p. 78
30. ibid, p. 79

# Chapter Three

# THE DEVELOPMENT OF A NATIONAL STATE 1821-1940

Although independence did not come until 1821, it was some twenty-five years earlier, in November 1796, that the first signs appeared of the ending of the Spanish Colonial domination in Central America. José Domas y Valle, at the advanced age of 96, and the President of the Audiencia de Guatemala, presided over the first public meeting of the 'Economic Society of the Friends of the Country'.[1] This Society enabled the educated group to engage in discussions for the first time in almost 300 years about the new régime, that would be required when self-rule was obtained. The early years of the 19th century found Spain embroiled in the turmoil in Europe of which Napoleon was the centre. The effect was felt in the isthmus as well as in Spain itself. Insurrection in Mexico in 1811 was followed by similar outbreaks in 1811 and 1812 in El Salvador and Nicaragua and again in El Salvador in 1814.[2] These, however, hardly affected Costa Rica where any ideas of liberty barely existed. Indeed such ideas were not very prevalent in Latin America generally, despite the efforts of Bolivar, Morelos and others.

In 1812 a Constitution and some liberal measures had been prepared by the Cortes in Spain, in the preparation of which delegates from Central America had taken part. Following the revolution in Spain in 1820, events moved quickly. Two newspapers appeared in Central America which, although not espousing the cause of breaking with Spain, urged freedom of trade, more representation in the Spanish Cortes and other liberal themes of the day.[3]

In April 1821 came news of Agustín de Iturbide's declaration of independence in Mexico. Although Gabino Gainza, President of the Audiencia de Guatemala, urged loyalty to Spain, Iturbide's proclamation was supported in other places. On 15th September, Gainza called a public

29

meeting in Guatemala City, at which Pedro Molina, editor of one of the newspapers, and his friends raised a cry for independence but were opposed by Archbishop Casaus and some others. Next day the Governor, Gainza, declared provisional independence with himself as head of the government and suggested a representative congress of the several provinces to make the final decisions. The document he used was prepared by a lawyer, José Cecilio de Valle, the publisher of the other newspaper, who had also spoken strongly in favour of freedom from Spain.[4]

Conflict arose between those who objected to union with Mexico and those who favoured it; there was opposition in other parts of the isthmus to domination from Guatemala. In Costa Rica this conflict was between those who favoured an imperial structure, similar to that to which they were accustomed, and others who favoured a more democratic regime. In April 1823 civil war broke out between what can be described as the 'republicans' of San José and the 'monarchists' of Cartago. The former emerged victorious and the capital was changed to San José.[5] Iturbide's attempts to include the provinces of Central America in his empire were not successful and, with his abdication and the departure of Gainza for Mexico, the isthmus was in possession of its own destiny.[6]

The declaration of independence made in Guatemala City in September 1821 did not reach Costa Rica until the following month and in November a provincial *Junta* replaced the Governor of the province. On 1st December the *Junta* proposed the adoption of a *Pacto de Concordia,* a fundamental social pact which is regarded as the first Constitution of Costa Rica. By this the province assumed full sovereignty and absolute liberty to decide whether or not to unite with any other government in the Americas'.[7]

Following Iturbide's abdication and the break up of his empire, the provinces and cities of the isthmus, many of which had issued their own declarations of independence, were ready to co-operate with Guatemala, so a National Constituent Assembly was formed and first met in June 1823. A second declarationi of independence was issued in July 1823 which confirmed the earlier declaration and now used the name 'United Provinces of Central America'. The five provinces or states forming the Assembly included Costa Rica in the form of the old 'Gobierno' with the addition of, in 1825, the province of Nicoya or Guanacaste, which seceded from Nicaragua.[8] This area is substantially that of present day Costa Rica. The Constituent Assembly became the basis of a federal system on which preparations could begin for a return to a united Central America. A President was appointed for the Federal Republic and each State had a Chief or Head of State. The first Chief in Costa Rica was Juan Mora Fernández (1784-1854), a well-adjusted man respected for his democratic principles; he was a most suitable man to initiate and guide the development of a political movement. There was apprehension about having strong men who might manipulate the political system, and this led to a preference for strengthening the legislative assemblies with the consequent weakening of executive power. Because a large number of people were concerned, decisions were delayed which hampered and retarded the solution of the tasks of administration.[9]

The National Constituent Assembly's first task was to produce a Constitution, which it did in November 1824. This provided that each State was to be independent in its government but that the Federal Congress should legislate in matters of common interest and impose taxes to support the federal government. A President, Senate and Supreme Court were to be elected and special rights of nobility and clergy were abolished – as was slavery. Although there were several guarantees of civil rights, Roman Catholicism was to be the only form of public worship. There were also proposals for making a canal through Nicaragua to provide a link between the Pacific and Caribbean Oceans and plans for elementary education for all. Subsequently the Church was regarded as being too closely identified with the old colonial system and freedom of worship was instituted.[10]

Quarrels soon arose and sporadic civil war was suffered from 1827 to 1829. The Union was finally brought to an end following a war which began in Guatemala in 1837. Francisco Morazán, who had been elected President in 1830, had aroused opposition by his vigorous leadership and although he won several victories against those who rebelled against him, he was finally defeated. In May 1838 the Congress decided the States might do as they pleased in regard to continuing to adhere to the Union. Costa Rica with Nicaragua and Honduras withdrew by the end of that year and Guatemala followed soon afterwards. Morazán returned to Costa Rica from Panama in April 1842, seized power and prepared an army but was soon defeated and was executed in September 1842.[11]

There were many attempts later to bring about the union of the five countries but all failed. There was a semblance of a union in the 1850s, but this was of a miliary nature when the peoples of Central America joined together to resist attempts by William Walker of Tennessee to establish himself as President of Nicaragua.[12] There were two attempts by Walker and his confederates during this period. One of Costa Rica's national heroes, Juan Santamaria, gained undying fame by throwing lighted faggots into the building where Walker and his chiefs were gathered causing them to flee, several being killed, as was Santamaria. Statues of him with the faggot raised on high are erected outside the Congress House in San José and in the public square in Alajuela. Costa Rica's international airport is named after this young hero.

Following independence and the short-lived Central American Union, there had been a period of unrest with attempts by some of those holding office to take measures to make sure they retained it. One such, Braulio Carrillo, in 1841 made himself dictator for life, but this only lasted for one year before he was ousted.[13] Juan Rafael Mora was President from 1849 to 1859 and he also played an important rôle in helping to defeat Walker. Mora established order and maintained at least a semblance of democracy but sadly, following his defeat, he attempted an invasion in 1860 and was executed about the same time as the swashbuckling Walker,[14] in whose capture Britons had played a conspicuous rôle.

At the time of independence, Costa Rica had been the poorest and most backward province in the 'Kingdom' of Guatemala. It seems the conditions under which the people lived during the Spanish colonial rule had brought about a lethargy from which society had to be awakened to realise it was the owner of its own destiny. Braulio Carrillo, President between 1835 and 1842, worked to establish a stable economy based on coffee production and he saved the country from the difficulties from which neighbouring states suffered for a very long time.[15] The coffee plantations undoubtedly made the most important contribution towards the improvement of economic life and, although there was some mining, mainly in the Aguacate Mountains, this was of minor relevance.

Because the coffee was cultivated in the area where most of the population lived, i.e. in the Central Valley, and where ownership of the plantations had been well distributed, the social benefits were widely shared. The construction of roads to the coast facilitated the development of foreign commerce, and accordingly production increased. As early as 1820 there had been exports to Panama, by 1832 coffee was being exported also to Chile and, in 1843, to Britain.[16]

This helped to bring about a change of mentality, giving the people knowledge of the existence of a world very different from that of the Central Valley. New ideas appeared and new attitudes were evolved and, although society continued to be fundamentally patriarchal, the condition of women was improved.

A Constituion of 1859, which established a period of three years as the term of office for Presidents, was rewritten some ten years later but the latter survived barely three years. The Constitution of December 1871, however, endured, with one short exception, until the civil war of 1948. By the Constitution the President, Tomás Guardia, yielded office in 1876 but remained as chief of the military and took over as President once more a year later. He held office until he died in 1882 and it is to him the country is indebted for the construction of the railways linking the Central Valley with the two chief ports, Puntarenas on the Pacific and Limón on the Caribbean.[17]

A term of four years for the office of President was now established and a single chamber Congress, half of whose members were elected every second year. During the Presidency of Bernardo Soto (1886-1890) there was the impetus for a free and compulsory public education system which has had such an important impact on the development of modern Costa Rica. Politically and historicaly there was a great step forward in 1889 when Soto's party was defeated in the election. They accepted defeat without question and it has been said this was the country's first peaceful transition from a group in power to a successful opposition and that only Honduras of the other five Central American republics has shared this experience.[18] For many years the democratic tradition prevailed, with only relatively minor attempts by Presidents to secure the election of chosen successors or their own re-election. This materially aided the development of the country's economy, based chiefly on coffee and bananas, in contrast to the neighbouring republics. Political parties operated freely and, although the owners of the larger coffee plantations and the leaders of commerce constituted an aristocracy which, in many cases, secured their sphere of influence in political activity and thus power remained with the wealther classes, the expansion of general education throughout the urban centres ensured the eventual triumph of democracy.[19]

In January, 1917, there was a rebellion which brought a temporary hitch in the democratic process. President Gonzáles Flores, appointed rather than elected in 1914, had attempted to control the mid-term elections to Congress and to place more of the burden of taxation upon the rich. His Minister for War, Federico Tinoco Granados, seized power, managed to get for himself the office of President, and had a new Constitution prepared in June 1917. Only two years later, however, Tinoco resigned and the Constitution of 1871 was restored.[20] The period from 1924 to 1936 was regarded by many to be a 'golden age' of Costa Rica. Ricardo Jiménez Oreamuno was President for two terms, 1924 to 1928 and again 1932-36; the intervening four years were served by Cleto González Viquez: both men had served in this capacity in earlier years. They respected the democratic traditions and supported progressive measures within the general framework of their 19th century society; although the former has been referred to as an 'intellectual dictator'. He was instrumental in securing the formation of a National Bank of Insurance (later called the National Institute of Insurance) which gave Costa Ricans better protection and also kept funds within the country. This created a monopoly of the different types of insurance the Bank was able to handle as it continued to develop. It was during Ricardo's final period as President that Costa Rica's first minimum wage was established. In 1935 the United Fruit Company gave to the President a quarter of a million acres of land to be distributed in small holdings to some of the landless.[21] This once again emphasises the difference between Costa Rica and its neighbours; strengthening the independence of its inhabitants and contrasting with the gigantic landholdings and subjection of the peasantry to little more than labouring serfs in the other republics.

During these years (1924 to 1936) appeared for the first time the dis-satisfaction of the mass of the people with the poor life prevalent in all the republics of the isthmus. Over forty years of general education now enabled the people to be aware of the possibility of measures being taken to improve their lot. In 1929 a Communist Party was formed, organised by Mora Valverde, a law student, only 19 years of age. Much more was heard of him in the eventful years of 1940 to 1948. By 1934 the Communists were strong enough to secure the election of two members to Congress and also to lead a strike in the banana industry around Limón. This resulted in the banana workers there obtaining a minimum wage higher than that prevailing in the rest of the country.[22]

In the political arena there were also substantial and important changes. It had been traditional to form groups simply to support one candidate in one campaign but the example set by the Communists of continuing political activity between election campaigns was now followed. A National Republican Party had been formed to secure the election of Ricardo Jiménez Oreamuno in 1932. This party continued its existence and won a clear victory four years later when León Cortés Castro was elected President, followed by a landslide success in 1940 with its nominee Rafael Angel Calderón Guardia.[23]

The latter's studies in Europe had promoted a concern for the welfare of his people and his country. He was anxious by his governmental programme to improve the economic, moral and cultural condition of the working people. A biographer describes him as 'an emotional and intellectual giant amongst dwarfs . . . devoted only to the most elevated realms of thought, highly cultured, brilliant, patriotic, democratic, indefatigable, an architect of social welfare, exemplary and of profound spiritual depth . . .'[24] As will be seen, the events of 1948 and 1955 do not justify such a panegyric.

Cortés had been able to introduce moderate reforms, notably in the banana industry along the Pacific coast and government stabilisation of prices, but the contributions of the Calderón era were more far reaching. His influence in the politics of Costa Rica undoubtedly resulted in the epic and courageous measures almost a decade later when the army was dissolved and the Constitution amended to make a standing army illegal.

## NOTES TO CHAPTER 3

1. Parker, p. 75
2. ibid, p. 76
3. ibid, p. 76, noting 'Escritos del Doctor Pedro Molina' and 'Obras de José Cecilio Del Valle' the respective publishers of the Newspapers.
4. ibid, p. 77
5. ibid, p. 260
6. ibid, pp. 77/8
7. Melendez, p. 95
8. Parker, p. 78
9. Melendez, p. 96
10. Parker, pp. 78/9
11. ibid, p. 80
12. ibid, p. 80 Melendez, p. 100
13. Parker, p. 260
14. ibid, p. 261
15. ibid, p. 281
16. Melendez, p. 102
17. Parker, p. 261
18. ibid, p. 262
19. ibid, p. 262
20. ibid, p. 263
21. ibid, p. 264
22. ibid, p. 263
23. ibid, p. 264
24. Colorado, p. 25, referring to Fernando Ferres Vincinzi's 'lyrical paean'

# Chapter Four

# CALDERÓN GUARDIA'S REFORMS 1940-44

The eight years from 1940 to 1948 were momentous and it is necessary to deal with these in some detail to understand how Costa Rica, which cherished a historical tradition of a stable society, a high rate of literacy, democratic institutions and almost, if not quite, general and peaceful transfer of political power, could be brought to a situation of revolution. Professor John P. Bell in the Preface to his excellent book *Crisis in Costa Rica* confesses to being intrigued by a successful armed uprising taking place in a generally stable and pacific nation. It is convenient to divide this period into three chief sections: post-election 1940 to the end of 1943; 1944 to 1947; and the events of 1948. The last mentioned will, undoubtedly, call for examination in depth with

(1) its election fracas leading to revolution and open armed conflict
(2) the unexpected and dramatic dis-solution of the army by Figueres, who only months earlier had led the great parade of the victorious fighters through San José
(3) the election of a Constituent Assembly and
(4) the invasion from Nicaragua of the earlier defeated Calderón Guardia and his supporters.

It should be remembered that Costa Rica's development had been almost entirely in isolation from its neighbouring republics, primarily because it was somewhat isolated.[1] The Spaniards who settled came as farmers and not to gain wealth and profit from exploiting a native population. This meant there was no aristocracy or class enjoying privilege and domination. Most families lived separated from others and worked their own land. Although some inevitably prospered more than others, there was a frugal but equal existence and a form of agrarian democracy. Thus was developed the individualism and equality which

36

undoubtedly formed the basis of the democratic tradition which distinguishes Costa Rica from its neighbours. Even with the advent of an upper class, by the cultivation of coffee on a large scale, as has been noted, those who became rich had a strong sense of social co-operation.[2]

At the time of independence, in 1821, the population was around 60,000[3] and this had increased tenfold by 1940. In the ten years between 1930 and 1940 the increase was about 27 per cent.[4] The pressure of the population increase was a major factor in the social problems, more especially in the capital, San José, where basic facilities were lacking. Unemployment and, more particularly, underemployment, limited earnings; malnutrition and endemic diseases affected many. A Chilean journalist, Tancredo Pinochet, when asked to comment on the equitable distribution of land, caused a scandal by remarking 'what is well distributed in Costa Rica is poverty'![5] Those not directly affected excused themselves and minimised the problem by reminding each other that Costa Ricans lived better than their neighbours and indeed, better than most Latin American peoples, but education, coupled with the endeavours of the Communists, made poverty a prime political issue. Although there was a relatively high standard of living, Costa Ricans ranked only tenth amongst Latin American countries in three important categories; the *per capita* consumption of total calories, grams of daily protein and annual consumption of milk. It is however, important, to observe that in Central America only Honduras was in advance of Costa Rica in these respects.[6]

Lack of adequate housing was a major factor in the social tension; small farmers and farm labourers were said to be living with their large families in one room without any sanitary facilities. Even as late as May 1944 the newspaper *Diario de Costa Rica* produced a two page study depicting the conditions in which the urban poor existed in and around the capital. This referred to the absence of hygenic facilities, the consequent prevalence of tuberculosis, intestinal parasites, other health hazards and that 'all social evils abounded'. This study, however, was produced by those opposed to the governing party.

Politically the National Republican Party basked in the glow of its candidate, Calderón Guardia, who enjoyed phenomenal success in the election of February 1940 when he obtained almost 93,000 votes out of 102,000 cast.[8] Retiring President Cortés alleged links with communism on the part of the former National Republican President, Jiménez, whose support, although including that of Mora and his Communist Party, was predominantly non-Communist. It was considered Cortés had not maintained the ideals of a retiring President and persecution by him had decimated the opposition to Guardia. There is, however, little doubt that

Calderón Guardia, a medical doctor, enjoyed great personal popularity throughout the country. There was a general opinion he was strong enough to win the election against the opposing coalition without Cortés' intervention. An unexpected and interesting result emanating from Cortés' departure from the traditional idea, was the gain subsequently made by the *Bloque de Obreros y Campesinos* (Mora's group) in popular esteem. They were able to capitalize on the Costa Rican traditional belief in democratic practices and encourage influence and respect for their party by condemning Cortés' actions as limiting the freedom of the ballot. The general acceptance of a communist party was due, in large measure, to the quality of its leadership. Mora was recognised as an active and respected member of Congress and by responsible citizens as a 'watchdog for injustice'.[9]

In 1941 Cortés broke away from the National Republican Party and founded the Democratic Party.[10] He did so because he opposed the social reforms being effected by Guardia; this defection was a grievous loss to the government and had most serious implications. Cortés, being widely known and in some quarters respected, was able to attract to the new Party many of the élite who were opposed to social change of any description.

The most significant feature of this period was the founding of the *Centro* by young professional and white-collar workers and students. It was derived from an association of law students and its members came almost exclusively from the upper and middle classes.[11] The Centro group led to the formation of the Social Democratic Party after the 1944 elections and played a significant part, along with Figueres' party, *Acción Demócrata,* in spear-heading the opposition to Picado's government of 1944-48 and in the events which resulted in the revolution.

The political scene of the 1940s cannot but include mention of José Figueres Ferrer, a well-to-do, self-made agriculturist. He was born in 1906 in San Ramón, Costa Rica, to which his parents had emigrated from Barcelona only a short time before. There was conflict with his parents when they insisted he attend a secondary school run by a religious order after which he left for New York. There he worked for four years and learned English. On his return he began to develop a plantation in a remote area south of San José; it is not without significance that he named his *finca* 'La Lucha sin Fin' (the Struggle without End). His biographer suggests the name represents Figueres' philosophical conception of life, due probably to his study of Herbert Spencer, his major inspiration.[12] He came into prominence on 8th July 1942 when he delivered over the radio a virulent, scathing attack on the Government of Calderón Guardia, which he alleged was in the hands of the Communists. There was a scuffle in the broadcasting studio when police arrived and arrested Figueres. He was

38

exiled, the first since the Tinocos in 1917. He was accused of disclosing military secrets, collaborating with Germans and assisting some of them to avoid confiscation of their property. It was even suggested the United States government had pressed for him to be exiled; although Guardia's government had more prominent critics, none but Figueres was exiled, and at that time he was comparatively unknown.[13]

His exile and the government's conduct made Figueres a confirmed rebel. In a pamphlet written in Mexico but published in Costa Rica, Figueres wrote:

> 'Man lives in society and sustains a regulating state for his own benefit. From the moment in which that state prejudices him or disrespects his person, the contract is broken and the society ceases to exist.[14]

His opposition to the government became of paramount importance: he was resolved to found 'the Second Republic'. This was to be a most important facet of future events. It was whilst he was in exile that he met exiles from other nations and this again played a not unimportant part in the revolution of 1948. He conceived the idea that his cause was larger than that of this 'little Costa Rica' and encompassed the struggle for the liberty and democracy of all oppressed peoples of the American continent. In a letter written from Mexico City he urged honesty in government, liberty for the people and a professional civil service. He added that the state should assume gradually the direction of all economic activity with the objectives of a greater production of wealth and more equity in its distribution.[15] His absence enabled his supporters to create an almost legendary figure; a self-made man, a capitalist coffee grower but a socialist, a philosopher-politician, a revolutionary supporting all opposition groups but exclusively identified with none. Figueres did not return to Costa Rica until after the elections of February 1944.

Calderón Guardia when he became President in 1940 faced an almost insuperable task. There were four major issues, the most serious being the social question, but the problems of the electoral process were of scarcely less significance. Doubts were arising in the traditional belief in the efficacy and adequacy of the democratic provisions and the vote. The growth of communism represented by Mora's Bloque de Obreros y Campesinos was looked upon by the élite as a threat to their way of life which, understandably, they identified as Costa Rica's way of life. The élite were devoted to preventing the communists from taking any prominent part in the democratic process, much less in the government. For their part the communists set out to expose the defects in the system and establish their claim to be entitled to use the traditional democratic channels. The result could only be to increase the citizens' doubts about their part in the making of decisions. The communists' success in organizing the strike in the banana plantations as early as 1934, and their skill in drawing attention to defects in the social provisions, added considerably to their prestige and support. The fourth major issue, with which Guardia had to contend, was that of mismanagement and financial corruption, which his opponents constantly alleged during his four year term as President.[16]

At the outset of his term Costa Rica was suffering, as have so many of the under-developed countries, by its being an agrarian society seeking to retain its traditional way of life in a world that was rapidly changing. In general it suffered from poverty and all the evils that result from large numbers of the population living below subsistence level. Whilst all deplored the poverty, the élite, who had controlled the government, took refuge in the comfortable thought that life in Costa Rica was a good deal better than it was in neighbouring republics. The growth in population and the activities of the communists were the two major factors making the issue one which could no longer be ignored. Guardia immediately accepted the challenge and in his inaugural address he proposed measures to aid the social, economic and cultural development of Costa Rica. These included a revision of the taxation system so that those best able to contribute would bear a larger share; the provision of rural credit and a programme of land distribution; improved development of the Atlantic region which had been almost entirely abandoned by the 'colonial empire' of the United Fruit Company; a low-cost housing scheme, the founding of a national university to promote the general progress of the country: to provide for the welfare of all, he proposed to establish a system of social security, similar to that already operating in Mexico.[17] By this means he hoped to negate the attacks of the communists and yet persuade his wealthier supporters of the necessity of his proposals to enable the state as they knew it to continue to survive. To ensure their support he pledged that there would be no government involvement in any direction where private interests could be established. In this he was only partly successful; as has been pointed out, his staunch supporter, the previous President, León Cortés, was unable to accept the radical social programme of Calderón Guardia and, in 1941, broke away from the National Republican Party to establish the Democratic Party.[18] This seriously weakened the government as Cortés attracted the support of many of the élite, especially those who were not prepared to countenance any social changes that threatened their mode of life. Cortés was careful, having regard to the widely accepted desire for reforms, to put forward proposals to ensure the continuation of the legislation already in being. His appeal was to follow the established ways and to return to the domination of the large coffee interests, oblivious of the fact that these had seriously undermined the position of the smaller farmers who, in many cases, had to reinforce their meagre subsistence by working also for the larger groupings.

A second major factor which seriously affected Guardia's programme of social and other reforms, was the involvement of Costa Rica with the United States in the Second World War. Already the country had suffered as a result of trade with Western Europe being dislocated, but now there was pressure from USA to increase exports to Panama and the Canal Zone. Being cut off from some of its sources of imports resulted in shortages of capital goods, manufactured articles and some foodstuffs and brought about inflation. This was intensified by the construction of the section of the Pan American Highway which came through the country, which, though subsequently it has had beneficial results by facilitating access and thus promoting tourism, was designed to aid the defence of the Western Hemisphere, and, more especially, to protect the Canal Zone. The cost of this construction was the largest single factor in the financial crises the government had to face and loans for this and other essential purchases from the United States contributed substantially to the serious fiscal problems that followed. In 1981 the colón depreciated to one-fifth of its value against the dollar and other linked currencies (and subsequently depreciated further) and the cost of servicing the National Debt has since overtaken Education as the highest cost item in the Budget. During the Second World War Costa Rica was also required to have a more professional army, accept a military training mission as well as an air detachment from the United States because of its proximity to the Panama Canal. Most controversially, it had to suppress its German residents. More than two hundred Germans were deported, and others placed in a concentration camp. Farms and businesses owned by Germans were expropriated or placed under national administrators. Criticism was directed more against Guardia and his government than it was against the United States. In addition to hampering the proposed social reforms, the war gave rise to an unaccustomed interference by the government in the Costa Rican's life-style. The regulation of prices, construction of the Pan-American Highway and other public projects to create employment as well as the increased military activity, all enabled the opposition to increase its criticism of the government and allege a 'terrible' intrusion into private affairs.[19]

There was, however, one quite unexpected and unforeseen result of World War II. As the Soviet Union was now an ally of the United States and other Western democracies, national communist parties were encouraged to collaborate with their democratic governments. For

Guardia this had the important effect of off-setting the loss of Cortés and his influential group by the gain of Mora and his devoted workers for the advancement of communism and the improvement of social conditions. This alliance was made the more respectable by the Chief of the United States Military Mission participating alongside Communist leaders in an anti-fascist demonstration at United States Independence Day celebrations on 4th July 1942.[20] Although Guardia had, during his first two years of office, represented his social reform measures as being necessary to combat the growth and influence of communism, he now welcomed Mora's support to ensure his programme succeeded. There were no Ministerial posts offered to the communists, who pledged their assistance if Guardia would quicken the pace of his reforms and make even greater efforts to improve the plight of the workers.

Despite the additional pressures by reason of the demands of World War II, Guardia's government made very considerable advances, spurred on from 1942, as indicated, by the alliance with the communists. Legislation was introduced to protect tenants from eviction and to freeze rents, to provide low-cost housing, to promote new industries and encourage diversification of commerce, to establish a Labour Code, create a Social Security System and revise the Land Law. There was even provision to ensure needy children had free shoes to protect their feet from parasites.[21] Figueres in his radio attack on Calderón Guardia caustically said:

> 'My peons do not have shoes, nor clean sheets, nor milk for their children, but Social Security guarantees them an old age without privations; Gentlemen of the Government, let us finish the comedy; assure the Costa Ricans a good burial and let them die of hunger.'[22]

His letter written from Mexico a year later, which has previously been referred to, shows something of a change of perspective.

The revision of the Land Law, referred to as 'The Law of the Parasites', was necessary because of the number of what are usually called 'squatters'. Of the total area of about 23,000 square miles, there were 10,000 square miles of uncleared forest and about the same area of unoccupied grassland; this was the estimate made in the mid 1940s. Small farmers and farm labourers had been accustomed to seeking out, occupying and cultivating land which was not being cultivated. Although there was no acknowledgement of their right to do so, their efforts constantly added more land to that producing much needed food. Although disparagingly referred to as 'parasites' – hence the name given to the new Land Law – their numbers became large enough for them to be recognised as a distinct group. In cases where the land was registered in the name of someone else, the state paid compensation to him as the land became the property of the 'squatter'. In addition to bringing uncultivated land into production with a minimum of bureaucratic effort, the practice relieved pressure on the Central Valley, where 70% of the population lived, and also the number of small farmsteads increased, thus strengthening a basic feature of Costa Rican democracy.[23]

Guardia's Social Security System, established in 1941, was the first in Central America. It was based on the Chilean scheme and experts from that country gave help and advice. Insurance was compulsory for all under sixty years of age working in agriculture or industry or domestic service as well as self-employed artisans working at home. Employees, employers and the state were all required to make contributions to the insurance fund which was invested under the supervision of a Board which included the managers of the National Bank of Costa Rica and the National Insurance Bank. The law provided for the scheme to be extended to cover everyone.[24]

A year later came what was perhaps the most basic of Guardia's reforms: the amending of the constitution so that Social Guarantees might be included and the social function of property asserted. The President had based his proposals on encyclicals pronounced by Pope Leo XIII and Pope Pius XI and he reaffirmed his Christian outlook. These 'Social Guarantees' included the right to establish co-operatives, to set up a Social Security System, regulate working conditions, provide a minimum living wage, bargain collectively in labour disputes, and to establish Labour Courts, and also confirmed rights of equal opportunity for urban and rural workers, and preferential treatment in hiring practices for Costa Rican workers as against other nationals.[25] It was understood the amendments constituting the Social Guarantees had no legal force but were indicated as basic principles leaving the substance to be defined by Congress and the Courts to interpret them.

As if the foregoing legislation were not enough for the élitist opposition to swallow, Guardia introduced in August 1943 his Labour Code. This provided for a Labour Ministry, made collective bargaining mandatory in disputes between management and labour, guaranteed labour the right to organise and made provision against arbitrary dismissal. Labour Courts were also created and there were specific rights for labour to form a collective conscience but not to instigate class warfare.[26] There were other measures to assist the poor and needy which did nothing to commend the government to the élite who claimed that Calderón Guardia and his supporters were indistinguishable from Mora and his Communists. Perhaps Guardia miscalculated the strength of the opposition to his social changes, taking the view that 'men of wealth and power in poor nations . . . must lead the fight for those basic reforms which alone can preserve the fabric of their own societies.'[27]

One attempt only was made to reform the electoral law but this was roundly condemned by the opposition who claimed it was a device to place more control in the hands of the chief executive and would thwart the popular will. As the main demand for electoral reform ceased when the Communists changed from opposing to supporting the government, Guardia withdrew the proposal from Congress and made no further attempt to implement the promise he had made in his inaugural address to introduce a more effective electoral law.

Although the allegations of fiscal mismanagement, graft and corruption were not as serious as some of the other factors, they did alienate many of the younger men and contributed to the climate of opinion which brought about the revolution. Cortés had made the issue of corruption a principal reason for his defection from the National Republican party and thereafter the attacks made by him upon the Communists were switched to fall upon Calderón Guardia. The Ministry of Public Works was alleged to be letting out contracts without first seeking tenders and, in view of the government's large scale public works programme, coupled with the construction of their section of the Pan-American Highway, opportunities for corruption substantially increased. These activities of necessity meant an increase in the number of government appointments which, the opposition alleged, enabled Guardia to 'reward' his friends; 'jobs for the boys' as it is often termed. As previous governments had usually been able to balance their budgets and Guardia's was seriously in deficit, his critics had an excellent area in which to persuade citizens the government was indulging in corrupt practices. It had been the practice for those in public office to be rewarded with the esteem of their fellow-countrymen rather than by financial gain.[28] Several Presidents in past years had sustained considerable financial loss as a result of spending four or more years in office; one indeed was said to have been reduced to penury. The considerable increase in government activity, consequent upon the social reform programme of Calderón Guardia, required a corresponding increase in the number of civil servants, some of whom needed specialised training. The fiscal rewards of earlier regimes were inadequate, especially in a time of rapid inflation, with the result that measures, illegal as well as legal, were taken to supplement earnings. Wartime shortages, allocation of scarce commodities, and substantially increased government spending, all contributed to the problem and provided opportunities for mis-use of power. Perhaps Guardia's chief defect in this area was a complacency induced by his colossal victory in the 1940 election; the absence of any substantial or serious opposition encouraged a laxity in his administration and lack of control of his subordinates. It was not until several years after his term as President came to an end that he admitted some members of his government had not been honest.[29]

Despite the many allegations of fiscal malpractices made by members of the opposition and in the newspapers opposing the government, little was proved. The opposition further weakened its case by claiming there were excessive payments made for special services. Unfortunately for the opposition, one such payment had been made to Alberto Martén who was a University professor of economics. He was also a close personal friend of Figueres and, by strenuously defending the payment made to him, he cast doubts on the validity of claims that such payments were evidence of a corrupt government. This was further supported by reports emanating from the United States Minister to Costa Rica, Robert M. Scotten. He referred to government mismanagement and widespread allegations of graft, but went on to recommend to the US Department of State that favourable consideration be given to negotiations with the Costa Rican Financial Secretary. He further implied he did not consider Guardia to be corrupt as he had readily accepted help from American experts to find solutions to unprecedented fiscal difficulties of his wartime government. Guardia, however, seriously damaged his public image when, towards the end of his four years as President, he decreed an amnesty for some of his supporters who had been found guilty of electoral offences and complicity in financial mis-dealings. The Supreme Court had no hesitation in declaring such an amnesty unconstitutional.[30]

It is not without significance that Calderón Guardia appears to have made no attempt to introduce a system of taxation of incomes. This, despite his pledge in his inaugural address on being elected President that he would introduce measures to revise the system of taxation so that this was based on the capacity to contribute. Perhaps he was discouraged by the mounting opposition to his social programme and the accentuation of Costa Rica's difficulties due to World War II. The financial position of the country was indeed grave as of the three chief sources of government revenue, customs duties, export taxes and receipts from the liquor monopoly, only the latter had not been seriously affected by war-time conditions. Loans escalated enormously in the three years after October 1939 when the first loan was received from the US Export Import Bank.

By the mid-term elections of 1942, the National Republican Party was already losing some of its popular esteem. It must be remembered, however, the mid-term elections were for part of the Congress only and the personal appeal of the President was not a factor enlisting support from the voters. In February 1942 Calderón Guardia had lost the support of Cortés and his personal following and had not yet gained in return the backing of Mora and his Bloque de Obreros y Campesinos. The latter increased their share of the vote by over 50% i.e. from about 10,000 to over 16,000. Other smaller parties and independents polled over 20,000 votes, so the voting strength of the National Republicans was much depleted from the approximately 93,000 votes cast for their candidate two years earlier.[31] Only after 1944 was the opposition recognisable as a united and cohesive force.

In 1943, the Communists changed the name of their party to Vanguardia Popular in an endeavour to gain support from non-Communist workers. Archbishop Sanabria assisted their cause soon afterwards when he stated publicly there was nothing in the programme of Vanguardia Popular which need preclude a Catholic worker from joining and working for that party.[32] He went further and said it was the only party in Costa Rica which offered workers an opportunity to air grievances calling for redress. The Archbishop's pronouncement indicated the respectability attained by the communists at the time they decided to support the Guardia government.[33] Despite the appeal of Vanguardia Popular and of a new labour organisation, Rerum Novarum, promoted by Father Benjamin Nuñez, Guardia continued to attract support from the ranks of the workers, particularly after the publication of his Labour Code.

Thus began the run up to the election of 1944.

## NOTES TO CHAPTER 4

1. Parker, p. 259
2. Bell, p. 5; referring to Mario Sancho 'Costa Rica: Suiza Centroamericana' p. 9
3. Parker, p. 256
4. Bell, p. 21, quoting Time, Jan. 1, 1945
5. ibid, p. 20, quoting Mario Sancho 'Memorias'
6. ibid, p. 24, referring to Lawrence Duggan 'The Americans – The Search for Hemisphere Security'
7. ibid, p. 21
8. ibid, p. 16
9. ibid, p. 50
10. ibid, p. 34
11. ibid, p. 14, quoting Alberto Canãs 'Los ocho años' (the eight years).
12. ibid, p. 87
13. ibid, pp. 88/89, referring to sources, including La Tribuna
14. ibid, p. 90; referring to José Figueres Ferrer 'Palabras gastadas'
15. Parker, p. 266
16. Bell, pp. 17/18
17. ibid, p. 27
18. Parker, p. 264
19. Bell, p. 26
20. ibid, p. 43
21. ibid, p. 29
22. Parker, p. 266, quoting Arturo Castro Esquivel 'José Figueres Ferrer: el hombre y su obra' (the man and his work), San José 1955
23. Bell, p. 8
24. ibid, p. 30, quoting La Gaceta, Nov. 14, 1941
25. ibid, p. 31, quoting International Labour Review 46 (Nov. 1942)
26. ibid, p. 31
27 ibid, p. 33, quoting Arthur M. Schlesinger's 'A thousand days' and attributing the principles to President John F. Kennedy
28. ibid, pp. 64/65
29. ibid, p. 70, quoting El Social Demócrata, Nov. 22, 1947
30. ibid, pp. 71/73, referring to Surco, no. 47, May-June 1944
31. ibid, p. 110, referring to La Tribuna, Feb. 19, 1942
32. Parker, p. 264
33. Bell, p. 43, referring to International Labour Review, 50, 1944

# Chapter Five

# THE STORM CLOUDS GATHER

Costa Rica, like the United States of America, holds an election for President every four years. The Administration completes its fixed terms of office, and does not have the right to choose an auspicious moment to go to the polls, or consider whether an issue on which it has been defeated is sufficiently serious to occasion resignation – as with the British system! Along with the President was elected one half of the National Congress, the other half being elected in the mid-term elections. Calderón Guardia was ineligible under the country's Constitution, to stand for a consecutive second term and his friend, Teodoro Picado Michalski, was the candidate for the National Republican Party. That Party, having been formed as long before as 1932 with the intention, which was successful, of securing the election of Jiménez, had seen its candidates Cortés in 1936 and Guardia in 1940 sweep to victory, the latter with a vast majority. Why then should it doubt sucess in 1944? The Democratic Alliance formed in 1940 to back Jiménez, although having the support of Ulate Blanco, of whom much will be heard in the events of 1948, and Mora, had dissolved, having been to some extent crushed by the out-going President, Cortés, who used his office to make vehement assertions about the 'reds' and taint even Jiménez, a former National Republican candidate, with the label of communism.

In 1944, of course, Cortés himself had changed sides having left the National Republican Party in power to form the Democratic Party, and he was chosen to put himself forward for a second term. Mora and his Communist faction had also changed sides and now supported the National Republican candidate. It is more accurate to say that Picado was the candidate of the Bloque de la Victoria, an alliance formed to fight the election by the Vanguardia Popular and the National Republican Party, the latter being dominant so far as numbers and influence were concerned. Cortés was encouraged by additional financial support coming from many employers who opposed the Labour Code introduced by Calderón Guardia. There had been many dismissals of workers

48

immediately before the Code became law and opponents denounced it as being politically motivated and communistic. Once again Cortés maintained his allegations that the opposing party were not only dominated by communists but were communists themselves. The epithets 'caldero-communismo' and 'picado-communismo' speak for this manoeuvre,[1] which, now that the communists were backing Picado, had more validity than it bore in 1940. Mora and his group were, however, too well known in the sparsely populated country for any allegations of adherence to international communist aims to be given much credence by the majority of the people. Besides, were not the United States and the Soviet Union still allies in the common cause against Nazi Germany?

The young men in the Centro were in something of a dilemma. They posed as an apolitical group dedicated to postulating the need for social reforms and how these might be secured. Their criticism was directed not so much against Guardia's programme as against the man himself and, accordingly, against his party and Picado in the 1944 election. The urban middle classes had gained little, if any, relief from the social measures passed which were not only severely criticised by them as being politically motivated but also were to have serious political repercussions. There was even a hint at this period of an armed uprising plot but this came to nothing as it did not have the full support of the Right.[2] The subsequent political alliance of the élite, which saw its leadership rôle being diminished, with the Social Democratic Party emanating from the Centro, to spearhead the opposition to the National Republican Party was a major factor leading to the revolution of 1948.

There was a substantial amount of violence during the election campaign of 1943/4 when Opposition rallies and leaders were continually harassed. It was said that workers favourable to the Picado cause manufactured blackjacks (a type of club) in the Ministry of Public Works workshops and used them to intimidate opponents. On the Sunday before the election a demonstration was being held in San José by Cortés and his supporters. Many people were brought into the city from the surrounding country with the result that in clashes in the streets one person was killed and no less than forty-eight were injured. During the last week of the campaign Guardia, as President, actually prohibited Picado's supporters from staging any more rallies. Nevertheless the government endeavoured to ensure Picado's success by using official vehicles to transport his supporters and even allowing police to intimidate those attending Cortés' rallies.[3]

On the day of the election violence continued and four people were killed. Picado had a majority of almost 30,000 of the 137,000 votes registered. This compares with the 102,000 votes cast four years earlier; the population had increased of course. Whilst not comparable with

Calderón Guardia's phenomenal victory in 1940, it was nevertheless a substantial success and indicated the National Republican Party still enjoyed a large measure of popular esteem. In fact the Party had succeeded in securing the election of 28 delegates to Congress against 13 Democrats and 4 from Vanguardia Popular.[4] Scarcely had the election votes been counted before those who had opposed Picado alleged there had been widespread fraud and chicanery. There is no means of ascertaining whether this had been on a scale sufficient to deprive Cortés of victory but the opposition certainly asserted it had, and continued to clamour for electoral reform.[5]

Leaders of the main political parties realised the country was facing a serious political situation. Calderón Guardia left for New York where he practised medicine for some two years; Cortés advised his supporters against insurrection and refrained from active participation for some time. Picado also made attempts to quieten and pacify public anxieties by promising to introduce measures to increase fiscal integrity and to prevent dishonesty in government. The allegations of fraud had much more far-reaching effects and was the main basis upon which the parties in opposition could unite.[6] It was immediately recognised that, unless the strength of those opposing the National Republican Party could be reflected in support at the polls, there was going to be a return of Calderón Guardia as President in 1948 and that was unthinkable. Although there were serious differences – for instance while the élitist group objected to most, if not all, social reforms, which they saw as interfering with their established domination and the young men of the Centro group favoured social reforms, which they recognised as not only desirable, but equitable, for the poorer classes – they were in entire agreement in condemning Guardia as communist and charging him with fraud.

Events moved fast; within a fortnight of the election appeared a newspaper, *Acción Demócrata,* under the editorship of Alberto Martén, who had accompanied Figueres to the radio station on the night of the fateful broadcast. The paper was the voice of a newly-formed political party which devoted much of its space to building up Figueres' image. The first number carried as its editorial theme 'La Lucha sin Fin', the name of Figueres' first ranch, and went on to assert it was 'a weekly of battle, battle without end'! Succeeding numbers related the speech which had occasioned his exile, reviewed his latest publication and anticipated, and reported, his return from exile in May 1944.[7]

Later in 1944 was formed the National Union Party in order to support Otilio Ulate Blanco, the owner and publisher of *Diario de Costa Rica.* Ulate, like the young men of the Centro, had remained somewhat in the background during the 1944 elections, and he represented very much the conservative element in the country. Ulate undoubtedly had his eye upon the Presidential election of 1948 but there was much to be done before he could be a candidate with sufficient backing to present a challenge to Calderón Guardia, who still maintained a considerable public following. It was almost a year later, in March 1945, when the Acción Demócrata Party joined with the Centro to form the Social Democratic Party; this was an event of supreme importance in the political events leading to the 1948 election and the subsequent revolution. Acción Demócrata originated with a group of young activists in Cortés Democratic Party and were to the right of the Centro group.[8] The latter were more concerned with social issues and favoured a governmental programme to ensure economic and social development but the Acción Demócrata concentrated on politics and, whilst accepting the state had a role in regulating the economy, it was predominantly capitalist. It was during 1945 that a cohesive Opposition was organized consisting of Ulate's National Unionists, the Social Democrats and the Democratic Party; they prepared for the mid-term elections of 1946.[9]

The Opposition was careful not to charge the National Republican Party as a whole with being communists; in a country of less than one million inhabitants, the leaders were too well known for such an allegation to bear credibility. Instead they concentrated upon attacking Calderón Guardia in an attempt to minimise his popularity amongst the non-communist workers and emphasised his apparent subservience to, and reliance upon, the support of Mora and his fellow-communists in Congress to carry through his programme. It was convenient at this time to overlook the considerable contribution made by the communists in educating and leading the working classes to secure improvements in their working conditions – to which even Ulate had paid testimony before he became violently anti-communist.[10]

Following the ending of World War in 1945, the Opposition benefited considerably as the coalition between the United States and other Western democracies and the Soviet Union for the purpose of prosecuting the struggle against Nazi Germany degenerated into the 'Cold War'. Costa Rica was closely identified with the USA and, as the fear of communism grew, the Opposition were able to identify their cause with that of the country's powerful ally. It was not difficult to represent communism as threatening the traditional Costa Rican way of life of the small farmer and to spread what amounted to hysterical anti-communism, oblivious of the fact that large scale farming had been the factor most threatening such tradition. It was possible to represent Mora and his party as an alien movement and a threat to the Catholic religion, which the majority of Costa Ricans profess.[11] Mora had always argued that, because the Communists were able to participate in the democratic processes prevailing in Costa Rica, there was no need for violent revolution as they could institute a peaceful transformation of the system.

The Vanguardia Popular had, however, resorted to violence during the 1944 election and this provided the newly formed Opposition with the opportunity and excuse to follow similar tactics. The population had become somewhat accustomed to political violence and the Opposition were able to use terrorist tactics without general condemnation. It is well said that 'violence breeds violence'. The Opposition attempted to brand the government of the National Republican Party as a dictatorship and even compared it with the detestable regimes of Somoza in Nicaragua and Trujilo in the Dominican Republic. This exposed the weakness of their case as there was in fact freedom to a degree unusual in Latin American: newspapers even printed personal attacks upon the President, the Courts maintained their independence, there were rights of organisation and assembly, no secret police, no arbitrary arrests and no political prisoners. Only Figueres had been exiled in over 25 years and he was away only two years. There was no conscription and a small military force led by non-professional officers could hardly maintain in power even a semblance of dictatorship.[12]

President Picado was only too conscious of the need for electoral reform, the demand for which came from all sides, including the communists who had a self-interest, realising their co-operation with the National Republicans was not likely to last indefinitely. In 1945 Picado's draft code was received acceptably by all parties and, although approved late in that year, it was not possible to put it into effect for the 1946 mid-term elections. Picado however, used the new code as a guide and there were few disputes. In one instance at the request of the Opposition, the President decreed a re-election in one district. His endeavours received favourable comment – even from the Acción Demócrata.[13]

The movement away from the National Republicans continued, not to be unexpected after their gigantic success in 1940, but in the mid-term election of 1946 they still held about 50% of the vote and elected eleven of their candidates. The Opposition were able to record success for ten of their number but, as Vanguardia Popoular had two successes, the government could still claim it had a majority of popular support.[14]

Immediately after the elections Cortés approached Picado in an endeavour to persuade him to break the alliance between the National Republican Party and Vanguardia Popular and assured him not merely of his personal support but also of ample backing from the business community. Perhaps there might have been a very different story to tell had not Cortés died early in March. Discussions continued between leaders of the Democratic Party and Picado along with Calderón Guardia's brother, and Ulate also made approaches to Picado. The talks were of no avail and only served to cause recriminations between members of the Opposition. Figueres and the Social Democrats were totally against any suggestion of a compromise with the government; for them it was not a simple political issue; the regime was 'bad' and had to be obliterated completely.[15] The attempts to seek a compromise were in accordance with the spirit of democracy and tradition long enjoyed by Costa Rica. Although there was some talk of revolution, Picado did not believe this would be possible nor did he believe the Opposition nor anyone else seriously advocated it.

In an endeavour to embarrass the government more seriously, the Opposition boycotted the sessions of the Congress in an endeavour to cause a lack of the required quorum. The effect was to cause the National Republicans to rely even more heavily upon the members of Vanguardia Popular. The Opposition newspapers now intensified their propaganda against the communists even to the extent of publishing 'open letters' to the people of the United States (there is a considerable US colony in Costa Rica) and the US Ambassador warning of the serious threat of Costa Rica becoming communist. The international situation was identified with the domestic situation; the 'good' people were the USA and its allies; the 'bad' were the Soviet Union and its associates. Accordingly the 'bad' people in Costa Rica were the members of the Government and the 'good' those of the Opposition. It was even argued that the 'bad' Costa Ricans no longer should enjoy their rights to the democratic institutions of the country and that the 'vanguardistas' were not entitled to be treated with reason or decency. Thus the political scene degenerated.

Towards the end of 1946 Picado introduced a measure to tax incomes; this induced the Opposition to end its boycott of Congress in order to promote every effort to oppose the proposition. This was indeed a bold step for Picado to take when one considers the effects such a proposal had had on previous régimes. As early as 1917 President Flores had introduced such a measure, which substantially caused the coup by Tinoco. Jiménez was a most popular President, but he did not continue with his income tax proposal in 1924, although backed by a 'Reform' Party. Cortés during his term of office (1936-40) commisioned an expert from Chile to draw up a law which was placed before Congress, but Cortés very speedily withdrew it. In 1946 the majority of the Opposition leaders bitterly objected to a direct tax on income and property. So Social Democrats found themselves in a dilemma. They had espoused a socialist ideology which included preference for direct as against indirect taxation. They managed to reconcile their position by claiming the Picado government was using the bill to obscure real issues and endeavouring to stave off impending bankruptcy threatened by its progressive activities.

They remained united in opposition! There was much public debate both in favour of and against the proposed tax which, despite the strenuous efforts of the Opposition, was carried by Congress which, of course, the National Republicans still controlled. When the measure was passed, the Opposition quickly recognised it had wide support and accordingly they reverted to their allegations of graft and fiscal mismanagement on the part of the governing party.[16]

Mora gave the Opposition another excellent opportunity to intensify its propaganda when he organised demonstrations against United States for giving aid to Greece and Turkey.[17] In the light of the 'Cold war' climate then existing these actions enabled political opponents of the government to increase their endeavours to discredit it. Ambassadors representing the United States in Costa Rica had been changed so that one believed to be favourable to Guardia was replaced, and an expert in Communist affairs was subsequently appointed. Picado even considered breaking the alliance with Vanguardia Popular but could not ensure adequate support from the capitalist sector which had, understandably, been opposed to his taxation reform.

In Feburary 1947 the Opposition held a Convention with the intention of agreeing upon a single candidate whom all could accept in the election of a President to take place a year later. Otilio Ulate, José Figueres and Fernando Castro were put forward by their respective groups and the former was successful when, on a third ballot, students and young intellectuals who had supported Figueres switched their votes.[18] Perhaps this again demonstrates the Costa Ricans' love of, and tradition for, democratic procedures and institutions when, despite Figueres' dynamic and intensive campaign against the government, he still could not inspire with his talk of 'revolution' enough of the young who were disillusioned with the 'old guard' to give him their support as candidate for the Presidency. Ulate responded by appointing Figueres to be his campaign manager.

The National Republican Party immediately held their convention in which they purported to invite the public to participate and help choose their candidate; in effect, the object was to seek confirmation of, and support for, Calderón Guardia, who had already been selected. Even at this late stage further efforts were made by the National Republicans to reach a compromise with the Opposition. Guardia offered to withdraw if the Opposition would offer someone as a candidate who would be acceptable to him. Although Ulate's newspaper carried a report of the possible compromise, Ulate denied he knew of it. The Social Democrats would have none of any such compromise and, despite the efforts of some members of the alliance, the views of the younger men prevailed.[19]

In the early months of 1947, Ulate carried on an intensive campaign to discredit Calderón Guardia alleging constantly that he was a communist. He encouraged others to join this campaign, one example being the senior employees of the United Fruit Company who paid for a two page advertisement in the *Diario de Costa Rica* stating

'For the Salvation of Costa Rica'
'Calderón is a Communist'
'The Opposition will accede to Power'[20]

Guardia retorted he was not, never had been and never would be a Communist and reminded Ulate he had approved of Mora in the past. Guardia could not, of course, deny he had accepted the help of Mora's party in carrying through his social reform programme nor the political alliance which had helped to elect Picado in 1944. Calderón Guardia later in the year tried to turn the tables on Ulate by representing him as one who was seeking to involve the United States and implicate Costa Rica in the international confrontation instead of treating Costa Ricans as being capable of deciding their own future. It is not, however, without significance that the alliance of the National Republican Party with Vanguardia Popular, which had been so successful in 1940, was not renewed in the 1947-8 campaign. This was just as well, as in October 1947 the communist party issued an official declaration of adherence to the Comintern and coupled this with an attack on the United States. Much was made of this by the Opposition even to the extent of pressing for a special session of Congress to declare the Vanguardia Popular outlawed.[21] President Picado continued to display his moderate approach to this as to other political problems and pointed out that in Costa Rica all political parties enjoyed equal legal protection. Such a procedure would have been unconstitutional in any case. Allegations were then made that Picado would not act against the communists as he owed his position to their support and Ulate joined in by using his paper to ask the direct question 'Is the government pro-Soviet?'. He was very careful to observe that, if he were elected President, the Communist Party would have complete freedom – but not special consideration as afforded them by Picado. The issue continued to be used against both parties and Calderón Guardia and to allege against the latter participation in an international conspiracy, as though his previous alliance with Mora threatened the whole continent. The distortions were such that a relatively placid democratic nation was being changed into one where hysteria, fear and violence prevailed. There were even attempts to assassinate both Calderón Guardia and Manuel Mora.[22]

It was still hoped there would be a fair election under the terms of the new Electoral Code which established an Electoral Tribunal, consisting of three leading citizens chosen by the three branches of government and a substitute selected by Congress. At first, all political parties agreed the men nominated inspired confidence and that the election was going to be a fair contest. The Social Democrats, together with Ulate, later continually questioned that the election could be fair and that the Electoral Code was adequate. After threatening to resign unless the government established conditions necessary to ensure a free election, the Tribunal secured concessions and more financial support than any government had previously sanctioned. Guzmán, the nominee of Picado to the Electoral Tribunal, ascertained not only that, at the Civil Registry, the applications of the National Republicans' supporters were receiving priority, but also there was evidence of fraud on their part. Conversely, the office of the Electoral Registry was under the direction of Benjamin Odio, a known supporter of José Figueres.[23]

And what of the firebrand Figueres? What had been his activities during these turbulent years? He returned from exile on the 23rd of May 1944 and was acclaimed at a rally organised by his friends. He immediately established his ideas on the future of Costa Rica when he spoke from the balcony of Ulate's newspaper building. He attacked Calderón Guardia and his party as not respecting the right of suffrage, compared the plight of Costa Rica with that of occupied France, asserted that political action would not bring about a transfer of power and that the only way to oust the government was by military action. He repeated his demand for the establishment of a Second Republic. This theme and his plea for 'Battle (or 'Struggle') without End' (the name he had given to his ranch) were repeated in succeeding days as he undertook an extensive speaking tour in the country; the first task, he reiterated, was to overthrow the government and existing institutions. He was supported by the Acción Demócrata which reported his speeches and his appeal to the youth of the country. His plain call to arms was reported in several editions as follows:

> 'It is not behind a desk that the Allies fight for democracy. It is with their hands on a rifle and in battle to the death with the enemy. It is not in family conversations or in comfortable discussion groups that we have to save our Fatherland. Co-operate in this decisive battle.'[24]

Despite this, and identifying the government with neighbouring dictatorships, as well as urging the youth of Costa Rica to emulate the struggles of students and others to overturn those dictatorships, Figueres was not again exiled nor even arrested. No doubt Picado and his Party believed the traditional democratic base of the Costa Rica nation was sufficiently sound to enable such vituperation to be ignored, but where else in the world but in Costa Rica could such excesses have been tolerated? Figueres was a member of various groups with the object of achieving his revolution and he gathered around himself in the newly formed Social Democratic party a small terrorist faction. The Social Democrats' position within the Opposition was not unlike that of the communists in the government; influence but not power. Their manifesto clearly indicated their objective in the words:

> 'the party organises and arms itself not for a battle but for a war. In the ultimate combat we will triumph and we will renew the Fatherland to its very roots.'[25]

They had realised their only hope of achieving power was by an armed uprising.

The first attempt came about four months after the mid-term elections of February 1946. In this Figueres took no part and considered it misconceived. It depended largely upon the help of some Nicaraguan mercenaries but their support failed to materialise. The government captured about 200 prisoners and considerable quantities of arms and ammunition. Picado saw that the rebels were freed; he still believed the traditional Costa Rican *ambiente* would be adequate to resolve the critical issues.[26] Figueres and his group feared the possibility of some compromise being attained between the government and the Opposition; there had already been the talks between Cortés, Ulate and others with the leaders of the National Republican Party. He stressed to his supporters the need to work in three chief directions. Firstly, because most of the Opposition still believed in the efficacy of elections, political activity had to continue, but the idea of the futility of elections and the need for revolution had to be inculcated. Secondly Figueres' small groups were to dedicate themselves to terrorist and propaganda methods and accuse the government of dictatorial and militaristic practices when it responded. Thirdly, contact had to be strengthened with the Caribbean faction dedicated to the overthrow of dictatorships in the area, so that trained professional military men and an adequate supply of arms would assist the revolutionary campaign.[27]

Violence escalated; Mora's house was partially destroyed by an explosion and there were the attempts to assassinate both Mora and Calderón Guardia. Gangs of youths calling themselves 'the resistance', in response to the comparisons made with occupied France, attacked not only communists and members of the National Republican Party but also the police. In early May 1947 workers returning to Cartago from a celebration in San José were stoned by a large group of youths and this led to an exchange of shots following an attack on the Vanguardia Popular

Club. There were serious differences in the police hierarchy and the chief, who favoured the youths, was forced to resign. Reinforcements were brought from San José which enabled the opposition to inflame still further local pride and resolution. In July there was open rebellion in Cartago and a virtual battle between the police and the 'resistance'; two were killed and about fifteen wounded. This led to a general strike (the strike of 'fallen arms' in which very large numbers joined)[29] and hopes were entertained that this would be successful in bringing down the government as had been the case only a few years earlier in both Guatemala and El Salvador. Figueres even attempted to obtain a supply of arms from his Caribbean connections but only a small quantity was received. More violence erupted in San José a few days later when workers from the coasts arrived to take part in demonstrations supporting the government and the communists; some businesses were attacked for taking part in the general strike. The government interpreted the strike as a prelude to an armed rebellion and took extreme measures to have the streets patrolled by police and the military. Early in August a body of women marched to the palace of the President to petition him to guarantee that the elections would be free. Instead of receiving them, Picado had them dispersed by force, which did more to discredit the government.[28]

These events, however, led to the government, the official party and the Opposition reaching agreement and accepting the demands of the strikers: a 'Pact of Honour' was entered into. This not only placed the police under the National Electoral Tribunal for any matter pertaining to the election and guaranteed free elections but also stipulated that during the last week of the campaign there was to be no public political activity by anyone, that in this period the Electoral Tribunal would be in charge of the electoral process, and its decision as to the result of the election would be accepted.[29] Sadly the violence continued after August 1947 as the terrorist group intensified its efforts and government supporters retaliated. Figueres, realising he had not been able to achieve a successful general strike, pressed his claim to arms with President Arévalo of Guatemala, under whose control was an arsenal ostensibly belonging to a group of Dominican rebels. Arévalo's intention was to have the arms used to overthrow dictatorships in the area and establish a Central American Union. Figueres was able to convince him the battle should commence in Costa Rica and in December 1947 they signed, along with other exiled leaders, the Pact of the Caribbean. Men and arms were now likely to be available to Figueres when he decided the moment for revolution was propitious.[30]

# NOTES TO CHAPTER 5

1. Bell, p. 111
2. ibid, p. 39
3. ibid, p. 112
4. Parker, p. 265
5. Bell, p. 112, expresses the view Cortés most probably was defrauded of victory
6. ibid, p. 113
7. ibid, p. 93
8. ibid, p. 84
9. ibid, p. 37
10. ibid, p. 50, quoting *Acción Demócrata*, Apl 26, 1947
11. ibid, p. 47, referring to Mario Sancho '*Memorias*'
12. ibid, p. 114
13. ibid, p. 116, quoting *La Nación*, Feb. 20, 1946 and *Acción Demócrata*, Feb. 16, 1946

14. ibid, p. 116
15. ibid, p. 118
16. ibid, p. 76/77
17. ibid, p. 55
18. ibid, p. 119
19. ibid, p. 120
20. ibid, p. 57
21. ibid, p. 59, referring to *La Nacion*, Oct. 28, 1947
22. ibid, p. 58
23. ibid, p. 122
24. ibid, p. 94, quoting Acción Demócratia, Dec. 16, 1944
25. ibid, p. 96, quoting Acción Demócrata, Feb. 3, 1945

26. ibid, p. 97
27. ibid, pp. 97/8, considers the first objective was successful when the opposition diverted part of their campaign funds to Figueres to prepare the revolution and when the latter was accomplished under cover of the chaotic electoral situation in March 1948
28. ibid, pp. 99/103
29. Parker, p. 267 and Bell, pp. 103/104
30. Bell, p. 105

# Chapter Six

# THE STORM BREAKS

In Costa Rica it had long been resolved that the only legitimate means to power was by election based on universal manhood suffrage. (As in Switzerland, with which Costa Ricans often compare themselves, there was no vote for women in 1948.) Professor Bell refers to Charles W. Anderson's *Politics and Economic Change in Latin America* where, on pages 108/9, the question of governmental legitimacy is discussed and Costa Rica is stated to be one of the few exceptions in that only an electoral victory gives an accepted claim to office.[1]

There is little doubt that the success of Ulate Blanco in the election of 1948 very considerably, and probably materially, enhanced Figueres' success in promoting his revolution. He was, therefore, able to attract and secure popular support, which would otherwise have been denied him, had he not been able to claim his cause embraced Costa Rica's long adherence to the democratic process.

Whilst elections invariably caused great activity and almost a year of preparation, there was always such mutual recrimination; the events leading up to that of 1948 greatly accentuated the antagonism. Each party accused the other of seeking to prevent the free expression of the people. Whilst the Opposition continued to allege the Government had perpetrated frauds in the elections of 1942, 1944 and 1946, the Governing party responded that the Opposition was trying to divert public attention from the real issue, i.e. the social question, and that the allegations of fraud had never been substantiated.[2] The campaign was fervent and stormy. Calderón Guardia had the backing of the governing party and the army and also had access to large campaign funds. The programme of Ulate and the united Opposition parties was hampered by lack of money but Ulate, well known as the publisher of the newspaper *Diario de Costa Rica*, was widely respected and popular.[3]

Surprisingly, the election held on Sunday, 8th February 1948, was peaceful enough on the whole, although there had been serious difficulties because of the new Electoral Code. Sufficient differences were discovered between the registers and the voters' identity cards that, during the afternoon of polling day, the Tribunal felt obliged to dispatch telegrams to the polling stations instructing relaxation of the regulations so that all citizens producing identity cards should be allowed to vote. The telegraph offices were unable to handle such a great number and many of the outlying districts did not receive theirs until after the poll had closed. The Opposition tried to prevent opponents from voting by advising their supporters to vote in the morning but to return again in the afternoon and impede those in the queues waiting to register their votes.[4] The tactic was perhaps more successful than at first admitted, as the number of votes cast, as will be seen, was less than in any election since 1936; hardly credible. Unofficial returns at the end of the day indicated Ulate had won the Presidential election by a margin of around 10,000 votes.[5]

The Electoral Tribunal was required by the new Code to scrutinise the whole voting process not merely to recount the totals sent in from the districts and to make a provisional declaration on February 25th. A special session of Congress was convened for 1st March to make the final declaration of the result. The National Republicans came to the conclusion there had been serious frauds in the electoral process and that the President's anxiety to ensure there was no repetition of the frauds alleged to have been made by the National Republicans in 1944 had resulted in a reversal for their party. Were they annoyed to find they had been beaten at their own game? René Picado, Public Safety Officer and brother of the President, had said at the close of the election he believed it had been fair and free; he reversed his opinion the following day. Calderón Guardia had prepared a statement acknowledging defeat, but was persuaded not to publish it by some of his supporters who claimed there had been massive frauds. There were certainly ample grounds for suspicion as, despite a rapidly growing population and greater interest occasioned by the parties' campaigns, the total of votes registered was much reduced, being particularly so in the areas where the government and Vanguardia Popular were strongest. There were complaints in many districts that supporters of those two parties had been deprived of the franchise because of purely technical reasons but the Electoral Tribunal declined to consider the charges of fraud made by the National Republican Party.[6]

The work of the Tribunal proceeded slowly and it was soon obvious they were not going to be in a position to make the required declaration on the 25th February. Their work was further impeded by demonstrations outside their office and there were times when they might have been personally attacked. It has been suggested the Tribunal was hoping the parties would come to some agreement which would have the effect of satisfying public opinion and reducing the tension but the public regarded the declaration by the Tribunal as essential and final. It was during this period that Odio, director of the Electoral Registry, departed to join Figueres. He became an officer in the Revolutionary army and later a Minister in the Figueres' administration. Attacks were made upon his impartiality which were strenuously defended, but it would seem he should have informed the public of the difficulties he was finding in his work at the Electoral Registry.[7]

Demonstrations by 'calderonistas' claiming they had been denied their right to vote reached almost riot conditions. Guardia was considering the possibility of reaching some agreement with Ulate, perhaps leading to neither of them being President and relinquishing their claims in favour of someone less controversial. Although at first Ulate had indicated his willingness to enter into discussions with a view to reaching a compromise, he announced in his newspaper on February 18th he was no longer prepared to do so. As the National Republicans still held a majority in the Congress and it was known a majority of the army officers favoured them, the voices of moderation were ignored; the Congress could, if the majority so decided, over-ride the announcement by the Tribunal. By the 25th February it was understood the Tribunal had only been able to examine one-third of the votes cast; they were further impeded in their decision by some of the voting materials being burned but it was never ascertained who had done this. In order to comply with the Electoral Code, the Tribunal officially closed their scrutiny of the votes and declared themselves in secret session.[8]

At length a provisional declaration was made on February 28th by two members of the Tribunal, the third member, Koberg Bolandi, withheld his opinion as he considered the count incomplete. It is interesting to note that Koberg was the nominee of Congress, and the other two, José Maria Vargas and Gerardo Guzmán had been appointed to the Tribunal by the Supreme Court and President Picado respectively. It is understood the provisional declaration was made largely on the basis of the count of the votes submitted by telegrams from the many polling stations. As the count had been carried out by the *fiscales* (which may be translated as 'district attorneys') of the Unión Nacional[9] (Ulate's Party) it is not to be wondered at that the National Republicans were sceptical. The declaration showed that Ulate was credited with 54,931 votes against 44,438 for Calderón Guardia. The total being less than 100,000 compared with the 102,000 of 1940 and over 137,000 in 1944; well might there be complaints of interference with voters and allegations of fraudulent practices. Despite the delay by the Tribunal in issuing its provisional declaration there had not been sufficient time for consultations to take place between the parties, even if they had been in the mood to consider any such. On the one hand, Ulate (having announced in his *Diario de Costa Rica* on February 18 that he would no longer even discuss a compromise) pointed to his victory at the polls and claimed the Presidency as being rightfully his, whilst Guardia regarded the apparent frauds of the Opposition and the manner in which the Tribunal had counted the votes, as justifying his claim that the election was not a genuine one.

On March 1st Congress met to consider the Tribunal's decision and proclaim officially the result. *La Nación*, now the country's foremost newspaper, carried this report on its front page the following day:

## CONGRESS ANNULLED THE PRESIDENTIAL ELECTION BY 27 – 19

We are going to make a brief resumé of the historic and momentous session yesterday in the Legislative Assembly. We are not going to reconstruct the speeches of the National Opposition deputies since the noise of the procedings on the benches did not allow the resounding speeches of the deputies to be heard – Lawyers Don Fernando Volio Sancho, Fernando Lara Bustamente and Otto Cortes Fernandez.

We had understood the session would proceed without barracking and that had been agreed, but the result was that it proceeded without Opposition barracking. Deputy Volio Sancho spoke for about an hour defying the insults and threats of the barrackers. His speech, which the public heard over the radio, has been greeted with warm congratulations, as was the case with Bustamente's.

### BEFORE THE SESSION BEGAN

Hours before the Session began, the Congress building was completely filled by the communist and calderón forces, backed by the military. 15 minutes before 2 p.m. the group of deputies composing the Opposition party arrived and soon afterwards came the vanguardista section. The representatives of the Republicano Nacional were arriving one by one. General René Picado arrived at 2.15, accompanied by his general staff. The barrackers applauded them, just as they did those of the official party.

### THE SESSION OPENS

Successively were read the agreement of the Executive Power convening the Assembly to have cognizance of the elections and the provisional declaration of the National Electoral Tribunal, together with the explanation of the vote of Señor Koberg Bolandi.[10]

The Majority report was discussed and it was Resolved:
Article 1.
Through various defects of the poll affecting the legitimacy of the popular Juntas convened to elect the President of the Republic on 8th February last, the vote taken on that date to elect the numerous officials is declared null, and in consequence the provisional declaration which, by simple majority, the National Electoral Tribunal took, is null and void.
(Then followed the names of the delegates voting for and against).

## MOTION IN THE NAME OF CUBILLO
to hold elections again.
Deputy Alvaro Cubillo sought to explain his vote on the report, declaring that he voted as he did (in favour) so that there should be new elections and he drew up a motion in that respect. But his initiative was rejected, only Sr. Cubillo voting for it. The session was closed.

## SO WHAT FOLLOWS NOW?
Everyone will be wondering after this decision on the conduct of the election procedure given by Congress – so what follows now? And the question arises all the more urgently as armed incidents follow each other and unprecedented unrest reigns throughout the country.

This parliamentary news item, like others in the same edition of the paper, has been restricted to limits set by the circumstances.

We greatly fear that these circumstances will worsen to such an extent that we shall find ourselves obliged to suspend publication.

The last were prophetic words indeed; it is unlikely *La Nación* knew any better than anyone else the course events were to take, and during the next two weeks endeavours were made to avert a catastrophe. They might have been sucessful: but the moderates of both sides were no longer being listened to, and, despite the obvious weakness of their position, the pro-government forces believed they had the strength necessary to prevail. It seems their intention was to let matters lie in abeyance until May 1st when the new Congress would assemble: on which occasion they would elect Calderón Guardia as first designate to the presidency and, in the absence of anyone having been declared elected President, he would serve for a term of four years. There is no doubt however, that by not recognising the Tribunal's verdict, as they had agreed in August 1947 when they signed the Pact of Honour, the National Republicans not only

64

lost a great deal of sympathy and support in the nation but also the people were incensed by their disregard of the democratic processes to which the nation was accustomed. Neither was their cause assisted by attacks made upon the three members of the Electoral Tribunal, nor the subsequent resignations of the two who had made the provisional declaration. Koberg Bolandi telegraphed the President on 29th February seeking protection for the other two and on 2nd March *La Nación* printed a copy of his telegram along with a statement by him urging that offences should not multiply.

On the same day the newspaper carried a report that two deputies had been forcibly prevented by official forces from attending the session of Congress on March 1st. Another of the deputies repeated the condemnation he had pronounced in the Congress and described the act as 'more barbarous and savage than anything we Costa Ricans are accustomed to'.

Great as was the political blunder by Calderón Guardia and his party in refusing to accept the decision of the Tribunal, it seems to have been exceeded by the events leading up to the arrest of Ulate. The following account is taken from copies of telegrams sent by the USA Ambassador to his Secretary of State.

'Two hours before Congress met on March 1st, some fifty uniformed troops and police with armoured vehicles, machine guns and rifles surrounded house of Dr Carlos Luis Valverde, prominent oppositionist where it is well known Ulate has been staying. House riddled with bullets; Valverde seriously wounded, one other slightly. Ulate and several companions have presumably taken refuge in a neighbouring house. Entire area surrounded by police and irregulars with imminent possibility further bloodshed unless some means worked out remove him to refuge in Archbishop's palace or friendly legation. Understand Archbishop actively endeavouring effect such arrangement.

Official version Ulate opened fire on police who had come to search for arms. I witnessed preparations for attack and some firing but did not see who shot first.

Valverde taken to hospital in critical condition. At urgent request hospital surgeon I appealed to President permit Red Cross ambulance and personnel evacuate other wounded. Permission granted no wounded found but two government dead in street.'

After referring to an offer from the Brazil Legation of asylum for Ulate, that a radio broadcast stated the President had decreed the closing of banks for two days and the press threatened suspension if opposition called general strikes, the telegram continued

### 'FOLLOWING FACTS CLEAR

(1) uniformed government troops under command Major Tavio [Minister of Public Security] with overwhelming force surrounded and fired into house where Ulate publicly known to be
(2) despite predictions press radio no suspension of guarantees had been decreed and Calderonista version does not claim troops had search warrant
(3) attack occurred during Congress debate and before vote while galleries patio and street filled with Calderonista crowd demonstrating for annulling election;
(4) a prominent citizen seriously wounded perhaps killed by government troops under order

### FOLLOWING UNDETERMINED

(1) whether police intended search for illegal arms as alleged
(2) who fired first shot
(3) whether Tavio had orders from superiors or acted on own responsibility. Of significance is that he or his men obeyed order from President to pass ambulance.'

The account given by Professor Bell in his book *Crisis in Costa Rica* varies but slightly. This account says Tavio, the Cuban born chief of police, who had less scruples about using force against Costa Rican nationals, was acting without authorisation and against the expressed wishes of René Picado. Figueres had left the house shortly before the police arrived. The two policemen were killed as they climbed over the garden wall. Valverde was shot as he stood at his front door signalling for the firing to cease.[11] Ulate escaped to a neighbouring house but was captured next day and imprisoned.

A second telegram from the US Ambassador at 5 p.m. on the 2nd March expresses anxiety for the safety of American citizens in the area as René Picado had threatened to open artillery fire if Ulate did not surrender. He also reported most business houses were shut, there had been some bombings in neighbouring towns and some air flights were suspended.

Telegrams from the same source the following day indicated Ulate and his party had agreed to surrender and be taken to the artillery barracks under protected escort in preference to going to the Venezuelan Legation which had offered refuge. At midnight 2nd March the Archbishop had contacted the US Ambassador urgently saying the President had decreed Ulate only was to be immediately released at which the Archbishop had protested saying to release Ulate alone and unarmed at night invited assassination. Was that the President's purpose? The Ambassador had gone with the Archbishop to the President, and they were assured Ulate would remain in the barracks until next morning.

*La Nación* on 4th March announced in letters three inches high for Otilio Ulate's name, that he and his six companions had been released unconditionally the previous day at 12.30 p.m. (proceedings having been taken under the Law of Habeas Corpus). The Ambassador's telegram at 4 p.m. on March 3rd indicated they had all made statements before a civil judge and then been accompanied by the Archbishop, the Ambassador and some of Ulate's friends to his house where they were cheered by the crowd which had assembled. Although a few calderonistas were present and cheering for their candidate there were no disturbances. The Ambassador also reported he had been told later by the Archbishop that the opposition had agreed not to call a strike and that Congress was to be summoned on 4th March when both parties would agree to a mutually satisfactory President.

Immediately after he had reached home safely, Ulate left for the Hospital where his friend, Dr Valverde Vega lay dying. *La Nación* later showed picutres of 'thousands and thousands' of people queueing to pass by the coffin and pay their homage to the 'illustrious departed'. There is no doubt Dr Valverde Vega was held in high respect and his death in the circumstances in which it was caused did a great deal to reduce popular support for the National Republicans and further increased Figueres' adherents in the struggle which followed. In addition to the many pictures concerning the incident, the homage and the funeral, there were testimonies paid, resignations of medical personnel and a widespread condemnation of the assassination.[12]

The situation deteriorated rapidly: there was almost complete commercial paralysis, many shops being boarded up in San José and many shopkeepers working on credit (the Banks were closed) could not keep that up for long. An attack on the electricity power plant occasioned considerable damage which the Company said could cause a suspension of current for several months. The Court had to remind the prison authorities they must allow lawyers to see their clients without being obstructed in any way. The printing in the newspapers of a message from the University Student Council that the country was living in the climate of dictatorship and that the security of the citizen was in conflict with international communism, resulted in the military occupying the University building, at which the Rector published a vehement protest.

Meanwhile the Archbishop of San José, Dr Victor Sanabria, made renewed efforts to try to get the political parties to reach agreement. It was now recognised that the riot and ferment could escalate into civil war.

Ulate was prevailed upon to delay reading a message he proposed to deliver to the nation and the Archbishop asked radio broadcasters to abstain from broadcasting inflammatory comments – for twelve hours! The newspapers reported this was done on the supposition a decision would be reached but there were no indications to encourage any hopes. Legally a second election could have been required under the provisions of the Electoral Code but on 2nd March in *La Nación*, Lawyer Zúñiga, general manager of the Electoral Roll, had published a letter he had written to the Secretaries of Congress in which he expounded the difficulties faced in correcting and bringing the Roll up to date and maintained this could not possibly be accomplished in the space of a few months. It was clearly quite impossible to organise and carry out another election before Congress was due to meet for its next session commencing 1st May.

The proposal by the Archbishop that the controversy should be submitted to arbitration by him as Head of the Church in Costa Rica was accepted by Ulate but not by the National Republican Party. *La Nación* in its edition of March 6th carried a detailed report of the attempts made by the Archbishop; the proposal he had made and a counter proposal by Ulate: Mora had sought and had a private interview with the Archbishop after Ulate and his friends had asked for more time. After waiting all night an unknown person had given the Archbishop a memorandum from the National Republicans and Vanguardia Popular declining his proposal, which had by then been accepted by Ulate, whereupon the Archbishop said he would cease his efforts. The newspapers printed a declaration from Ulate saying he was willing for the Archbishop to mediate and accepted his proposal that propaganda should cease; also a memorandum from Mora saying, if the parties did not really want to spill unnecessary blood, they should attune their minds and appoint a Commission with representatives of the Political parties under the presidency of the Archbishop, which should produce an acceptable solution within 48 hours. A memorandum from the National Republican Party considered any effort was justified which prevented civil war but the formula of arbitration could not be accepted without consulting the Party's deputies and that was not possible in a short time.

The situation was confused – or there were changes of mind – as, on 5th March, the US Ambassador had telegraphed to his Secretary of State that the Calderón-Vanguardia group was definitely known not to be averse to a compromise, but it was Ulate and those surrounding him who remained adamant, believing that by biding their time they could eventually achieve their objective.

On the 7th March *La Nación* carried in headlines on its front page

THE ARCHBISHOP WITH GREAT PRUDENCE AND WISDOM OBTAINED THE
TOTAL SUSPENSION OF POLITICAL PUBLICATIONS AND PROPAGANDA.

This was based on a declaration made by the President, which went on to state that the Association of Bankers had joined with the Archbishop in an endeavour to secure the continuation of the negotiations. The Bankers had met from 9 a.m. until 10 p.m. and had produced a memorandum which they sent to the President urging the heads of the parties for the sake of the peace of the country, to continue negotiations. Ulate and Guardia indicated they had agreed.

The headlines on 10th March announced that the negotiations were on a good footing and that rumours circulating the previous day that hopes of reconciliation had been abandoned were unfounded. The truce arranged earlier was to be prolonged; the banks remained shut. The Bankers Association had been in continuous session all day Monday (8th March), through the night until 7 p.m. on the Tuesday evening. Various suggestions had been forthcoming and had been communicated to the two Presidential candidates. The news on the 11th March was that it looked as though an acceptable formula had been reached and, if not altered, it could be a solution. Calderón Guardia had made a hopeful response but the paper contained no mention of Ulate. There were large headlines on the 12th March to announce that negotiations were to follow directly between the two Parties. Three delegates from each Party were to begin conversations that same day in order to decide how agreed plans already well advanced could be executed. If a formula were agreed, the Banks would open next day (Saturday) and remain open on the Sunday.

They had reckoned without José Figueres; it will be noticed there had been no mention of him since he escaped just before Dr Valverde Vega was assassinated. He had taken no part apparently in the negotiations and had been at his ranch where he had been joined by his band of revolutionaries and others sympathetic to his cause. *La Nación* on Saturday, 13th March, had in almost four inch letters EXPLOSION! It reported a revolutionary movement had started in the region south of San José (where Figueres' ranch was situated) and there were risings in four other areas. There had been fighting on the Pan-American Highway with dead and wounded on both sides. The Government was sending reinforcements in order to control the situation; the radio stations of the Opposition had been closed and many opposition elements detained throughout the Republic. The paper was careful to point out the information was exclusively from official sources as it had been unable as yet to receive bulletins or establish contact with revolutionary forces!

'Guarantees were suspended', meaning, presumably, a declaration of martial law, by the Executive Power.

The inside pages contained reports of rumours that a group of men from Figueres' *finca* (ranch) had taken up arms and moved out to block the Pan American Highway; that three Taca planes had been detained by the police and fighting had broken out between passengers and the authorites as the planes were carrying arms for Figueres. (These three planes were probably the three seized by Figueres' men and sent to Guatemala to pick up men, arms and ammunition, making nineteen flights for this purpose.)[13] United States personnel working on the Highway reported armed persons had taken tractors and other heavy machinery being used there and, when an army detachment had been sent to restore the vehicles, it had been fired on as it reached a barricade and five men were wounded. It is interesting that in the same issue appeared a displayed paragraph by Dr Valverde's widow criticising the irresponsible authorities of the calderón-communists who had caused the assassination of her husband, thanking those who had sent commiseration and those who were fighting to rid the country of Calderónes, Picados and Tavíos.

During the conditions of abnormality, the newspaper announced, it would be circulated at mid-day; it was not published again until the 23rd of April!

The refusal by the National Republicans to accept the decision of the Electoral Tribunal, especially after specifically agreeing to do so in the previous August when the Electoral Code was signed, the arrest of Ulate and senior, influential members of Unión Nacional and perhaps, most significant of all, the blatant assassination by Government forces of Dr Valverde Vega, gave Figueres' revolutionary stance the essence of acceptance and support, if not respectability, by many who had previously had grave doubts. This only serves to confirm the Costa Ricans' general adherence to democratic ideals and their desire to resolve political, and indeed international, differences in an orderly manner. As will be seen, there were even further attempts at compromise and the principal opponents reached agreement even whilst the fighting was taking place. It was the attempt by the National Republicans to retain power by all means possible that vindicated Figueres' opinion that the only way to oust them was by military measures. Testimony to Costa Rica's democratic tradition was paid by US Secretary of State, George Marshall, when he telegraphed his Embassy on March 12th:

> 'to inform President Picado of this country's deep concern over situation and express our hope that problem may be solved within limits traditional constitutional processes in observance of which Costa Rica has justifiable pride.'

The rebels gained two important initial successes; the first on the late afternoon of March 12th when, from well defended positions, they inflicted heavy casualties on the government forces and on the following day when the government forces attacked La Lucha sin Fin. Figueres had only the night before received some additional military equipment flown in from Guatemala and the government troops were routed.[14] The armaments which were obtained by Figueres as a result of his connections when exiled and the professional contribution supplied by the men from abroad who joined him (later they became known as the Caribbean Legion) undoubtedly played a decisive rôle in the success of the revolution. It is doubtful if without them Figueres could have succeeded.

The response of the government was weak, partly because there was a small army of only three hundred men (according to the official records this figure is correct and included tailors, barbers and the like for each detachment). Also President Picado, anxious to avoid bloodshed, thought the presumably greater forces at the command of the government would easily contain the rebellion. He and his colleagues seriously under-estimated Figueres' determination and the strength of his international connections. Volunteers of workers' militias, whilst supplementing and strengthening the regular troops, enabled allegations to be made that the government was in the hands of the communists, with disastrous results so far as help from the USA was concerned.[15] As early as March 9th Ulate, when thanking President Truman for the help afforded him by the US Ambassador, had pointed out that arms furnished by the USA were in the hands of the communist party which, with the official political party, had staged a *coup d'etat* against the result of the elections. On the 19th March Costa Rica's Ambassador in Washington had represented Figueres as being of the extreme right, Ulate's party and most of the Republican Party as the centre and Vanguardia the extreme left. He accused Guatemala of supplying arms to the revolutionaries but was keen to distinguish between that and his Government seeking assistance from Nicaragua. When the Ambassador asked about military support being available from the USA he was told this was a hypothetical question.[16] By 26th March USA officials were saying the communist influence in Costa Rica was out of proportion to its numbers and that its influence on the government was paramount. The US Embassy in San José considered 'Vanguardia as being both directly and indirectly responsible for the state of chaos and uncertainty in Costa Rica'. In the armed forces, communist elements were said to constitute 70% of the police and army and 'have spread a reign of terror unparalleled in Costa Rican history'.[17]

On 5th April Costa Rica's Foreign Minister complained bitterly to the

US Ambassador that, although Costa Rica had expelled Germans at the request of US Government during the Second World War, the latter had behaved in a most unfriendly way by blocking all attempts to get arms to fight the revolution. When the Costa Rican government had attempted to purchase arms from Nicaragua, Honduras and elsewhere the USA had intervened each time. The United States was trying desperately hard to appear to be neutral and constantly reiterated its attitude of non-interference in an internal dispute. They had remonstrated with both Guatemala in regard to their supplying arms to the rebels (to which President Arévalo had responded that, although he sympathised with Figueres, his policy was one of neutrality and non-intervention) and with Somoza, dictator of Nicaragua. It had been stated the latter was sending 1,000 troops into Costa Rica to intervene in the disturbed conditions in that country. The Nicaraguan Ambassador when telephoned in Washington had claimed his Government's action was only in response to a request to assist a 'friendly' Government and did not constitute intervention. He also reiterated several times that the Communists in Costa Rica had turned against the President and that the assistance from Nicaragua was intended to protect both his country and Costa Rica from Communism (a good stance to take at that time with the USA). The position of Nicaragua is most interesting as the dictatorship of Somoza was, as just indicated, vehemently opposed to communism but, on the other hand, he feared Figueres because of his alliance with other Caribbean rebels and their pact to overturn all dictatorships in that area. When the US Official told the Nicaraguan Ambassador their information did not support the contention there was discord between Picado and Mora, the Ambassador took time to consult with his Government and later said their policy would be 'hands off', despite Picado's request. President Picado had admitted some Nicaraguans were serving with the Government's army but countered that Guatemalans and others were assisting Figueres. He denied asking Somoza for any men and said both arms and planes had been requested but refused.[18]

Picado maintained the US Government did help the rebels and, in addition to quoting occasions when there had been refusals to issue permits for the export of arms and reductions in numbers of arms authorised, said Ulate had been treated with great affection by the US Government, the military attaché of the US Embassy had frequented opposition circles, that their Public Roads Administration had helped the rebels and even that Figueres had obtained a plane in the Canal Zone.[19]

The fighting continued and, in a thirty-six hours battle for San Isidro del General, government troops succeeded in capturing the town but could not hold it when their supplies ran out. There were other battles, whilst the revolutionaries remained generally on the defensive. On 10th April they commenced offensive tactics and on the 11th captured the Port of Limón, repulsing government forces sent next day to recapture it. Also on the 12th Figueres led a force of some 600 men against Cartago which he took (except for the barracks) with little resistance.[20] Now the rebels were within a few miles of San José which Mora prepared to defend with a force of around 1,500 vanguardista workers; if necessary by house to house fighting.

President Picado was now completely dispirited; around 500 political prisoners had been confined in San José and some of them were his friends. Mora proposed to place them at the tops of the buildings to ensure the revolutionaries did not bomb the city.[21] Further attempts at compromise had almost been successful at the end of March as, despite disagreement between Ulate and Calderón Guardia as to whether an appointed President should have political experience or not, they, along with Mora, had finally reached agreement that Dr Julio César Ovares should become President.[22] This proposal had failed owing to opposition from Figueres and his group. Although there were some grounds for believing San José could be successfully defended and even Cartago retaken, this would have meant a state of unrestricted civil war. Nicaraguans had already invaded the country in the north and there were reports of United States troops being on stand-by in the Canal Zone ready to ensure the country was not taken over by the communists, as they considered San José had already been.[23] Events in Bogotá only a few days earlier had made the United States government even more apprehensive about the spread of communism in the Western Hemisphere.[24] The President accordingly increased his pressure on the United States to intercede but they continued to decline until the onus was placed on the Diplomatic Corps. Some Ambassadors agreed to act, including the one from the United States Embassy, and negotiations began.

It was most unfortunate that, just as a cease-fire was about to be arranged on 13th April, the most serious battle of the revolution occurred. A large contingent of government troops was returning to San José from a few miles south of Cartago, not realising only the barracks there were still held by some of their forces, and that the town itself was in the hands of the revolutionaries. The latter thought the government force was advancing upon Cartago and moved out to establish themselves on the plaza at El Tejar, a small town nearby. There was terrible slaughter with over 200 government troops killed and almost as many seriously wounded. The rebels were said to have lost only 14 men.[25]

In addition to sending his troops into the north of Costa Rica, Somoza had sent for President Picado to meet him in Managua. The terms upon which Nicaragua would assist were specified and Picado was given a letter which he was to issue asking Nicaragua for help against Figueres and communism. Mora became aware of this proposal, called on all forces in the nation to be prepared to resist any invasion by Nicaraguan troops and told Calderón Guardia and the President he would join arms with Figueres to defend Costa Rica.[26]

There were several meetings between the Diplomatic Corps representatives and Figueres and his emissary, Father Benjamín Núñez, before terms were finally agreed. At first Figueres proposed that he should be first choice for President and two of his chief supporters should be substitutes. Picado had meanwhile asked Santos Leon Herrera if he would take over the office as President, as he was the third designate (presumably after Ulate and Calderón Guardia). Although at first Figueres was insisting upon his terms, he finally accepted Herrera,[27] when it was pointed out to him the government forces would be unlikely to accept him as President, and that he could control Herrera.

Figueres was an astute politician and was trying to ensure support from all sides. He had broadcast twice to the people explaining the significance of the revolution and urging a campaign of civil disobedience for those not actually fighting. He was at pains to say his National Liberation movement was not a 'rightist' group as had been alleged both by the government and in the foreign press. Although he said he would honour the election of Ulate as President, he said his objective was not to restore the old liberal democracy but to establish the Second Republic. He even went so far as to say his régime would be socialist and the social welfare provisions of Calderón Guardia and Picado would be extended not diminished. He had to be warned by one of his senior aides to be more cautious as some of his supporters in San José were far from enthusiastic about his socialist expressions or even the social welfare schemes. The statements were accepted for the time being as they tended to counter support for the government from the workers and peasants.[28] On April 17th, however, when negotiations were proving difficult even after the cease-fire had been attained, Figueres threatened to march on the capital if the communists continued to resist and he stated that no concessions would be made to conflict with the anti-communist policies of the United States.

The negotiations were proving difficult because, as the US Ambassador reported to his Secretary of State on 15th April, the government was still trying to salvage something from the wreck. They were claiming 26 seats in the Congress against 20 for the Opposition, although it had previously been agreed they would have 23 seats each.[29] Vanguardia Popular had 8 and it seems the government was by no means certain of

74

continued support from the Communists. Whilst the only difference between the two sides now appeared to be as to the appointment of Figueres, and his two associates as substitutes, to the Presidency, the diplomats had learned of a meeting held between Picado, Guardia and Mora with Somoza's representatives on 20th April. Even at this late stage it was feared the government was trying to arrange terms upon which Nicaraguan forces would enter Costa Rica and fight to restore the régime of the National Republicans. Mora, however, assured the US Ambassador he had told Picado and Guardia he would fight with Figueres against any incursion by Nicaraguan troops. He also said Guardia, though tempted by the suggestion of help from Somoza, was hesitant, and, if agreement came promptly, all elements, including Guardia probably later, would give in and not invite Somoza to intervene.[30]

It was then learned that army units from Nicaragua had invaded Costa Rica and established themselves at three points. When challenged about this, Somoza said the action had only been taken to defend Nicaragua as a large body of revolutionaries, many from Guatemala and Venezuela, was approaching the fronter between the two countries. Even as late as 18th April it would seem that Picado and Guardia especially were flirting with the prospect of help from the Nicaraguan army to assist their cause. The US Ambassador describes a meeting on the morning of that day with Picado, Guardia, Mora, Núñez (Figueres' representative) and other senior government officials present, as well as the Diplomatic Corps concerned with the negotiations. Picado was challenged with a telegram from Somoza saying he had been invited by Picado to send his army into Costa Rica; Picado declined to give a definite answer to this, even when he was pressed and referred to an old standing agreement for border guards. Whilst the President left to consult his military leaders, Guardia and Mora were noted to be in close conversation – presumably about accepting help from Nicaragua. When Picado returned he gave a categorical denial of Somoza's claim and produced a telegram to the Costa Rican Minister in Managua requesting immediate withdrawal of Nicaraguan forces.[31] The Ambassador's telegram to his Secretary of State next day states:

> As the President was visibly disconcerted when aware we had text Somoza's telegram, I believe only that factor made him apparently reverse decision to accept Somoza's help.

Finally on 19th April at 3.20 p.m. the President and Núñez in the presence of the Diplomatic Corps signed a final agreement, which was not, by any means, a victor's demand for unconditonal surrender as will be seen from the terms which included the following:

(1) Resignation of presidency, delegation of power to Leon Herrera and nomination Brenes[32] as Secretary of Public Security.

(2) Secretary of Public Security take all pertinent means to secure retirement of government-armed forces.

(3) Government to assist the departure of certain persons, not signifying, however, their expatriation.

(4) Figueres' forces to refrain from taking any armed action while final details were arranged.

(5) Usual guarantees life and property.

(6) The social rights and guarantees of all employers and workers to be respected and extended.[33]

(7) The government to take all judicial and diplomatic means possible in accordance with existing treaties, in defence of national sovereignty, i.e. against Nicaraguan intervention.

(8) Vote of thanks to Diplomatic Corps for its actions.[34]

There can be no doubt whatever that the Pact saved the people of Costa Rica from an even more costly and bloody civil war. The government had not been completely prostrated and still controlled most of the country. Had there been an arrangement to secure the assistance of Nicaraguan forces on a larger scale it is probable that the Army of National Liberation would have been defeated and Calderón Guardia returned to power. His National Republican Party remained the largest single party in the nation. The Pact provided for a negotiated peace, without limiting the basic rights of the defeated, but this was not borne out by subsequent events; sadly there was a good deal of persecution. Many members of the National Republican Party and Vanguardia Popular were exiled, imprisoned and dismissed from employment: in some cases their goods were confiscated by Special Courts established by the *Junta* (Administrative Council) outside the judicial system. A Professor at the University, in 1981, spoke of his father who had been forced to leave his appointment at one of the hospitals and worked for some years at a mental institution. This was contrary to the law as well as the Pact: eventually on 22nd June 1948 the *Junta* declared the Pact dissolved. Vanguardia Popular was proscribed.[35]

The number of casualties remains a complete mystery; estimates vary from a few hundred indicated by a University Professor and a Canadian diplomat, to five thousand suggested by a representative of *La Nación*. Most of those interviewed and other authorities give a figure of two thousand, although a spokesman at Union Party H.Q. said three thousand, and Biesanz considers it could have been as high as four thousand. What is certain is that the number of casualties of Figueres' force was significantly lower than the government's; the highest number suggested is one hundred. There were evidently several ambushes when the government forces suffered heavy losses. No help is gained by consulting the official statistics which show the following surprising comparisons:

Deaths per thousand of population

| | |
|---|---|
| 1946 | 13.9 |
| 1947 | 14.9 |
| 1948 | 13.2 |
| 1949 | 12.7 |
| 1950 | 12.,2 |

Even with a small population of approximately 800,000 the figures would appear to reflect no exceptional deaths from the revolution. It is difficult to believe only, or mainly, Nicaraguans were killed on the government side (where the losses mainly occurred) and thus were not registered in Costa Rica. In an interview with the author in 1983, José Figueres, whilst agreeing the casualties sustained by the government's troops very substantially exceeded those of his 'army', considered the total would be around 2,000. He expressed the view that many were peasants from Nicaragua and that others were not 'declared' or registered when people did not claim pensions. (Could this be so as to avoid identification with the National Republican cause and consequently freedom from victimisation or even persecution?)

On 20th April President Picado resigned and the next day he departed with a large party for Managua, Nicaragua. As he had transferred his Presidential powers to Santos León Herrera it was anticipated no difficult questions of any succeeding government being recognised would arise, although this was raised by one Government representative at the Organisation of American States.

In April 1983, José Figueres related to the author the gist of an interview he had with Manuel Mora, to which no other reference has been found. This took place as Picado and Calderón Guardia were fleeing to Nicaragua. Mora suggested their two armies should join to fight any incursion of USA marines from Panama and the Nicaraguan invaders already on Costa Rican territory. 'No' replied Figueres, 'the men have been fighting each other, and would continue to kill one another.'

77

Mora then suggested there should be a joint government but Figueres considered this neither practicable nor acceptable. 'What do you propose?' asked Mora, to which Figueres replied, he would continue the social legislation already provided. 'Will you end Income Tax?' queried Mora. 'Hell, no, I shall increase it' was Figueres' response. Mora there upon disarmed his men and San José was occupied by the Army of National Liberation without any fighting or damage to lives or property, which would undoubtedly have been considerable.

## NOTES TO CHAPTER 6

1. Bell, p. 106
2. ibid, p. 107
3. Area Handbook, p. 26
4. Bell, p. 123
5. Parker, p. 267, referring toNew York Times, 2nd March 1948
6. Bell, pp. 124/5
7. ibid, p. 125
8. ibid, p. 127, referring to Cañas 'Los ocho años'
9. ibid, p. 127
10. Koberg Bolandi was the member of the Electoral Tribunal who had withheld his consent to the declaration of the result of the election on the ground the count was incomplete.
11. Bell, p. 129, saying the best account of the events surrounding the death of Valverde appears in the Diario of Costa Rica of December 1952.
12. La Nación, the details which follow are translations of reports from this daily newspaper published in San José.
13. Lundberg, p. 145, relating how six of Figueres' men commandeered the three planes by a simple ruse.
14. Bell, pp. 136/7, Don José Figueres told the author that the revolution had been 'a war of successful ambushes'.
15. ibid, p. 139
16. US Foreign Relations, pp. 496/7
17. ibid, p. 502
18. ibid, p. 500 and 505
19. Bell, p. 142, quoting Picado's 'Commentario sobre 'Como y Porqué'.
20. ibid, p. 143
21. ibid, p. 146
22. ibid, pp. 153 and 135 where reference is made to Teodoro Picado's pamphlet 'El Pacto de la Embajada (Embassy) de Mexico'.
23. ibid, p. 150
24. ibid, p. 149 stating a good account of events in Bogotá on April 9, 1948, giving rise to the dramatic increase in such USA apprehension is to be found in Vernon L. Fluharty's 'The Dance of the Millions: Military Rule and the Social Revolution in Colombia'.
25. ibid, p. 148
26. ibid, p. 146/7, saying the most complete account appears in Comisión Politica de Vanguardia Popular.
27. US Foreign Relations, pp. 511, 512, 513 and 514.
28. Bell, pp. 144/5
29. US Foreign Relations, p. 515
30. ibid, p. 517
31. ibid, p. 518
32. Miguel Brenes Gutiérrez, who had the respect of both sides
33. Bell, p. 151, observes Mora's influence was particularly important for the inclusion of this point of the Pact.
34. US Foreign Relations, p. 523
35. Bell, pp. 157/8

# Chapter Seven

# THE JUNTA RULES

On 24th April *La Nación* announced that at 4 o'clock, break of day, that day, the troops of the Army of National Liberation were to enter San José. A force of disciplined police would take charge of vigilance in the Capital and put an end to restrictions on all movement of pedestrians and vehicles. The paper also set out as its main feature the names of leaders of the revolution who, with Herrera as President, would govern until 8th May. The previous day, however, the same paper had noted in a small paragraph, 'official sources' had stated that in no way would any member of the said Army take part in the government which would end on 8th May but that from the date the take-over by the army would be decisive and total! This came at the end of a report of a journey made four days earlier to the Army's H.Q. in Cartago, describing in eulogistic terms the leaders who had been seen (including Benjamin Odio, who had almost been taken prisoner several times) and the Priest, Benjamin Nuñez. The reporter described the great quantity of guns and ammunition captured from the government troops, which, he said demonstrated the fighting had all the realism and horror of modern battles.

On the same page was a report of an interview with José Figueres which had taken place on 22nd April. This stated there had been precisely defined military plans but no planned policy at the civil level. The intention was to bring down the unhappy regime (of Calderón Guardia) but they did not consider what would happen after that. Figueres was reported as saying as the campaign advanced the leaders met during the night and realised Costa Ricans wanted institutional renewal, such as the founding of study centres to consider the country's potential and aspirations. A desire for material improvements was also noted and linked with the regime of Léon Cortes (a popular era). The 'banditry' of the calderonistas had put an end to all hope of institutional life, especially with its disregard for the law and suffrage (a reference to the allegations of fraud in the 1944 election). Figueres claimed that the First Republic had ceased to exist on 13th February 1944 (when Picado became President)

79

after which Costa Rica had lived the life of an 'occupied country' (a comparison with France in the Second World War). A new Constitution, essential for the founding and development of the Second Republic, would be half a century ahead of its time instead of behind the times (a reference to the then Constitution established in 1871). A commission of lawyers and economists would be nominated to draw up a design for the new Constitution, after which a Constituent Assembly would have the final say. Until then the victorious organisation would assume command with its principal task the preparation of the dawning of the Second Republic. On Page 1 appeared a Press Notice to a similar effect under the name of José Figueres, Commander in Chief.

In its Editorial that day under the title 'National Renewal', *La Nación*, having been suspended from publication for a period by the 'military hand', identified itself with the young and honourable combatants of José Figueres who had defeated the forces of evil. It agreed that the Second Republic must be founded and continued 'We do not know yet what the exact form of the future government will be. But whatever it is, we retain confidence in the patriotism of Costa Ricans coming once again into play, and we are sure the country will begin her political, economic and moral revival with firm and sure steps.'

Although comparisons have been made with the *coup d'etat* of 1917, the only other occasion this century when violence has played a part on the Costa Rican political scene, there is a significant difference. The earlier occasion was to maintain the *status quo*, whereas in 1948 the revolution was to bring a new group to power following victory in the election.

The Ambassador of the USA reported to his Secretary of State the entry of Figueres' forces into the City in the early hours of 24th April but that there had been some firing the previous evening apparently relating to the search for arms. The Ambassador referred to a statement published by Figueres that it was regretted certain steps taken by force of circumstances had created an impression of an intention to instal a military dictatorship but that nothing was more removed from the temperament and inclinations of the leaders of the liberation movement.[1]

Whilst there is little doubt José Figueres and his group could have held power which they had won by defeating the government, they would have incurred the wrath and opposition of a considerable majority of their fellow countrymen; not only the remaining supporters of Calderón Guardia who, as will be seen by successive election results, were a large number, but also Otilio Ulate and his backing of wealthy coffee growers and business men. Nevertheless it can only be described as an act of great statesmanship and foresight that Figueres did not attempt to establish a military dictatorship but ensured an orderly and equitable return to political democratic equanimity.

The Ambassador's telegram also indicated that the Acting President (Herrera) had declared he had assumed power 'to conserve until the last moment the principle of constitutional legality of our institutions and maintain them until their legal end'. He had continued to define his position as 'serving as a bridge between the fallen regime and the new regime which the triumphant revolution possessor of the force and the arms, will instal.' No reference, the Ambassador pointed out, to any form of a future government.

Happily any tendency to continue violence in San José was very short lived. A noted criminal alleged to have been armed by the previous government and who had transformed his house in a fortress was reported captured on 23rd April after an exchange of fire and on the same day Miguel Brenes Gutiérrez, appointed Secretary of Public Security, announced his resignation as he had completed his task of disarming the marauding groups roaming the city and ensuring that all public forces, the garrisons and police were in the hands of the new government. There remained a few incidents, mostly on the border with Nicaragua, despite Somoza ordering the withdrawal of his troops reported to be about 50 miles from the capital, and a raid in the south when about 100 of Mora's fighters were responsible for killing a dozen people.[2]

*La Nación* reported on 27th April, quoting from official sources of the Army of Liberation, that as soon as Figueres reached San José, he had met Ulate Blanco and invited him to form part of the Cabinet which was to control the country from 8th May and indeed to undertake the functions that might be assigned to a President. At that time Ulate had not responded but shortly afterwards he tactically decided not to accept until a Constitution had been agreed. It was suggested later he had sat back and let Figueres make all the necessary unpleasant pronouncements. The paper's report indicated already some differences of opinion were being encountered: some, presumably Ulate and his party, had interpreted the revolutionary struggle as defending electoral rights but Figueres and his group took a wider view, saying the struggle was to defend the whole life of the country, of which electoral rights were a small part only. The official sources had made it quite clear a Junta would take control on 8th May and govern with full powers until constitutional life was restored. The newspaper called everyone, including 'the opposition' to join unitedly in the post-war battle which it pointed out was as important, or more so, as the war which had just been won.

On another page was reported an interview with Gonzalo Facio, who had exchanged his uniform for the striped trousers and jacket of an Under

Secretary of Foreign Relations. Facio emphasised his intention to work to increase the bonds existing between all the countries of the Hemisphere and develop a policy of frank and loyal co-operation with all the nations of the American Continent (no doubt he had relations with Nicaragua in his mind). He made it clear Costa Rica was to be identified with the USA in the division between east and west and linked their defence of democratic principles and the dignity of man with the objectives of the National Liberation Army.

The 28th April saw what was described as a Brilliant Parade of the Victorious Army through the streets of San José. One of President Carazo's Aides in 1981, although indicating some sympathies with the Guardia regime, recalled seeing it when he was a youth and described it as 'very impressive'. Homage to the dead was linked with the names of León Cortes and Dr Valverde, the latter's assassination, it will be recalled, having done much to reduce the support for Calderón Guardia in March 1948. It is especially noteworthy that homage was paid to the 'poor mariachis' – as the previous government's troops were termed – who were the 'victims of a monstrously irresponsible decision'. Figueres called for a not excessive alcoholic celebration both that day and in the future; 'many times I have tried to make you understand this is not from a puritanical point but a practical convenience.' He went on to say it had been made patent to the world what happens when two armies confront each other in combat and one is of sober men and the other is an army of drunkards! A former soldier who claimed to have fought with the Army of National Liberation – but, being in the army, it may well have been he had fought with the government forces – said Somoza had sent prisoners to fight with the latter and many of them had drunk excessively. He also said the army was divided, some having fought with Figueres but there is no confirmation of this from any other source. Otilio Ulate was present, of course, and gave testimony to the brave soldiers and their chief, José Figueres.

Now began the real task of the *Junta* – to win the peace as well as win the war. On 1st May they received a message from the acting President, León Herrera, who spoke of the ordeal through which the country had passed and the determination to continue the democratic tradition of Costa Rica. Most important, however, on that day was the Agreement signed by Ulate and Figueres defining the political situation as follows:

(1) The Revolutionary *Junta* is to govern without Congress for 18 months commencing 8th May and, if necessary, may request 6 months extension from the Constitutional Assembly.

(2) The *Junta* will call elections on 8th December for a Constitutional Assembly.

(3) The *Junta* immediately to designate a commission to formulate a draft constitution.

(4) The *Junta* recognises and will immediately declare Ulate as legitimately elected President on 8th February last.

(5) The *Junta* will request the Constitutional Assembly to ratify the election of Ulate to exercise power during the first constitutional period of the second republic.

(6) The *Junta* will integrate the national electoral tribunal.

(7) Both signatories to the agreement formally obligate themselves not to undertake any electoral activities for a period of six months from that date.[3]

The eleven man *Junta* took up its powers as the *Junta Fundadora de la Secundo Republico* thereby confirming the intention was to establish a new regime and not resuscitate and revive the old. Their aim was to fit the nation into the theoretical framework they had designed for it. Immediately legislative and executive powers were assumed and a good deal of judicial power. Incumbent justices of the Supreme Court were dismissed and replaced with the *Junta*'s own partisans. Many Courts were established outside the orbit of judicial power, including Courts of Immediate Sanctions; it was these Courts which were used to punish the supporters of Calderón Guardia, many of whom were workers and peasants. New local governments were established. The governing *Junta* at once declared the Constitution of 1871 was null and void except for provisions that bore on individual, national and social guarantees. Later it was declared the 1871 Constitution was 'without effect' instead of being nullified. The anulment on 1st March by the Congress of Ulate's election was over-ruled. Although Ulate's election was now declared lawful the effect of these decrees was to postpone his taking office whilst the *Junta* governed.[4]

Four days earlier the Chiefs of Diplomatic Missions in Costa Rica had been called to the Foreign Office when Gonzalo Facio read a statement vindicating the Guatemalan Government and its local diplomatic representative from the charges made by the previous administration that the Guatemalans had supplied the revolutionaries with arms. No doubt José Figueres had his tongue very much in his cheek on that day, knowing that if arms had not been supplied to his forces it was unlikely there would have been the opportunity of delivering such a vindication.

There had been serious criticism of the United States Government for supplying arms to the Picado Government, especially when Ulate's supporters were endeavouring to promote a general strike. It was even alleged the United States would be responsible for any bloodshed should the arms be used during any such strike. During the peace negotiations some of Figueres' officers had jocularly remarked to the U.S. Ambassador they had captured most of the arms so supplied. The Ambassador was equal to the occasion and remarked that would make it easier for him to present to the rebels, when they succeeded to the reins of government, the unpaid bill! The occasion arose when Figueres spoke to the Chief of the US Military Mission to Costa Rica about a supply of arms and possibly other military equipment for the 'new' army being planned which was to comprise six hundred officers and men. (It can be pointed out this was approximately double the size of the army in March 1948.)[5] The Ambassador observed his Government would require assurances about the nature and mission of the new army, i.e. whether it was to include municipal police, constabulary and customs guards, or be a strictly military force integrated into hemispheric defence plans – the Embassy was not prepared at that time to discuss arms questions.[6] Cozean reports the New York Times of 17 June, 1948 under a heading 'San José sets Army Goals', stating that shortly after the end of the revolution Figueres had announced plans to replace the regular Costa Rican army of about 5,000 (sic) men with 500 highly trained men from his National Liberation Army. Under Figueres' reorganisation, the force was to be strictly professional, with new uniforms and a much higher pay. All other soldiers would be returned to civilian life.[7]

A Professor at the University in 1981 gave as his opinion that Figueres had wanted to legalise his army but the strong wealthy group of coffee growers did not trust him and he was not of that group. They resisted his intentions and, being a powerful group, they prevailed. The National Guard, he said, was equipped as a para-military force and was larger than the previous army.

There was clearly a good deal of apprehension in regard to the possibility of trouble with Nicaragua. Early in June 1948 the Costa Rican Ambassador in Washington had been complaining that some Latin American countries had obtained from USA arms and ammunition which they did not really need.[8] At the end of that month the Nicaraguan Ambassador in USA was maintaining that revolutionary activities in Costa Rica might result in an invasion of his country. He was told there had been reports of flights of Nicaraguan planes on reconnaissance over Costa Rica and reminded that one thousand troops had been sent from Nicaragua to aid Picado in his fight against the revolutionaries. It was also pointed out to him that it was

> thoroughly undesirable that action taken by one country outside its own frontiers should be disguised as defence measures.[9]

About a month later the Costa Rican Ambassador was again exploring the possibility of arms being made available to his country. A list of those considered necessary had been prepared by the US Military Mission in San José and submitted by the Costa Rican Embassy to the US Government. This had been received sympathetically but an indication given that nothing could be supplied owing to the lack of arms available and the USA's own rearmament programme! The report contains the following paragraph which again underlines the approach of the Costa Ricans in regard to armaments:

> The Ambassador expressed himself most emphatically as being sick of the whole armaments mess and very discouraged over what he regarded as the necessity of his Government to arm the country to a level beyond that formerly held essential to the national safety. He said that he did not like having arms brought into Costa Rica and especially did not like the financial burden they imposed but that there seemed no alternative at present in view of what he described as obvious preparations on the part of General Somoza for aggressive action.[10]

The Arms Policy Committee of the USA Government having rejected the list of arms required which had been presented by the Costa Rican Embassy, further attempts were made to persuade the USA to ensure arms were available and arrangements were made to facilitate purchases through commercial channels. The Costa Rican Ambassador reiterated his Government's apprehension that the Nicaraguans had the intention of invading Costa Rica and said a substantial number of exiles was being trained near the border across which frequent incursions were being made, as well as flights over his country's territory by Nicaraguan war planes.[11]

On the other hand, reports from Nicaragua indicated apprehension of invasion by rebel elements with support from both Costa Rica and Guatemala. No doubt this related to fears of the activities of the Caribbean Legion, the group pledged to the overthrow of dictators in that area. It was being said that, while Figueres was reluctant to permit the launching of any revolutionary attempt from Costa Rica, he was determined to support the Nicaraguan revolutionaries on the best possible basis as soon as they had formulated their plans. US Embassy officials in Managua believed it was likely Somoza might invade Costa Rica alleging 'self-defence' unless he could be satisfied Figueres was not permitting plotting by the revolutionaries in Costa Rica.[12]

There appears to have been no significant change in the situation until November when, on the 25th of that month, the US Ambassador in Costa Rica had a conversation with Figueres in which the presence of the Caribbean Legion in that country was referred to as constituting a threat to the restoration of confidence in the area. Two days later the disbanding of the Legion was announced and President Figueres paid glowing testimony to the important role its members had played in the successful revolution earlier that year. He continued by praising no less their gesture (in disbanding) which he described as endeavouring to obliterate the disquiet which the composition of the group had given rise to in various countries. The report continues:

> When it was pointed out to Mr Figueres that General Ramírez (the military leader of Figueres' Revolutionary Force) would perhaps have a certain reluctance to returning to the US where he is under indictment, Mr Figueres said he had been unaware of that factor and asked what the reason for his difficulties might be. When it was explained that it involved a violation of the arms export regulations, Mr Figueres laughingly remarked that such activities were entirely honest.[13]

The significance of this date will be apparent as the events of December 1948 are told.

Meanwhile the *Junta* was issuing some of its several hundred decrees which appeared during its eighteen months rule. During the first month came the nationalisation of the banks, an extraordinary ten percent tax on private capital, and the organisation of a National Council of Production followed by the establishment of a state-owned Electric Power Institute to develop the nation's power resources but without eliminating private firms in the industry. In the debate on the nationalisation of the banks Figueres said:

> It is the banks which distribute and administer the financial resources by which agriculture, industry and commerce are fed . . . The administration of money and credit ought not to be in private hands, any more than the distribution of drinking water or the services of the post office. It is the State, political organ of the Nation, to which correspond these vital functions of the economy . . . This is a public service, and public should be the ownership of the institutions which manage it.[14]

The capital levy did not affect anyone with an income of less than US $10,000 and accordingly only the wealthy were affected – mainly Ulate's supporters.

These measures reflected Figueres' socialist inclinations and at once seriously disturbed his relationship with those who were influential. The weakness of his position is apparent when it is realised that the sucessful revolution had weakened the left and fortified the right of the political scene. The elimination of the National Republicans and members of the Vanguardia Popular left the Social Democrats (the basis of the National Liberation forces) as the only important representatives of a radical group pursuing objectives of social reform. What is even more to the point, the resistance to the reform programmes of the Guardia and Picado regimes was intensified because so many had made sacrifices for the revolution. Their privileges were being threatened even more by the *Junta* than had been the case with the calderonistas. The *Junta* was seriously threatening established interests with the result many who had formed a substantial part of the Opposition to Guardia and Picado now became strongly anti-Junta.[15]

An important effect of the revolution, along with the political crisis which preceded it and the programme of the Junta, was the rededication of Costa Ricans to the maintenance of civil government, the peaceful transfer of power from one popularly elected candidate to another, and a perfecting of the electoral process. Figueres, the Junta and the Constituent Assembly all contributed to strengthen these convictions. The bitterness engendered by the whole process of the revolution proved anew to the Costa Rican people that, even though representative government can be slow and at times unresponsive, it is an effective safeguard against governmental excesses. All subsequent governments have worked to make elections as nearly perfect as possible. The Electoral Tribunal has become a permanent and adequately financed body, one not likely to invite improvisation or to fall into the abuse which handicapped its efforts in 1948.[16]

# NOTES TO CHAPTER 7

1. US Foreign Relations, p. 524
2. La Nación, 23.4.48
3. US Foreign Relations, p. 524
4. Official Publications; British Museum Library
5. National Archives Records, San José. It is not possible to indicate an accurate figure, although 'about 300' was mentioned by several of those interviewed. By examining the figures of expenditure for 1947 (not surprisingly figures for 1948 were not available) which compared satisfactorily with those of the immediately preceding years, the following facts could be established:

| | Colones. |
|---|---:|
| Commander, officers and 150 men Barrack | 344,280 |
| Commander, officers and 150 men Artillery | 344,280 |
| Some military personnel (unspecified) | 34,800 |
| Some military personnel (unspecified) | 18,300 |
| Military administration | 29,400 |
| Military bands | 504,960 |
| Military bands – sundry payments | 32,640 |
| Armaments, freight and travelling expenses | 88,500 |
| Food, laundry, medicine, etc. | 280,778 |
| Personnel at USA Military Mission | 11,340 |

Expenditure under the heading 'Public Security' included Police and prisons as well as the military and amounted to 7.6% of total expenditure. This compares with 10.98% (average) shown in a table for the three years 1946-48.

6. US Foreign Relations, p. 526/8
7. Cozean, p. 32
8. US Foreign Relations, p. 528/9
9. Ibid, p. 531
10. Ibid, p. 532
11. Ibid, p. 533
12. Ibid, p. 534
13. Ibid, p. 536
14. Parker, p. 268, noting the spech was made on 19th June 1948
15. Bell, pp. 158/9
16. Ibid. p. 161

## Chapter Eight

# DISOLUCIÓN DEL EJERCITO

1st December 1948 is one of the most important dates in the history of Costa Rica – if not of the world. The newspapers published in the afternoon had a bonanza: *La Hora* with headlines over one inch high shouted:

DISOLUCIÓN DEL EJERCITO
(Dissolution of the Army)

*La Prensa Libra,* more sober with headlines about half an inch announced:

DISUELTO EL EJERCITO NACIONAL
(The National Army Disbanded)

Only next day were the morning dailies able to join in!
*Diario de Costa Rica* with headlines almost an inch repeated

DISUELTO EL EJERCITO COSTARRICENSE
(The Costa Rican Army Disbanded)

*La Nacion,* having been clearly left at the post, contented itself with a slightly larger than usual headline saying:

We consider it is sufficient for the security of our country to have a good Police Force.

The announcement is the more significant because it was quite clearly completely unexpected. The two afternoon papers referred to the 'sensational announcement', whilst the morning *La Nación* on 1st December had contented itself with the publication of correspondence between the Director of the National Museum and the *Junta* when the former had made a suggestion that the Army Barracks be converted into a National Museum to which the *Junta* had responded favourably. The morning of the 1st December was the occasion of a formal ceremony during which the keys of the barracks were to be symbolically handed over by the Minister of Public Security to the Minister for Education.

First, we are told, came the parade with representatives of the schools, the colleges of higher education of San José and the provinces and delegations from universities; then there were various corps of the National Army, the Public Security Police and the Fiscal Guard. President José Figueres and all the members of the Governing *Junta* followed. At the Bella Vista Barracks awaited them the Diplomatic and Consular Corps, specially invited for the occasion, many prominent citizens and foreigners, amongst the latter being senior members of the North American Military Mission.

After the singing of the National Anthem, the Minister of Public Security, Colonel Edgar Cardona, made his speech which contained the most sensational announcement that the Army of Costa Rica was to be dissolved and that in its place will be a splendid National Police; an announcement applauded and supported by the people of Costa Rica. His speech, with that of Professor Gámez and the one delivered by President Figueres, were printed in full.

Colonel Edgar Cardona said:

> In my own name and that of the Public Force which I command, I greet this great gathering of distinguished visitors. It is a great honour for me to address you on the occasion of this event which represents the handing over – and symbolic destruction – of the Buena Vista Barracks to the Ministry of Education and the Director of the National Museum.
>
> This act is symbolic too of the profound democratic feeling which it expresses. The Public Force hands over what has been a fortress to be used in the service of the education of the country.
>
> But it is evident that such an act demonstrates that the *Junta* firmly believes in its deep-rooted popular approval. For those who seized power by force of arms can only dispose of this fortress if they know they have the support of public opinion.
>
> This morning we have witnessed a parade of students and soldiers which makes me think that the students will feel that those soldiers are no longer the ones who at one time wanted to suppress public opinion, but that they are now the base and support of the public and its security and protection.
>
> This would be the right moment to state the ideals of the *Junta* if the President had not already expounded them on various occasions. But I want to use this opportunity to refer to a matter which is of great importance to me. The Ministry of Education has been attacked for its high budget. But that is unjust and does not take into account the esteem in which education is held by a people of civil and cultural traditions like ours.
>
> I believe, on the contrary, that each Ministry must contribute in some form, even if it means sacrificing some of its own functions, in

order to help to solve the problems of our educational budget, and the Ministry of Public Security wishes to be the first to give support, by offering the remainder of its budget which is available in consequence of the abolition of the army – a measure which I have presented for consideration by the Governing *Junta* and which deserves its approval.

Only a few hours ago have our soldiers heard of the decision to abolish the army. But like good Costa Ricans and patriots, conscious of the needs of their country, they have offered me their cooperation and have confirmed what they have shown before, namely, that when the country demands it they will unite as one, with desire and feeling, ready for the greatest sacrifices in order to make the country great and defend its institutions.

I have expressed my gratitude to all officers of the army for this unselfish and patriotic attitude which I hope will be recognised in its wide implications by all who are capable of valuing it.

I close by praying for the traditional peace of Costa Rica, but I want to add that I am certain that, if peace were disturbed then, as at la Sierra, el Elpalme and San Isidro, we Costa Ricans will again reform an army ready for sacrifices and full of fervour and patriotic enthusiasm.

The reports say his speech was greated with considerable applause; was he being ingenuous or not? Cozean interprets the reports as indicating that Cardona was advised of the decision to abolish the army only several hours before the ceremony.[1] Perhaps the report meant to say 'we Soldiers' and not 'our soldiers'. His final reference to a reforming of the army is also not without some significance. What is, however, most important is that, only a few months later, as the head of a much larger armed force which had just been engaged in resisting an invasion by Calderón Guardia aided by Nicaraguans, he, Edgar Cardona, attempted a *coup d'etat;* is this consistent with a man apparently taking the gigantic step of disbanding his army – and claiming it as his idea? The newspapers seem to have had little doubt as to the real author and instigator: *La Prensa Libre, La Nación* and *El Diario* all carried in their headlines the announcement by the President of the *Junta* Government, José Figueres, that the army was to be dissolved.

Colonel Cardona was followed by Professor Gaméz, whose speech included the following:

Those men who fought for a free fatherland are today giving up these military headquarters so that they can be made into a sacred witness of our history. Here all people will be able to come and relive the whole life of our nation, the days past and present and the longings of a dream of the future. A special place in the museum will be occupied by the event we are now witnessing; the armed forces giving up their headquarters so that the forces of culture may triumphantly enter them.

The Minister of War and Public Security proclaims the abolition of the army in order to give more strength to the education budget . . .

Young compatriots . . . may you receive with hearts full of enthusiasm the camp which the army has handed to you so that those men who gave us liberty may be sure that we shall be able to apply the power which we shall use to cultivate our spirit, to our arms as well so that we shall stand shoulder to shoulder by their side if the fatherland needs us. By doing away with the army the Government is showing the country that it is relying totally on public confidence. We must become worthy of such trust and be ready to defend the fundamental principles of the Republic . . .

Then it was the turn of José Figueres, President of the Governing *Junta,* whose contribution was much shorter than the others:

The Regular Army of Costa Rica, worthy successor of the Army of National Liberation, is today handing over the key of this Army Barracks so that it can be converted into a cultural centre.

The founding *Junta* of the Second Republic officially declares the dissolution of the National Army and considers a good police force sufficient for the security of our country.

We, who have recently shed the blood of a peaceful country, understand the seriousness which these wounds can assume in Latin America and the need for their healing. We are not brandishing the dagger of the assassin, but the scalpel of the surgeon. As surgeons we are interested today not so much in the accomplished operation, but more in the future health of the Nation, which demands that the wounds heal quickly and that a healthy and stronger skin will cover the original tissue.

We want to uphold the idea of a new world in America. To the Fatherland of Washington, Lincoln, Bolívar and Martí we want to say today: 'Oh America; other peoples, also your sons, offer their great gifts to you. Our tiny Costa Rica offers you always, as now, its heart, its love of civil life, of democracy and an ordered way of living.'

Figueres' speech was constantly interrupted by the applause of the crowd.

At the end of this speech following the symbolic act, the handing over of the keys of the Bella Vista Barracks by the Minister of Public Security to the Minister of Education.

But then none of the cultural ceremonies was more moving than the final act, when the President of the Governing *Junta,* Don José Figueres, broke with one blow of a sledge-hammer the first block of stone of the wall to mark the beginning of the reconstruction of the building dedicated to the museum and a Panamerican garden.

Finally President Figueres embraced the members of the army who were present and the common soldiers who took part in the parade and other military personalities.[2]

Three of the newspapers had photographs of Figueres striking the wall with the sledgehammer, the *Diario* showing a very large one under the heading 'Emotional episode at yesterday's civic ceremony'. Although all of them, except *La Nación*, highlighted the event in extraordinarily large headlines, none devoted the whole front page exclusively to the occasion. *La Prensa Libre,* one of the largest in its size of page, had five other items featured on its front page. The *Diario*, reporting the event in its issue of the following day, although placing the photograph of Figueres striking the wall towards the top of its first page, had several other features and placed the large headline and introduction to the story of the disbanding of the army in the lowest quarter of the page. At the top of the page was a photograph of Ulate (proprietor of the paper) and his defensive statement in reply to an attack made upon him by a political opponent. Perhaps this is another comment upon the background and traditions of Costa Rica. Cozean, however, quotes the New York Times of 2 December, 1948 as saying:

> Figueres left his audience speechless by declaring that the army had been disbanded . . . the announcement hit the audience like a bombshell.[3]

Figueres, note, not Cardona.

*La Prensa Libre* the following day announced:
IN PARIS THE DISSOLUTION OF THE ARMY CAUSES A SENSATION.

> The Press of the French capital has comented favourably on the action of Costa Rica's Government. Our Consul in that city, Sr. Cañas Bourla, informs us of this.
>
> President Figueres has received a very large number of telgrams and cablegrams from Costa Ricans residing abroad, all congratulating him on the dissolution of the army, including one from our Ambassador at the United Nations Conference.

The same paper was also at great pains in a short article headed 'Render unto Caesar' to pay tribute to Colonel Edgar Cardona for being the one who had suggested and carried into effect the plan of suppressing the army. The paper posed the question 'What other Minister of Public Security could have been the architect of the idea of dissolving the Army when it is a very significant part of his own powers?' Four months later, in

April 1949, after the attempted *coup d'etat*, no doubt *La Prensa Libre* was taking a very different view of Cardona!

More importantly, the same paper had an article under the heading 'No Army', extracts being as follows:

> At the time of the military treason in Peru, we said that such things happened there whereas in Costa Rica a government, which has those who find solace in eliminating with reticence any dictatorial element, was preparing to transform a military fortress into a National Museum . . . But the Government went further, adding to that incalculable transformation the declaration that the Costa Rican army has been disbanded . . . Costa Rica has proclaimed before the world, and particularly before the nations of this hemisphere, its unshakeable devotion to civilian institutions. The people of Costa Rica will not be among those who can go boastingly paying homage to those who support tyranny. Our land will not be the place where barracks will arise nor where the ambitions of the military barbarians and infidels will awake, to seize power.
>
> We Costa Ricans have a political mystique, an adherence, renewed every day, to republican practices. We were born and educated beneath a republican banner, forswearing everything, so to speak, that means the introduction of arms into the decision of public life or the maintaining of public life.
>
> In those days immediately following the entry of the army of National Liberation into San José, there was in everyone sincere gratitude, warm applause and admiration for the members of that army. But, by a natural reaction, within two days a change came about in the soul of the people. Now we wanted to see those soldiers once again civilians. And they themselves were very soon shaving off their hairy beards and putting on peasant garb. There was no ingratitude, nor was there any denial of the merits, well gained in fierce struggle. That reaction was simply a phenomenon of Costa Rican idiosyncracy . . .
>
> These military men of ours today have no stomach to lead them to constitute a clan of the type that has just drowned the constitutional systems in Peru and Venezuela. They are military because the destiny of their own country brought them here when, to redeem it from infamy, it was necessary for them to take arms.
>
> We do not console ourselves with the dissolution of the army as a sort of academic question. That would mean unworthy forgetfulness of deeds accomplished by its members in achieving the restoration of rights that had been snatched away.
>
> For us the question has intimate value for citizens at the same time as being of solemn over-riding importance. That is to say it rebounds on our feelings, galvanises our sensibility, because we bestow upon it the over-riding value it possesses. There is no

94

escaping its great importance at this moment; we confront a plain lie of most perverse nature about bellicose intentions, ideas of invasion, on the part of Costa Rica. And for the future it rests assured of the solid civilian control of the country. If by great misfortune, it were again necessary to overthrow a régime that was shameful, the citizens of future generations would go to join the struggle to bring about that overthrow.

We no longer rely upon the Army, but we guarantee the survival of the civil order, fitting to our temperament and in conformity with our traditions.

Perhaps a copy of this article with the last two paragraphs heavily underscored would be sent to President Somoza in Nicaragua.

On its front page along with the announcement of the Army being dissolved, the *Diario de Costa Rica* on 2 December 1948 carried the following leading article – could it be from the pen of Ulate?

### THE CIVIL STATE

"The founding *Junta* of the Second Republic officially declares the dissolution of the National Army, considering the existence of a Police Corps sufficient for the security of our country. . . .
José Figueres."

Darkness has fallen on the horizons of the democratic life, freedom and culture of various American countries which find themselves subjected to the armed protection of military castes who have, with the arrogance of force, deprived the civil statesmen of their governing functions. At such a time it is profoundly significant – especially for the strengthening of civil life in our country – that the decision outlined in the words quoted above has been taken, accompanied by the symbolic act of handing over to the Ministry of Education the old barracks of Bella Vista for conversion into a museum of national art.

Some sceptics will say that there is an excessive romanticism in all that, and in practice the dismantled barracks in the heart of the capital of the Republic can easily be replaced by a new one outside the city.

But for us these acts are important for they are helping in no uncertain way to strengthen the existence of the Civil State of Costa Rica; and will bring new light of civilisation, progress and culture to our nation.

Take, furthermore, the importance of the fact that this measure has been introduced in absolute coordination with national sentiments which are unwilling to accept the militarisation of the country and which desire that it should occupy a preferential place in the nucleus of the civilised nations, not because of its generals, its colonels and military parades, but because of its moral and spiritual values, its schools and colleges and its love for education, order, peace and work.

There was a danger that, since the glorious achievement of the National Liberation Army and, above all, since the victory of the armies raised in the Southern mountains (how exact and profound was Napoleon's remark that victory is the most dangerous moment of the battle) the country could be subjugated to a military dictatorship temporarily or for good.

This danger existed because, after shattering events like our civil war, other parts of the world have experienced the phenomenon of the life of the country being subjected to a militarised order, and when the military seize power in a nation they generally keep it, because the privileges which power offers are more tempting for men of arms and routine disciplines than they are for citizens who consider government to be a function for the service of the country and not an opportunity for showing off and making money.

But Costa Rica has not cultivated its citizenship in vain; those who were in the battlefield transformed themselves from citizens into soldiers. But, once victory was achieved, they returned to civil life and to appreciate the beneficial influence of the country's anti-military tradition and the need to continue it, for it has given the Republic its civilian character of which it is proud, the character of a nation which seeks a tranquil democratic life where an official police organisation will be enough to guarantee public order and national security.

Symbolic as may have been the acts of abolishing the National Army and converting the old barracks into a museum of art – for we would never have had an army like the armies which the other Central American countries maintain at the cost of misery and oppression of their people – Costa Rica must be praised for the fact that so soon after the end of the military revolution, measures have been proclaimed – one could say unprecedented ones – which have allowed the country to return to a fully civil state.

We from our modest position of journalists have all the time indicated the need for the country not to succumb to the dazzling temptations of militarism . . .

With the same spirit we applaud the dissolution of the army and the plan to replace it by a National Police Force which shall be trained to the high standard which the running of the Republic's civil life demands . . .'

Some months later, after the invasion and the attempted coup, Ulate urged that the abolition of the army should be delayed until problems with Nicaragua had been solved. However, when he took over the Presidency at the end of 1949, he not only dropped the Ministry of Public Security from his Cabinet but also announced he would assume the

*Costa Rica's President Señor Dr. José Figueres meeting the then Prime Minister of the United Kingdom, Sir Anthony Eden, at 10 Downing Street, London, during an official visit in October 1956 – Photo: Topham Picture Library.*

La Nación, 13 March 1948, headlining the outbreak of the revolution.

*The border incident in October 1977 when the Costa Rican Minister of Public Security was bombed by a Nicaraguan helicopter as he inspected the frontier. Above, his boat makes for the river bank: Below, sheltering in the forest.*

# THE TICO TIMES

CENTRAL AMERICA'S LEADING ENGLISH-LANGUAGE NEWSPAPER

Vol. XXI No. 516     San José, Costa Rica, Friday, July 13, 1979     Price ₡1.50

## 'Yanqui Go Home'

*THE ARRIVAL of U.S. helicopters and a military transport plane in Llano Grande Airport this week provoked a wave of protests, when Ticos concluded that "The Marines have landed!" Demonstrators waving Sandinista flags and "Gringo go home" placards filled the streets in front of the Legislative Assembly, and after heated debate, the congressmen voted to oust the coupers — which the U.S. Embassy claimed were here on a humanitarian mission to evacuate U.S. personnel from Managua. The aircraft departed, but left behind bitter feelings and a clear victory for anti-US policies here. See story below.* Tico Times photo/ Katherine Lambert.

## Government 'Losing Credibility'

By Stephen Schmidt

COSTA Rica has "lost enormous credibility" during the last month because of its involvement in the Nicaraguan civil war, and mounting internal pressure is threatening to split apart the fragile Carazo government coalition, a well-placed government source told The Tico Times this week.

In addition, this country's unofficial support of the Frente Sandinista de Liberación Nacional is making "a joke" out of Costa Rica's reputation as a neutral, defenseless nation.

Speaking as a "private citizen," the high-ranking official said he was "absolutely amazed at the way Costa Rica and the United States have bungled things" during the latest — and possibly last — round in the Nicaraguan popular insurrection.

"IT'S gotten to the point where I don't believe anybody; not the administration, not the U.S., not the Sandinistas, and certainly not Somoza," he said, adding that the Costa Rican people have been

### Tico Times News Analysis

"thoroughly confused" by their government's actions during the past several weeks.

The confusion appears justified. Events here lately have taken on Kafkaesque overtones, bearing little relation to the well-hatched plans of rebel groups, provisional juntas or national governments.

● HELICOPTERS. On the surface it seemed innocent enough. Last Sun-

day, two U.S. Air Force HH-53 helicopters and a C-130 cargo plane quietly landed at Liberia's Llano Grande Airport, ostensibly to be on call in case the U.S. Embassy in Managua needed to be evacuated.

But the dust stirred up by the choppers' blades has not settled yet.

"Marines Land in Guanacaste," read the banner headline in one daily newspaper Monday, much to the horror of U.S. Embassy personnel. The local press — along with most of the Embassy and the Costa Rican government — was obviously unprepared for the "humanitarian mission," as the task force

was labeled in a hastily-written press release prepared late Sunday night by U.S. Ambassador Marvin Weissman.

But by then the military craft had already landed, and 35 Air Force Security officers had begun setting up camp just off the runway. The damage was done.

COSTA Rica's Constitution requires that all foreign military planes receive permission of the Legislative Assembly before landing here, but the choppers and the transport set down with nothing more than a verbal O.K. by free-wheeling Minister of Public Security Juan José ("don Johnny") Echeverría, who granted permission after a phone call from Weissman Saturday.

On Monday, Echeverría formally asked the Assembly to approve his decision, but by that time things had gotten out of hand. As hundreds of placard-carrying students shouted "Yanqui Go Home," an unusual coalition of the Liberación Nacional opposition party, Communists and a few defectors from Carazo's Unidad party voted 29-20

*(Page 4)*

## This Week

**'DEEP BELLY' AND 'COMANDANTE BIGOTE'**
— Pages 20 & 21

**LOS ANGELES – SAN JOSE CHARTERS SUSPENDED**
—Page 24

## Costa Rica Bombed As Peace Nears

As the bloody civil war in Nicaragua appeared to be heading towards a negotiated solution this week, tensions between Costa Rica and its northern neighbor threatened to erupt into armed conflict.

While Nicaraguan bombs fell on this country's northern border region late Thursday, U.S. State Department spokesmen said the United States has responded "favorably" to the latest proposal of the Nicaraguan Government of Reconstruction, which acceded to demands that the National Guard not be disbanded in a post-Somoza Nicaragua.

The proposal broke an impasse in the complex negotiations this week between the provisional government and special U.S. Ambassador William Bowdler.

LATE Thursday afternoon, in an apparent attempt to reach consensus on a formula that would lead to Nicaraguan strongman Gen. Anastasio Somoza's resignation, four of the five junta members met in Puntarenas with President Rodrigo Cara-

to, former Venezuelan President Carlos Andres Pérez, former Costa Rican Chief of State José ("Pepe") Figueres, and a representative of ex-Panamanian National Guard head Omar Torrijos. Pérez and the Panamanian reportedly returned to their countries after the meeting.

The meeting took place after both Carazo and the junta met separately with special envoy Bowdler in San José. Costa Rica, Panama and Venezuela have

*(Page 3)*

*Political flags flying from a car (Ulate's supporter) and a government poster during elections – Photo: D.A.S. Photo, Bisley.*

*Administrative Building of the University for Peace, Costa Rica.*

*Former President José Figueres leading a march through San José, the capital of Costa Rica, to celebrate the Sandinista victory in Nicaragua. The banner means "The Light of Liberty shines in Nicaragua" – Photo: Tico Times, 27 July 1979.*

position of commander-in-chief of the forces.[4]

It is of the greatest significance that there was no protest from any quarter against the decision to dissolve the Army. Were the people still very conscious of the terrible civil war of some eight months earlier when (as was said several times) 'brother killed brother'; was it that there had been no real army for many years; or was it that the people of Costa Rica had become so imbued with their traditions of civil rights and democracy – and so steadfast in their faith in those traditions – that the formal dissolution of the army was recognized and accepted as being in the very nature of those traditions?

In 1981, one of the University Professors considered Figueres had interpreted the mood and history of the country which had never known conscription, whilst another was quite definite there had been no objection from anyone when the army was dissolved. It was well put by a spokesman at the United Party Headquarters (Calderón Guardia's son being their Presidential Candidate in the 1982 election) when he said 'it wasn't just pulled out of a hat, it was an ongoing process; we felt better having no army'! A Lawyer, in charge of the University for Peace project, was of the opinion the first suggestion about disbanding the army had come in 1941 or 1942 from the National Centre of Studies but no trace of this could be found in any of their publications. He was also certain there was no opposition from anyone at the time the declaration was made. Another of the Professors confirmed there had been no protest, no meetings nor correspondence in the papers but he was also of the opinion the idea had been floating for some time before. He considered there had not been a real army previously; not as an organisation of any social or political importance: it had been considered a very junior profession. As Head of the Political Science Faculty he pointed out that from about 1890 the budget for the police began to equate the army budget and in 1910 the former became the larger and had continued to be so; as a result the army began to disappear. He considered that in the 19th century the social problems were not such as to require an army, except as regards other Central American republics. As the United States' foreign policy took charge of Central America, any need for an army with a potential for foreign activities disappeared. (But this has not been the case with the other Central American Republics!) Again a young man at *La Nación* who recalled the Victory Parade of April 1948 as being such a magnificent occasion, said there had been no letters or objections; no-one was afraid; everyone agreed with the proposal.

What is truly remarkable is the way in which the event has been virtually ignored in so many important publications, e.g.

'In 1948 the army was again done away with . . .'[5]
'Calderon's anticipated invasion did not come until late 1948, after Figueres had disbanded the army.'[6]
'In the reorganisation of the government, one of his first actions was to disband the army . . .'[7]
'. . . they had dissolved the Costa Rican army, leaving only a police force for protection.'[8]
'The great achievements of the Junta were . . . the dissolution of the army, . . .'[9]

The above quotations are the only references in the respective publications of this truly remarkable step. In the first quotation the word 'again' refers to the army being first formally abolished in 1848[10] – significantly just one hundred years earlier. This follows the comment that

'An effort to impose compulsory military service by Francisco Morazán, who had become chief of state in 1842, contributed to his downfall, and he was publicly executed.'[11]

There is no mention of the dissolution of the army in *Notes on Costa Rican Democracy* published by the University of Colorado in the 1960s and, what is even more remarkable, not a word in Carlos Melendez' *Historia de Costa Rica* published in 1979. What to most must appear to be an event of major historical importance is completely ignored. Why?

It is almost unbelievable such a dramatic step could have been taken when there was obviously considerable apprehension regarding the intentions of the Nicaraguan dictator, Somoza, who would be known to be sympathetic to Calderón Guardia's desire to avenge his defeat in the revolution and retake power. During the months immediately preceding 1st December there had been constant attempts to persuade the United States to provide arms for the Costa Rican army – and now that had been disbanded, as had the Caribbean Legion. Apart from idealistic considerations that definitely influenced the decisions, several practical factors contributed to making possible the elimination of the armed forces. It was clear that the country had no aggressive intent or military pretentions. This gave it a respected place in the family of its sister nations and generally tended to minimise tensions or hostile confrontations, although there were occasions when these occurred. A significant element was the country's relative isolation and inaccessibility, protected as it is by mountainous terrain and impenetrable jungles.

Cozean suggests many reasons for the abolition of the army and first sketches the background of the non-military tradition of Costa Rica. He points out the military was never important, the nation having had few military heroes and only three military presidents – a unique feature in

Latin America. As there were no Spanish interests to protect nor large masses of landless farm workers to exploit, no strong army developed. Even under the 1871 Constitution the army was to be subservient to the President and have no deliberative authority. In the years that followed, the military remained under tight civilian control and only the President and Secretary for War had the authority to remove guns and gunpowder from the arsenal. During the Great Depression of the 1930s Costa Rica was one of the few countries in Latin America that did not fall to military dictatorships. During the Second World War, however, the anxiety of the United States to protect the Panama Canal led to the first Military Mission being established and the supply of modern equipment and training to the Costa Rican army. Thus General Picado in the period 1944-48 was in control of the strongest army in the history of the country and many feared the army had begun to exert an important role in politics. The events surrounding the disputed elections of 1944, 1946 and, most of all, 1948, fully justified this fear. Ulate's *Diario de Costa Rica* had several inflammatory editorials attacking President Picado as being a puppet in the grip of forces more powerful than himself and saying 'the fight is now beginning and it is between the barracks and a people without a President'.[12]

There have been many reasons advanced as leading to the abolition of the army and, no doubt, readers – and writers – will select and give most weight to those which appeal most to their points of view and prejudices. Cozean is certain that basically the abolition was the work of one man, Figueres. The first reason, that the army was no longer needed, he justifies by quoting a letter he received from José Figueres in April 1966:

> The army of Costa Rica was abolished in 1948 in order to reaffirm the principle of civil government. We are convinced that countries such as ours do not need any armed forces other than a good police force. The army disappeared following its defeat in April 1948. Later the legal move was made of declaring it unconstitutional and symbolically the army fortresses were converted into museums.[13]

A few years earlier Figueres had told an interviewer, Gerald Clark, the reason was revenge, which has been regarded by several writers as the most fundamental, but Ted Szule, New York Times correspondent, doubts this, although he concedes the army's attitude in general must have given Figueres a lot of food for thought.[14]

It will be recalled the army had for several years prior to the revolution supported the Calderón-Picado regime and there had been several occasions when opponents had been harassed and even several deaths were reported. Was not the General at the head of the Army the brother of the President? When the successful revolution ended the army was discredited and symbolized the defeated regime. The list of its 'crimes' included:

1. Whilst the legislature was debating the election results (of 1948) the army began to dominate events by occupying key positions in the city.
2. When Ulate was declared the winner, it was the army that made the first move towards rebellion when General Picado refused to give up power.
3. The army was a participant in the attempt to arrest Ulate when his friend Dr Valverde was killed.
4. President Picado demonstrated the untraditional but increasing influence of the army by moving from the Presidential palace into the army barracks.
5. The army furnished most resistance to Figueres' Liberation army. (Mora and the Nicaraguans might not agree with this.)
6. The army had accepted help from the Communists and accordingly could be held responsible when the latter seized control of San José – the first capital to come under Communist control in the Western Hemisphere.
7. Even when the truce was signed, Mora had refused to surrender the Bella Vista Fortress.[15]

The army could, of course, have been replaced by some of the liberation force; was Figueres' intention to make the army's defeat the more ignoble by complete abolition? This would make an example of the hated Costa Rican army for the rest of the world to see. Gerald Clark reports Figueres as saying:

> "Why should a band of professional soldiers have taken upon themselves the right to annul the popular will as expressed at the polls?"

On the other hand, Figueres' biographer, Arturo Castro Esquivel, considers the abolition was influenced by noble motives and the President's idealism. Figueres has been a giant in standing up for what he believes and, therefore, his strong philosophical motives as factors contributing to the abolition of the army cannot be over-emphasised.[16] Having developed his *finca* with due regard to high and noble ideals, he embarked upon his political life with biting criticism of the then President, Calderón Guardia, for which, it will be remembered, he was exiled. He has stated:

> "The only justification for armed revolt is the denial of electoral rights, as in Cuba under Batista. So long as it is legitimately elected, a bad government is better than a good revolution."[17]

To demonstrate his deeply help opposition to tyranny of any type Figueres visited Castro's Cuba, but when he delivered an anti-Communist speech which again was abruptly ended, he was expelled and dubbed an agent of Yankee imperialism.[18]

Nor must be overlooked the fact that Costa Rica was planning to rely heavily on the various mutual defence agreements that had been signed; these included:

1936 agreement in Buenos Aires which declared defence a mutual obligation.

1938 conference in Lima which established methods for consultation in cases of dispute.

1940 agreement at Havana which established the basic principle that an attack on one was an attack on all.

1944 and 1945 United Nations agreements.

1945 Act of Chapultepec in Mexico City which expanded the concept of inter-American defence.

1947 'Rio Pact' signed in Brazil, working out the technical problems of reciprocal assistance. It provided for defence against direct attack or even aggression short of a direct attack.[19]

The Rio Pact was described by Senator Arthur H. Vandenberg, a USA delegate to the Conference as of the greatest significance when he said:

'I do not believe there has been a more important document in the life of the New World.'[20]

Costa Rica was indeed to discover how significant and important was this Pact within a few days of the historic act of abolition. As the Pact was applicable in cases of aggression emanating from within or without the Americas, and aggression short of an armed attack, as well as any other situation which 'might endanger the peace of the Americas', it would, theoretically at least, cover nearly every conceivable threat to Costa Rica's security. Such idealism fitted in perfectly with the general scheme of the Second Republic then intended to be created. On 1st December 1948 Costa Rica decided to demonstrate her absolute faith in international peace-keeping machinery and as Ambassador Woodward said

'Costa Rica simply decided to take all these defensive agreements at their word.'[21]

There can be no doubt this is fully in keeping with Costa Rica's anti-military tradition.

Cozean draws attention to a third general set of motives, *viz.* dis-satisfaction with the traditional situation prevailing in Latin America at that time. Figueres had a strong dislike of the military, influenced probably by the time he had spent in exile in Mexico, where the miltary had been brought under control by 1938. He considered one of the greatest evils was that the military siphoned off funds needed elsewhere for the welfare of the people. Even when he was commander of the National Liberation Army during the revolution he would not accept being referred to as General or Colonel: 'I am just a modest citizen' he would retort. His wife is on record as admonishing a friend who referred to Figueres as 'Excelentissimo General' by telling him 'My husband and I do not care for the military mind'.[22] There can be little doubt that Figueres was so popular after the successful revolution he could have become military dictator, but he was reported as saying 'Militarism is as grave a danger as communism'.[23] It is suggested that he felt something should be done to control the military in all of Latin America, and that one of the motives that led to the abolition of the army in Costa Rica was his protest against the then recent military coups in several Latin American countries. Of these there had been seven during 1947 and 1948, the two most recent being in Peru and Venezuela in October and November 1948. Figueres was also acutely aware that in neighbouring Panama and Nicaragua military dictatorships were established. The most biting criticism he could apply was to abolish the army.

There were also some positive realistic factors which would be taken into account. The economy of the country was vulnerable and there were many bitter enemies of him and his *Junta* still in the country. It has been recognised that the best time for a *coup d'etat* is just before or just after a change in government. An article in the USA publication *Newsweek* observed:

> 'There is only one absolutely sure way not to have an army revolt; no army.'[24]

Figures also knew his government was very unpopular in some important circles, especially because of the 10% capital levy and that an army could be a rival to his authority. He wanted to reduce the power of the executive over the other branches of the government; disbanding the army would, it was hoped, place the various divisions of government on a more even and democratic plane.

In addition, as the economic situation was critical the army would be a good place to start cutting expenses. He speedily realised if he only reduced the army he would face the terribly difficult task of selecting from many who had fought with him in the revolution, those who should continue in office. Figueres realised that a small country like Costa Rica would never become an important military force in the world nor be able to afford the increasingly costly technological advances being made in modern weapons.

In addition to relying upon the defence agreements already referred to, Costa Rica would recognise that only the United States had the atomic weapon and there was, in many parts, a belief that the USA would become an effective policeman. The Good Neighbour Policy was being revised to include an Inter-American security system with the intention of guarding the peace within the Western Hemisphere; communism had not in 1948 become a major problem in that part of the world.[25]

Would Costa Rica, however, be strong enough to restrain any local trouble? Whilst the conditions appertaining to its isolation, which had helped the country to repel any foreign intrusion still remained, e.g. the jungle and the absence of passable roads to either Panama or Nicaragua, advances in military techniques, such as aircraft, presented a threat of a completely different nature. The abolition of the army can only be regarded as a gigantic step forward taken in faith. But would an army be able to ensure the protection of the country? Whilst in 1978 several senior officials and diplomats expressed to the author the point of view that treaties and pacts were relied upon, many people said simply:

> 'Even if we had an army it would be so small it could not defend us – so why have one?'

## NOTES TO CHAPTER 8

1. Cozean, p. 32
2. La Hora, La Prensa Libre 1.12.1948 Diario de Costa Rica, La Nación, 2.12.1948
3. Cozean, p. 31
4. ibid, p. 33, quoting the New York Times Nov, 10, 1949.
5. Area Handbook, p. 258
6. ibid, p. 27
7. ibid, p. 27
8. Parker, p. 268
9. Bell, p. 160, (in his Epiloque to his book written chiefly about the Revolution and events leading up to it)
10. Area Handbook, p. 258
11. ibid, p. 258
12. Cozean, pp. 34/39, quoting many authorities and for the last sentence, the New York Times of Feb. 4, 1947
13. ibid, p. 45
14. ibid, p. 48
15. ibid, p. 48/49, quoting the New York Times of April 17, 1948
16. ibid, p. 42, observing Figueres gained the respect of a number of the Hemisphere's intellectuals including the late Adlai Stevenson
17. ibid, p. 43, pointing out Figueres later broke with Castro over the issue of communism
18. ibid, p. 44
19. ibid, p. 51
20. ibid, p. 52
21. ibid, p. 52/53
22. ibid, p. 53, quoting C. H. Calhoun in the New York Times, April 27, 1948
23. ibid, p. 54, quoting Christian Science Monitor, May 13, 1950
24. ibid, p. 46, quoting Newsweek, 13.12.1948
25. ibid, p. 50, citing William G. Carleton, 'The Revolution in American Foreign Policy'

# Chapter Nine

# ELECTION: INVASION

Immediately after the sensational announcement on 1st December 1948, Costa Rica was embroiled in the election of a Constituent Assembly. This was the body charged with the duty of producing an acceptable Constitution which it was hoped would assist the country to return to a completely normal situation and enable Ulate to assume the Presidency.

In his *Diario de Costa Rica* on 2nd December, as well as finding room to report the abolition of the army and his response to the attack upon him by Jíminiz, appeared his 'moving message from the President-elect to the farmers of Costa Rica' styled Otilio Ulate, the 'Costaricans' best friend'. The farmers are great and noble, he wrote, and his experience had led him every day nearer to them and further away from the politicans. It was his innermost conviction that the last revolution did not come from the politicans but from the farmers and that 'our own Costarican revolution' could be described as a rebellion of the farmers . . . Ulate would, of course, be well known to the business interests of San José because of his newspaper, hence the specific appeal to the many farmers.

On the 5th December, Figueres' party, the Social Democrats, had a whole page advertisement – in Ulate's paper be it noted – urging the electorate to vote and not abstain and setting out twelve points, the first of which, interestingly enough, was to ratify Ulate's election as President on the previous 8th of Feburary. This would seem to confirm the contention that Figueres was quite genuine in his endeavours to uphold Costa Rica's democratic tradition rather than to seek power for himself. Other points in the advertisement were:

to consolidate the work of the revolutionary government

to maintain and improve the rights of the worker

to reduce the Congress to 39 deputies (instead of 45)

to make the Supreme Electoral Tribunal an autonomous body with the exclusive right to declare the election of President

José Figueres, however, was not amongst the list of candidates seeking election to the Assembly but in extra large headlines at the foot it was announced that the Social Democrat Party was employing the figure of José Figueres to give to Costa Rica a new Constitution; coupled with a photograph of the man himself – in evening dress. Readers were reminded Figueres was their Liberator and that his name forms part of the country's history. For good measure it was added the Party would defend, in the Constituent Assembly of 1949, the revolutionary work of José Figueres.

The Constitutional Party advertised its programme of a Political Constitution and Democratic Institutions in almost a full page of *La Nación* whilst in about half a page voters were invited to ensure the future of the country by supporting Acción Cívica who offered only eight candidates. The Constitutional Party's advertisement made much of the need for a legal and suitable Constitutional charter that would endure, and contained the following rather pregnant sentence:

> This Party does not fly personal flags, nor does it wish to seize power and hand it over to one determined citizen.[1]

Were they looking in the direction of Calderón Guardia – or José Figueres?

*La Nación*, in its Editorial column, urged the need for everyone to vote and referred to broadcasts from over the mountains – presumably Calderón Guardia in Nicaragua – by public enemies who were recommending abstention. Being somewhat anti-Figueres the paper took the opportunity of questioning the need for a new Constitution, indicating that the re-establishing of the 1871 Charter would be adequate. The following paragraph demonstrates the paper's position:

> We have therefore recently demanded – against the notorious protest of those who claim to base their own whims on the will of the people – that the constituent committee should not only have the duty of approving a new constitutional charter, but also that it should be given concrete and immediate political power to lead the Republic back to the path of Law in the shortest possible time.[2]

*La Prensa Libre,* on the other hand, contented itself with a strong plea for everyone (men only at this time) to vote and said it was not an occasion when political parties were important. A very long speech by Lawyer don Everardo Gomez was reported in full in which he castigated the calderónistas (without naming them), paid glowing tribute to those who had sacrificed their lives in the epic struggle and stressed the call to vote by both Ulate and Figueres, identifying them with 'that great sacrificed figure called León Cortés'. Another political commentator took the opportunity to deliver a slashing attack upon communism with which he identified all the excesses of the previous regime.

Although *La Prensa Libre* reported Figueres and his Ministers being widely and enthusiasticaly acclaimed when they visited some areas immediately before voting day, the result was similar to that in Britain in 1945 – a crushing defeat for the popular and venerated war leader. The result was:

| | | |
|---|---|---|
| Ulate's Party, National Union | 60,796 votes | 33 deputies |
| Constitutional Party | 10,714 votes | 5 deputies |
| Figueres' Party, Social Democrats | 6,266 votes | 3 deputies |
| Several smaller parties polled | 4,372 votes | |

The total of 82,148 votes was much smaller than previous elections for President and the Legislature, and it has been said that many of Guardia's and Mora's followers were denied the opportunity to vote. In any event it is more than likely many would, for one reason or another, not take part.

Next day *La Prensa Libre* considered the abstentions had been less than expected and the keynote was that the result ratified Ulate's success on 8th February. It was keen to emphasise the election had been held in peace and lamented it could not say 'In peace and concord' as there was a latent division still prominent. Testimony was also paid to President Figueres and his Ministers for the conduct of the election and for restoring confidence to the population. On another page *La Prensa Libre* asserted:

> the fact that a group which has disaffected, or still better the declared enemy of the Power which today exercises its functions, could contest an election without let or hindrance, speaks clearly of what electoral liberty in Costa Rica is. It has been clearly seen that that disaffected party, which was overthrown through the efforts of an armed revolution and was yesterday able to exercise the vote in support of a party it considered most in harmony with its principles, that party enjoyed complete immunity without at any moment there being raised against it the slightest obstacle, or being made the victim of the slightest persecution. Its members competed freely without either the sword of the military or the blackjack of political partisan being brandished against them. And their votes were respected; they were examined and counted for the election to the Constituent Assembly.
>
> And whilst this freedom was given to the party opposed to the present régime, the side which said it came from the government or was the governing *Junta*, had to submit to third place . . . as if it seemed that it did not enjoy the sympathy of the same electorate.
>
> It turned out to be the best example of electoral freedom the country has experienced . . .

106

It had been a magnificent civic gesture of the Costa Rican people and has given the lie in the clearest and most absolute manner to those who asserted, malevolently, that freedom in Costa Rica was bound up with the interests and vanities of those who at present exercise the Power.[3]

It is difficult to understand how the paper could justify the first paragraph quoted above; the votes for the party under the name Popular Republican Movement polled only 668 votes! Compared with the 93,000 of Calderón Guardia in 1940 and the overall success of the National Republicans in the elections of 1944 and 1946, as well as the 44,438 for Calderón Guardia again in 1948, the vote in 1949 was miniscule. Nor is it clear which of the other main parties could have attracted their support although there is a suggestion the Constitutional Party had the backing of former calderonistas. Nevertheless, the newspaper's comments were at least partially justified as some of the former National Republican strength would be in the 82,148 who voted on 8 December 1948; not all the difference in support for the other parties could be accounted for by the increase in the population.

On 10th December, *La Prensa Libre* was at pains to publish a justification of Benjamin Odio (Director of the Electoral Register in February of that year) and interpret the election result now achieved as a complete refutation of the terrible lies and abuse to which he had been subjected.

Figueres, disappointed as he must have been, went on record as saying the many telegrams he had received indicated appreciation that the holding of proper and correct elections had been restored to Costa Rica. 'We have undone the moral damage of 13th February', he said.[4] He must have known that, with a Constituent Assembly so heavily weighted in Ulate's favour, the days of the Second Republic were numbered; so it was, the title gradually fell into disuse.

December 1948 was certainly a momentous month in the history of this little country. The dissolution of the army on December 1st, the election for the Constituent Assembly on the 8th and before the effects of the latter had been digested – invasion! On the 10th came reports that the rebel forces of Calderón Guardia were entering the north-west corner of Costa Rica with, it was believed, support from Nicaragua. Whilst it was known Guardia had been at Managua with the Nicaraguan dictator, Somoza, who was very much opposed to Figueres, the actual invasion seems to have been unexpected at that time. Perhaps the rebel forces had been encouraged by the announcement of the disbanding of the army and the Caribbean Legion a few days earlier. Alternatively, had Calderón Guardia paid due attention to the election of two days earlier, he would have realised the chance of his securing any substantial volume of support from any who had not left the country with him was very small indeed. No doubt the invasion had been planned for some time and it was merely coincidental that it occurred so soon after the events of the 1st and 8th.

It is not strictly correct to say there had been no warning of the invasion. *La Hora* on 3rd December carried on its front page a large headline

### INVASION OF COSTA RICAN TERRITORY

and went on to relate that the Ambassador in Mexico had reported reactionary and anti-democratic forces abroad intended to try to sabotage or impede the elections for a Constituent Assembly. The Ambassador referred to

> a violent and well synchronised campaign in the press against the government of my country. It appears they are trying to induce a favourable climate to undertake the invasion of the national territory and impede at all costs the elections for the Constituent Assembly. They are trying to confound the liberation movement of my country with the military blows that are destroying Democracy in Latin America.[5]

What is even more significant and illuminating is the story also on the same page under the headline:

### MANUEL MORA BEGS HIS FOLLOWERS TO ABANDON ALL INTENTIONS OF REBELLION AGAINST THE PRESENT GOVERNMENT

The paper claimed the message had been received from Mora, who was living in Mexico, and that it had been published in the clandestine paper *Work* circulating surreptitiously in Costa Rica. Mora's message said:

> A civil war in Costa Rica at this time would be the beginning of a conflagration in Central America with grave danger for the independence and sovereignty of all the peoples of Central America. It is natural that, after a struggle so passionate and so sorrowful, everyone is desirous of redressing the abuses of which we have been victims but my friends and I do not believe that will be the way.[5]

Perhaps the *Junta* and those in charge had been somewhat apprehensive in case an attempt were made to interfere with the election but, all was well, it had passed off without incident. On 11th December, however, the morning daily *La Nación* was asking in larger headlines than usual

### IS AN INVASION ON THE NORTHERN FRONTIER IMMINENT?

The paper reported the Government had received information of military movements threatening its territory and that armed units had been dispatched to the frontier. Also that references to Calderón Guardia's supporters were in reality references to Nicaraguan military forces. It was also stated that from Nicaragua cablegrams had been sent out to give the impression that chaos reigned in Costa Rica and that there had been risings of calderonistas. There were reports of other quite important items noted on Page 1 of *La Nación* that day!

*La Prensa Libre* in its leading article pointed out that, in view of the lack of support at the polls for National Republican and Communist ideas, any intentions to invade were absurd. The Costa Rican people would drop fleeting differences and present a solid front to the evil-doers. No foreign government would be prepared to support a gang of soul-less men and

> We believe, in spite of the scepticism we profess about international agreements – that the norms which regulate relations amongst American states will act as a barrier of some strength to prevent foreign governments interfering in our affairs. We do not think any Central American or Caribbean régime is capable of a dishonourable stab in the back against an unarmed, peaceful nation . . . Such an attack would be the most heinous attack upon Right and Justice and, although it is clear that the world seems used to similar outrages, we believe there must still be noble peoples and governments to defend the weak . . .

After observing that strife, and even the rumour of strife, impedes progress and that the news seemed to be simply rumour, the writer of the article suddenly discovered 'the barbarous crudity of facts had overtaken us . . . *the invasion is here.'* On its front page, *La Prensa,* claimed Calderón Guardia's forces were gathering in Managua and reported a representative of a Nicaraguan newspaper had telephoned President Figueres at noon and asked him if there had been internal military disturbances by enemies of the *Junta*, to which Figueres had smilingly retorted 'Yes, listen to the shouts "long live Otilio and the *Junta*".' In order to emphasise this he had put the telephone outside the window below which a large crowd was gathered. When asked how the invaders would be received, Figueres had replied 'With flowers'.[6]

Ulate's newspaper, *Diario de Costa Rica,* carried a different theme. It told how Calderón Guardia with his brother, had been to El Salvador and of their plans to establish a 'Government' in Liberia (a town in Guanacaste, the north-west province of Costa Rica). There was even the announcement of the appointment of an international adventurer, Julio López Masegoza, as Commandant of the CCCR (Constitutional Commander of Costa Rica).[7]

The United States Ambassador to Costa Rica reported being called to the Presidency at 3 p.m. on 11th December when he was asked about arms being supplied if the invasion were not speedily repulsed. In reply to the Ambassador's enquiry about the Caribbean Legion, he had been told it had offered the support of a unit of 600 men but this had been rejected although individual volunteers would be accepted. Arms in possession of the Legion's members would be forcibly taken if not surrendered that night. The President had said that, contrary to reports of support for the invasion, offers to aid the government were pouring in. Efforts were being made to detain Vanguardia leaders but all except one had gone into hiding. It was believed about 800 men had attacked La Cruz (a little town in the north-west of Costa Rica), of whom no more than 200 could possibly be Ticos (the name by which Costa Ricans refer to themselves). Instructions had been given to invoke the Rio treaty which had been signed the previous year but only become effective seven days before the invasion.[8]

This latter is of the utmost importance. On 11th December the Costa Rican Ambassador in Washington, USA had sent to the Chairman of the Organisation of American States (the Headquarters of which are in Washington) a note saying:

> That in the night of 10th December the territory of Costa Rica had been invaded by armed forces proceeding from Nicaragua

and invoking the Inter-American Treaty of Reciprocal Assistance.[9]

Fortunately for Costa Rica – and perhaps for posterity – the Council of the OAS moved extremely quickly. A meeting was summoned for 3 p.m. on 12th December at which

> Costa Rica charged Nicaragua with tolerating, encouraging and aiding a conspiracy concocted in Nicaragua in order to overthrow the Costa Rican government by force of arms and making available the territory and material means to cross the border and invade Costa Rica.

The Council decided to call a Special Meeting for 14th December. Nicaragua had denied it had any part in the events in Costa Rica and referred to the formation of a Caribbean Legion trained in Costa Rica and Guatemala.[10]

On that date the US Ambassador in San José reported the capital presented a normal Sunday appearance and people were on the streets in their usual numbers. Communication censorship had been imposed, a football game cancelled and Santa Claus would not be arriving as planned. Very few facts about the fighting were available as there was no road from La Cruz to Liberia (the Pan-American Highway had not then been completed in that sector) and the normal means of communication was not available as La Cruz Airstrip had been seized by the Calderón forces. Although there were no definite figures as to numbers involved, the total reported was considerably larger than the number of Costa Rican citizens known to have been in exile in Nicaragua. The Ambassador also expressed the opinion that the troops could only have come from the direction of Nicaragua. Morale in San José was excellent, messages of support were pouring in to the Government which had received no reports of any support for Calderón Guardia anywhere in the country. The Army barracks converted into a museum ten days ago was no longer a museum; about 600 men, chiefly members of the Caribbean Legion, were assembling there.[11]

An interesting and poignantly important interview with Somoza was reported by the USA Ambassador in Nicaragua. Somoza had attempted to treat the matter lightly but had been told it was very serious and, despite promises previously made, he had allowed an insurrection to organise in Nicaragua and proceed to attack Costa Rica. He also denied Costa Rican émigrés had been given uniforms, shoes and arms and that his Guardia Nacional had allowed groups of men in trucks to pass without his knowledge or consent. The report continues that

> Tacho (presumably Somoza) expressed no regret that incident had occurred and stated also that if this brought about an armed attack on Nicaragua he would welcome it indicating he felt able to cope with this situation by force of arms. His final attitude was rather belligerent and his final statement was that this situation would be brought to a head and that the US would bring pressure on Costa Rica as well as on him to the end that peace and quiet might prevail in the two countries.[12]

Somoza's attitude is the more surprising when it is compared with the explanation of Nicaragua's position given by that country's delegate to the Organisation of American States on 12th December which was as follows:

1. Nicaragua had no aggressive intentions against Costa Rica or any other nation.

2. Nicaragua had abided and would abide by 1928 Habana Convention regarding revolutionary movements within its borders against other countries

3. There is no conflict between the Governments of Costa Rica and Nicaragua.[13]

Meanwhile on 12th December, *La Nación* announced in letters almost three inches high the Country had been ATTACKED from the Northern frontier, the Government had protested most energetically to the Nicaraguan Government and that 300 Spanish Reds had been recruited in Mexico. Otilio Ulate was to join the Government during the emergency. The leading article most severely castigated Calderón Guardia and contained the paragraph:

> But he attempts it (the invasion) against his own country, adding to the chain of crimes against his country, the command of revolutionary forces. Does this poor fool not understand that since this episode of his life his name is going to be for ever accursed among Costa Ricans? Does he not sense that his fellow-citizens will never forgive him for throwing foreign troops against Costa Rica? Or does the well-deserved censure of his compatriots not matter to him.[14]

No-one at that time could have anticipated that a man so despised and reviled would not only return to Costa Rica but also be able to stand for election as President again – and get more than one-third of the votes![15] Truly Costa Ricans are a remarkable people.

It is not without significance the following announcement appeared in one of the daily papers:

> ... the Government of the Second Republic found itself confronted by the inevitable necessity, imposed by the compulsion of the moment, of imprisoning as a security measure those persons who had openly, in a campaign previously, put their strength behind the system of the old régime. Nevertheless, the Government wishes to avoid, even against its own enemies, the slightest interference, so that it has decreed the setting up of an emergency tribunal to undertake the detailed study of each and every one of such detentions so that if the case permits, it may proclaim the right measures – without diminution of national security – to set at liberty those individuals whose previous conduct justifies it.

On the same day, 15th December, *La Prensa Libre*'s editorial found considerable hope in the way the Organisation of American States had responded to the complaint made by Costa Rica against Nicaragua. After referring to its previous expression of scepticism about international treaties, it continued

> Putting to one side the Council resolution, in so far as it fits our interests, there is another important aspect for international life in the relations which must govern people to avoid conflicts. The capital interest of the Costa Rican appeal takes its origin in the fact that this is the first time the Pact of Rio de Janeiro has been put to the test. Leader writers, observers, international commentators have all agreed with this assertion which in short has concentrated

American international opinion. It was the unavoidable parting of the ways where international law would either be strengthened or weakened.

Yesterday's vote strengthens the American juridical organs. Nations like ours, although young, are honest and loyal. They have a more correct feeling about their duties and adjust to them with more decision. America comes with its attitude of yesterday by means of the group of nations which make it up, to say that it is possible to solve problems, avoid crises, grant to each one its own through the treaties, without appeal to force, that sullen spring of death and ruin.

Let us hope in confidence, counting on the support of twelve nations, that Costa Rica will emerge from the aggression she has been the victim of, that Justice will accompany her, and that at the same time, the prestige of America will come out free and without stain.[16]

It should be appreciated that 'America' from Mexico south refers to the Western Hemisphere and not just the United States. There have been cases subsequently where the OAS has been able to preserve peace between different American nations and, although sceptics may say this is because of the power and domination of the United States, records will show this has not necessarily been so. A recent illustration was in 1979 when the Sandinista rebellion was gaining the upper hand against Somoza's National Guard; the USA strongly urged the sending in of a combined OAS 'peace-keeping' force – believed to be largely to prevent a Sandinista government, suspected of having communist sympathies, from taking power. The USA proposal was, however, defeated by opposition from Mexico and other American nations. USA's own record in Nicaragua would also mitigate against any such scheme.

The same paper, *La Prensa Libre*, had a very practical editorial the following day. It was headed 'Help for the Country' but might better have been designated 'Pay up!' This was an appeal to everyone to contribute to the public funds and had the very pointed suggestion that clubs and associations of every kind should raise contributions from amongst their members for the defence fund. This would make it easier for individuals to contribute and encourage them to be more generous in order to add to the prestige of the club – it didn't say it would be more difficult to refuse when being pressed by another club member. It even urged prompt payment of all taxes – including income tax – so that the Government would not see its coffers emptying!

No Costa Rican who feels himself nobly patriotic, nor any foreigner who feels himself worthy of the hospitality he is enjoying, can now be in debt to the state.[17]

113

(Why should it need resistance to an invasion, or a war, to urge prompt payment of one's dues?) A special office under the title of General Treasury of the Army was opened by the Minister of Public Works for receipt of contributions for the National Army.

This, and similar instances, underline the fact that the Costa Ricans do not claim to be, and are not, pacifists. They have simply learned how to exist without the burden of modern arms, whether it be by relying on treaties, recognising they cannot be defended by any army they could maintain, or for a number of other equally valid and contributory reasons. Nor is their situation dissimilar from that of most, if not all, other countries.

At its Special Meeting on 14th December, the Council of the Organisation of American States had made important decisions:

1. To convoke a consultative meeting of Foreign Ministers to study the situation created between Costa Rica and Nicaragua. The place and date of this meeting to be indicated as soon as possible.

2. To constitute itself as the Provisional Organ of Consultation in accordance with Article 12 of the Inter-American Treaty of Reciprocal Assistance.

3. To name a commission to investigate on the spot the acts which have been denounced and their antecedents. This commission will be named by the Chairman of the Council.

4. To request all the American Governments and the Secretary General of the OAS to lend their full co-operation to facilitate the work of the commission, which should begin its task immediately.

Twelve countries supported the resolution, only one, the Dominican Republic, abstained. The United States delegate made it clear that this resolution should not and could not be interpreted as implying any judgement in regard to the situation or as prejudging the case of any country. The Council in general shared this understanding.[18]

At the earlier meeting on 12th December, the Costa Rican delegate had proposed the appointment of a commission as was agreed at the second meeting. He had also suggested the appointment of an international force to control disorder but no action was taken in regard to this.[19]

A Commission of five Ambassadors was named by the Chairman, being those representing Brazil, Colombia, Mexico, Peru and USA. The Peruvian Ambassador withdrew on instructions from his Government because it had not been recognised by the Costa Rican Government. They proceeded to Costa Rica and on the 17th December interviewed four Nicaraguans captured with 35 followers of Calderón Guardia on 10th December at Santa Rosa, which is approximately 50 kilometers inside Costa Rican territory. Two days later they interviewed the Commanding Officer and a Major and two other prisoners at Liberia, Guanacaste Province, as well as meeting with President Elect, Otilio Ulate, in San José.

Having spent three days in Costa Rica, the Commission moved into Nicaragua where, on 20th December, they interviewed the President, the Minister for Foreign Affairs and the Minister for War. The following day they met with Enoc Aguardo the political leader of Nicaragua and Teodoro Picado, the ex-President of Costa Rica.

The Commission made its Report to the Council of the Organisation of American States in its capacity as the Provisional Organ of Consultation on the 24th December; what incredible speed! La Cruz and El Amo (small towns about 20 kilometers inside the territory of Costa Rica) had been visited and gunfire had been heard there. Enquiries had been made to ensure the Caribbean Legion had been disbanded as Costa Rica had claimed. The latter had said measures had been taken to prevent groups organising on its soil, which measures the Commission found were adequate but the true value would depend upon the persistence and effectiveness of their application. There had been allegations of invasions by Nicaraguans in 1945, as well as in March and April 1948, and it was even claimed the Nicaraguan National Guard had invaded Costa Rica in 1944 and thrust Teodoro Picado as President upon them by force.

The Commission was in no doubt that the revolutionary movement was organised and prepared in Nicaragua and that the Nicaraguan Government had failed to take adequate measures to prevent the frontier being crossed. It found, what was of the utmost importance, that, after 10th December, the Nicaraguans began to take measures to prevent the rebels continuing to receive aid (the clear implication being they had received such aid previously). There can be little doubt but that the complaint to the OAS followed by its speedy action – the Report of the Commission was made to the Council only fourteen days after the invasion commenced! – was instrumental in securing the cessation of hostilities. By ensuring that aid in the form of supplies did not reach the rebels they had no alternative but to cease their activities. This must be one of very few occasions when diplomatic action has brought fighting to an end. It is evident from the early attitude of Somoza that a continuation of the rebel invasion could well have caused the conflict to escalate into a state of war between Costa Rica and Nicaragua with the result that a permanent armed force would be reintroduced into and remain in the former remarkable little country.

The two countries entered into a Pact of Unity prepared under the auspices of the Organisation of American States which, it was hoped, put an end to the differences between them and also recognised the obligation to submit all disputes that might arise to methods for the peaceful settlement of international conflict. Extracts from the records of the OAS relating to this incident are given in Appendix 1.

Cozean reports that many of the OAS Council members were disappointed that the first test case of the Rio Treaty was not more spectacularly reported but this was not the view of the hemispheric press. A number of editorial writers noted that at last an international organisation had effectively brought peace; the following are a selection:

> The peace machinery of the Western Hemisphere emerges with honour from its first test . . . a precedent has been established . . . all accomplished within 15 days, a remarkable record for any international agency.[20]

> The first major success of peace-keeping machinery set up in the Western Defence Pact.[21]

> the OAS action represented a new direction in Inter-American relations[22]

> the OAS intervention is a contribution to the spirit of the Pact of Reciprocal Assistance.[23]

> the OAS move was an important precedent for all the Americas.[24]

> the OAS action established numerous precedents[25]

> the OAS met its first test admirably[26]

> most Ambassadors were delighted because their action proved that the Rio Pact was a living instrument. It is a safe bet that in future cases of aggression they will be ready to act even more quickly.[27]

> Even though the Costa Rican affair did not provide a clear-cut case of aggression, it was an important precedent in 1948 . . . a time when this kind of international action being advocated by the United Nations was as yet mostly theory.[28]

## NOTES TO CHAPTER 9

1. La Nación
2. ibid, 7.12.1948
3. La Prensa Libre, 9.12.1948
4. ibid, 9.12.1948
5. La Hora, 3.12.1948
6. La Prensa Libre, 11.12.1948
7. Diario de Costa Rica, 11.12.1948
8. US Foreign Relations, pp. 536/7
9. OAS Library
10. ibid
11. US Foreign Relations, pp. 537/8
12. ibid, p. 539
13. ibid, p. 540
14. La Nación, 12.12.1948
15. Area Handbook, p. 31
16. La Prensa Libre, 15.12.1948
17. ibid, 16.12.1948
18. US Foreign Relations, p. 541
19. ibid, p. 540
20. New York Times, 26.12.1948, Section IV, p. 6
21. ibid, 20.2.1949, p. 20
22. Diario de Costa Rica, 19.12.1948
23. El Tiempo de Bogotá, Colombia
24. La Estrella de Panama, 18.12.1948, p. 4
25. United States Department of State Bulletin, 5.6.1949, pp. 707/12
26. Newsweek, 3.1.1949, p. 34
27. The Nation, pp. 63/66
28. A Survey of US-Latin American Relations by J. Lloyd Mechan, p. 182

# Chapter Ten

# RETURN TO A CONSTITUTIONAL REGIME

It is not surprising that, when it met on 15th January 1949, one of the first acts of the Constituent Assembly was to pass a Resolution to remove the portrait of Dr Calderón Guardia from the gallery adjoining the Congress Chamber. In this gallery hang portraits of all the former Presidents. The only amendment to the Resolution was to add the word 'immediately'. (The portrait has since been restored; what a forgiving people the Costa Ricans are.)

On the following day, José Figueres Ferrer, President of the *Junta Fundadora* of the Second Republic, presented his Presidential Address to the Assembly. He commenced by reviewing the events of the epoch 1940 to 1948 and invited the Assembly to say that León Cortés was elected the Constitutional President on 13th February 1944. He paid homage to those who had died in the National Campaign of those eight years, especially in the Revolution, which he termed the 'War of National Liberation'. No indication was given of the number killed in the fighting nor reference to Calderon Guardia or Teodoro Picado, by name; nor most surprisingly to the dissolution of the army and the handing over of the barracks to be a museum which had taken place only a little more than a month earlier. Perhaps the terror of the invasion which had only just ended and for which the army had had to be resuscitated and considerably expanded was too vivid a memory. He reminded his audience of the pact he had made with Ulate and the provisional government formed as the Founding Junta of the Second Republic and that this had been accepted by the Diplomatic Corps, whose presence he acknowledged. He spoke briefly of the recent invasion and of the seventeen who had been killed but made no reference to, nor acknowledgement of, the immense and vital contribution made by the Organisation of American States.

There were two vital tasks he said; first to return to a state of security for all the inhabitants of the country and secondly to prepare for the

118

arrival of a new order guaranteeing institutional life and civic liberties and promoting the well-being of the majority. It was also necessary to re-establish the law and a Judicial Power that would be absolutely independent.

> We have decided to substitute for the 1871 Constitution a new one in which will be combined the essentials of our political life with modern ideas and the founding of the Second Republic.

he announced and referred to the Commission which had been formed to undertake the delicate task of preparing the proposal for the Constitution of the Second Republic. The election of 8th December and the inauguration of the Assembly was a testimony of the desire to return Costa Rica to an institutional life, and that day's ratification of Otilio Ulate's mandate a proof of faith in the pact and the desire for the country to return to its republican tradition.

The Second Republic would put forward four principal objectives:

1. To re-establish morale.

2. The introduction of technical ability into administration and the elimination of political influences.

3. A social programme without communism.

4. Greater solidarity with other nations, especially those in the Americas.

In regard to the third, Figueres observed:

> We must search for social progress which will be the fruit of Christian and democratic philosophy and not communist and dictatorial ideological tendencies which we consider to be retrograde.

and continued to make some most interesting observations on this theme. In prophetic words he concluded:

> 'In this perhaps we shall part . . .'

Figueres has been said to be a liberal-socialist who ousted another liberal-socialist (Calderón Guardia) in order to instal a conservative (Otilio Ulate). He reminded his listeners that the evil of poverty continued to exist and it was essential that remedies were sought.

> But instead of communism which inflames fratricidal strife, we wish to have a social spirit for everyone to join us in the struggle for production of all. Instead of a bad patriarchical almsgiving which humiliates the poor, we want to have a scientific attitude which

119

enriches them and a superior concept of justice that gives them dignity.

He terminated his long address with these words:

'The hour to inaugurate the Constitution has arrived.
Those fallen heroes say to us "The door is open, enter!"'[1]

It was not long before Figueres had to face another most serious challenge. The army had been swollen to about 5,000 men, five times its pre-invasion strength and, although some were being discharged, many would be needed to provide border patrols. Cardona would, doubtless, enjoy commanding a large army and clashed with the President when it was decided to place several army leaders on retirement. Shortly afterwards a friend of Cardona was refused the appointment as Director of the Police. Conditions for a *coup d'etat* were favourable; the invasion had upset normal activity throughout the country which was in considerable confusion; the *Junta* was preparing to pass power over to Ulate, and was not Cardona in control of a large army? Amongst his supporters was Fernando Figueroa who planned to seize the Bella Vista Fortress whilst Cardona took the artillery barracks. This they accomplished early on the morning of 2nd April 1949 with only three casualties. Cardona then issued publicly two demands. He required Figueres should

1. Discharge the Minister of Finance and Labour and rescind the unpopular 10% tax and banking law.

2. Step down immediately in favour of Ulate.

Unfortunately for Cardona, however, his confederate, Figueroa, was demanding that the *Junta* should stay and Ulate be forced to resign. Furthermore, most of the army stayed loyal to the *Junta*. Figueres was equal to the occasion and sealed off all exits from San José and had the rebel fortresses surrounded. Ulate repudiated Cardona's offer and made it known that he completely supported the *Junta*. Cardona surrendered the following day but Figueroa held out until a heavy mortar bombardment of the fortress quickly brought the rebellion to an end. Although the crowd was howling for Cardona to be executed, the *Junta* decided upon his dismissal only, which did much to increase Figueres' popularity. He now decided to accelerate the disbanding of the army and to rely for security on a well-equipped and well-trained police force.[2] It has been said that soon after Figueres came to power a counter-revolutionary plot was discovered when a large cache of submachine guns was found and 220 communists were arrested but no exact date has been given and this was probably in mid 1948.[3]

Figueres and his *Junta* Government had a great deal less success with the Constituent Assembly which was monopolised by supporters of Otilio Ulate. The Assembly had no difficulty in declaring without effect the nullification of the Presidential election of 8th February 1948 – which had been decreed by Congress on 1st March 1948 – and adopted the view of the National Electoral Tribunal of 28th February 1948 that Ulate had been constitutionally elected to the Presidency. When this was offered to him by the *Junta*, Ulate rejected the offer and said under no circumstances would he govern without a Constitution. The Assembly recognised the authority of the Founding Junta of the Second Republic to exercise the legislative power until a constitutional Congress was installed but then proceeded to refuse to adopt the preliminary draft Constitution prepared by the Commission appointed by the *Junta*. This would have reformed the Constitution in a more revolutionary manner than Ulate's group was prepared to accept.[4] One of them told the author in 1981, the draft Constitution contained some extreme measures similar to those adopted in the USSR – they were socialist![5]

Although the Constituent Assembly decided to adopt as a basis the Constitution of 1871 there were a number of significant additions. The most important of these for the purpose of this work is Article 12, which says:

> The Army is proscribed as a permanent institution. The State will rely on the necessary Police Forces to maintain and be vigilant about public order. Only by international agreement or for national defence will military forces be able to be organised which, like the police, will always be subject to the civil powers and will not be able to deliberate or hold demonstrations or make declarations either individually or collectively.[6]

The Motion was proposed by Deputies Trejos, Esquivel and Montiel. With considerable difficulty, the author managed, in 1981, to trace Lawyer Ricardo Esquivel Fernandez who recalled the debate between those who favoured a return to the old Constitution of 1871 and the others who pressed for consideration of the draft prepared by the *Junta*'s Commission. The decison to use the earlier Constitution as a basis but revise it, was a compromise. He considered it was the Constitutional Party which had had the support of the calderonistas in the December 1948 election. There had been on the part of some members of the Assembly a lack of confidence in the *Junta* and Figueres because of his 'crazy' ideas.

He could not, however, remember whose idea it had been to put forward the Article proscribing the army; there had been a small group discussing the provisions of the new Constitution, or it may have been in the draft Constitution put forward by the *Junta*'s group. (He evidently did not recall Figueres' dramatic action the previous December which, at the time of the interview, the author had not traced.) Ricardo Esquivel recalled the history of the previous century when there had been no military corps, but one had been raised to resist the attempt of Walker to seize power. When men had returned with guns they had felt important and had exercised considerable influence. There had occasionally been a caste of military men who had installed a President and then removed him; he instanced Tomas Guardia, and Tinoco's *coup d'etat* against Gonzalez Flores, who thought Tinoco to be his best and closest friend.

In 1949 they wanted to end any possibility of military domination by a President and were very conscious of the need to keep the *Junta* under control. They had very much in the forefront of their minds the previous year's civil war and its cost in terms of lives, property and effort; they wished to prevent any such occurrence again.[7] Article 12 was introduced into the Assembly on 4th July 1949, only a short time after the attempted coup by Cardona and this also must have been an important factor in the decision to provide in the Constitution that there should never be a permanent army in Costa Rica. It should be noted that in the 1871 Constitution Article 22 said:

> The military force shall be subordinate to the Civil Power, is essentially passive and must never deliberate on political matters.[8]

When the proposal was put forward on 4th July, 1949, Deputy Gomez had enquired if this would exclude the organisation of a citizen's army on the Swiss model, which disciplined itself voluntarily and which did its utmost, under the control of the Ministry of Security, to come to the defence of the motherland efficiently. Esquivel, on behalf of the proposers explained that it did not exclude a citizens' voluntary organisation such as had been indicated because that would not constitute a permanent army of a military character nor would an organisation supporting national defence be excluded from the article under discussion. Gomez asked that the doubt which he had expressed should be clarified in the respective Act as a guideline to interpreting the said article in the future.[9]

A later discussion is of interest as showing the different factors influencing the Deputies in their deliberations. The Social Democrats had put forward a motion under the Title of Individual Guarantees which read:

> The right of association of inhabitants is recognised. All organisa-tions which employ military techniques or the use of violence as a means of action are proscribed.

In the debate which followed, it was suggested to the proposers they should add that nobody should be obliged to belong to any association. Deputy Gamboa said he would not vote for the motion as, in his opinion, instead of a guarantee it constituted a real and serious threat and danger in the hands of unscrupulous governments to proscribe, for example, a specific political organisation by accusing it of employing violence as a means of action. Volio Sancho pointed out the necessity of making it clear that association was permitted only for legal aims so that this wording should not come into conflict with the definite objective of the Assembly – which prohibited the organisation and the functioning of groups 'which intend to destroy the basis of our democratic organisation'. Deputy Arroyo demonstrated that the motion constituted not a guarantee, but a possible threat to Costa Ricans. The experience he had lived through in the eight years of earlier governments, was one which could well occur again in the country; and the proposed clause would be an effective weapon in the hands of an unscrupulous government, as the last two had been. Moreover it did not seem a good idea to establish prohibitions in a section dedicated to individual guarantees, which tomorrow might serve as a pretext for unscrupulous governments to eliminate some specific group or association of a political nature. It would suffice to proscribe illegal organisations . . . Deputy Fournier explained he thought that the citizen's rights were also defended by protecting him from such organisations which used military techniques or violent modes of action. 'We have suffered personally' Fournier continued 'the action of this type of association in the last campaign when so-called shock troops of Communists were formed into groups. This kind of association exists in other countries like the Ku-Klux-Klan in the USA. The motion proposed has been copied from the modern Italian constitution and was intended to forbid fascist-type organisations which have done so much harm in Italy. However, if a motion were considered dangerous it could easily be withdrawn provided that a new formula were approved with the acceptance of the Chamber.' He then put forward the following:

> The inhabitants of the Republic have the right to join together in association for legitimate aims. Nobody can be obliged to become part of any organisation.

which was approved.[10]

There were other quite important innovations introduced in the new Constitution. One of these was the provision of 'full untrammelled autonomy for the Supreme Electoral Tribunal[11] which was to have the absolute control of elections.[12] The Tribunal was to be formed by three Magistrates and three alternates selected at staggered two year intervals to serve terms of six years each. They were to be elected by a two-thirds vote of the Supreme Court of Justice which would designate two of the alternates to sit with the Magistrates for a period of eighteen months, being one year before and six months after each election. This Tribunal to be the final arbiter on all questions concerned with the conduct of electoral apparatus. It was understood this Tribunal had control of and authority over the different corps of Police before and during elections. Further, not only was primary education made compulsory but also secondary education was pronounced free and supported by the nation.[13] Women were given the franchise with full political rights.[14] The 1949 Constitution sought to replace the Presidential system, over one hundred years old in Costa Rica, with a modified form of parliamentary government,[15] and to provide important guarantees against disproportionate exercise of executive authority.[16] There was also provision for the contribution of government funds to political parties for campaign expenses.[17] There can be no doubt that, despite the rigorous rule of the *Junta Fundadora,* the election of 8th December, 1948 did not yield a majority which was subservient to *Junta* domination and that in its deliberations from 15th January to 7th November, 1949, the Assembly adopted important constitutional provisions which did not entirely represent the will of the *Junta.*[18] On the latter date, the *Junta* accepted the provisions of the new Constitution and on the following day Otilio Ulate assumed the office of President.

Shortly before, in October, elections had been held for the Legislative Assembly, when again Ulate's party of National Union secured 33 seats as it had in the Constituent Assembly. Figueres' party, the Social Democrats, lost one seat and were reduced to three only. After their eighteen stormy months in power Figueres and the *Junta* had not succeeded in transforming the nation according to their theoretical framework. Even with the power of a *de facto* régime, their concrete realisations in social and economic reform did not equal those of the National Republican governments of Picado and Calderón Guardia.[19]

The revolution and the *Junta* consolidated the reform programme of the previous eight years by moving the centre of controversy further to the left. The full meaning of the goals of the Second Republic, as revealed in the decree laws and the draft Constitution, so alarmed most of Figueres' former allies that the reform measures passed by the previous two regimes no longer seemed radical. Within a few years Calderón Guardia's programme became part of the accepted heritage of the past, although he himself remained a controversial figure. With the passage of time the *Junta* found that their plans for improving economic, social and political conditions in Costa Rica were generally complementary rather than antagonistic to those of the National Republicans.[20]

During Ulate's Presidency two revolts were attempted; one in August

1950, the other in February 1951.[22] He concentrated on stabilising the economy and improving the administration; his mission was to do well what had to be done rather than to look for new avenues of service. The national economy prospered under his rule, though most Costa Ricans remained very poor. The national deficits of the years 1940 to 1948 were changed into surpluses.[23] Within two years the nation's financial situation was basically sound and Ulate proceeded with development schemes, including the construction of a larger airport and the creation of a dam and power plant on the Reventazón River. He was aided considerably by the high price of coffee on the world market and the reopening of the Caribbean banana plantations.[24] He was able to improve border relations and during his term of office no major border clashes developed.[25] Ulate did not attempt to abolish the social welfare programmes of Figueres and, although he authorised two private banks to balance the national system, he left the entire provisions basically intact.[26]

At the time the army was disbanded Ulate had expressed serious reservations, saying it was dangerous to disband the army whilst relations with Nicaragua were still so delicate. He did not, however, seek to undermine the intent of Article 12 although he might have interpreted the phrase 'necessary police force' to include almost any sort of para-military force. Alternatively he had reason to declare 'national emergency' – especially having regard to the Nicaraguan situation – or he could simply have ensured the Civil Guard developed into the type of force which exists in Nicaragua and Panama by including the necessary funds in the annual budgets presented by the executive. Instead he demonstrated he was more interested in building schools than in rebuilding the army and gradually increased the proportion of the annual budget going to education at the expense of other functions. He even dispensed with a Minister for Public Security as a member of his Cabinet.[27]

In September 1952 there had been an allegation of police brutality and the Assembly voted for an investigation of the Civil Guard saying it had interfered in politics. Ulate and six of his seven senior security officials resigned in protest but after sixteen days the investigating committee cleared the Civil Guard and Ulate resumed office.[28] When he presented his final message to the Legislative Assembly on 1st May 1953 he expressed pride in having ruled with complete respect for the legislative authority and said his desire had been, to quote the Chinese proverb, to end his term

> with the sabre rusty, the plough bright, the prison idle and the granary filled.[29]

Figueres and his group were not content with the direction politics had taken after their success in the revolution. The Social Democratic Party

125

was brought to an end in 1951 and the Party of National Liberation formed. Figueres expounded its general position as follows:

> Within a hundred years, Americans . . . will not understand . . . how we, in the middle of the twentieth century, with our natural resources, with the present advance of science, and with two thousand years of Christianity, maintained the greater part of our population at an intolerable level of misery. But they will not be able to accuse the men of the Movement of National Liberation of Costa Rica, if some meticulous historian reaches the point of mentioning us, of having been retrogressive. We endure the present economic and social situation of the world, under protest.[30]

Figueres was chosen as his party's nominee for the Presidential election in 1953 and Ulate's party chose Echandi Jiménez, who had been Foreign Minister, to oppose him. The Democratic Party was reformed and chose Castro Cervantes, who received the backing of Ulate's supporters when Echandi decided to withdraw. Having regard to prior events, it is unbelievable that Calderón's group of National Republicans should join Ulate and support Echandi.[31] Despite his opponents endeavouring to discredit him as a Communist or Fascist, Figueres won a bitterly fought campaign by almost two to one.[32] His party won 30 seats in the Legislature, including three going to the first women deputies (women had voted in the elections for the first time) with Union National (Ulate) only one seat as compared with their previous substantial majority.

Figueres was President for four and a half years during which many changes took place, economic, political and social.[35] His term was intensely controversial. Those who favoured him contending his government was fruitful, laying the foundation of a new order in Costa Rica. His detractors insisted that his expensive policies brought the country little beyond inflation and economic instability.[34] He commenced by renegotiating the contract with the United Fruit Company and persuaded it to increase the share of profits paid to the Country to 35 per cent. In addition the Company passed over to the government free of charge all its housing projects, schools and medical facilities. Figueres then created a National Institute of Housing and Urban Affairs and worked to expand the public school system. His doubling the top levels of income tax and increasing the minimum wage would not endear him to his opponents.[35]

With the election of Figueres the future of Article 12 of the new Constitution was guaranteed. Ulate had already given the article four years of tradition. In one of his first public acts, President Figueres announced that he was reorganising the Ministry of Public Security with the basic aim of giving the Ministry an even greater civilian image. From the beginning of his term, Figueres wanted to make Costa Rica a symbol of anti-militarism. Yet from the time of his taking office in 1953 he had trouble minimizing the size of his armed forces. His own election was viewed as a real threat in Nicaragua as, whilst out of power, Figueres had continued his personal crusade against dictators.[36]

The animosity existing between Somoza and Figueres, the presence of Calderón Guardia and some of his chief supporters in Nicaragua, coupled with Figueres continued collaboration with the leaders of the Caribbean Legion pledged to oust dictators from Central America and the Caribbean,[37] all combined to bring about another attempt to seize power by armed force. Early in January 1955 about four hundred men invaded Costa Rica from Nicaragua. In addition to some calderonistas, there were supporters of the Presidents of Cuba, the Dominican Republic, Venezuela, Colombia and Nicaragua – all had denounced Figueres as a Communist.[58] They were commanded by Teodore Picado, a son of the former President of Costa Rica, who was employed as a secretary by Somoza. There can be little doubt that the latter knew about the invasion and had given his support. There had been an abortive attempt to assassinate Somoza in 1954, for which he held Figueres responsible.

Not only did troops enter the north-west corner of Costa Rica but also planes bombed San José and some of the other towns. Picado believed supporters of the former Guardia-Picado régimes would rise to join him and had planned for his supporters to rally others round them in San José, Cartago and elsewhere. Instead many Costa Ricans were incensed and flocked to the Government's call to resist the invaders. Figueres' response was firm; he closed down Ulate's newspaper[39] and had arrested and tried for treason, Mario Echandi Jiménez, his most outspoken critic in the Legislature and a known sympathizer of Calderón Guardia.[40] Once more the Costa Rican Government appealed to the Organisation of American States which followed the pattern set in 1948 and quickly appointed a Committee of Investigation. Although the Costa Ricans, probably because of the bombing, had requested military assistance as well as the intervention of the OAS, the Council of the latter asked other member Governments to place at the disposal of the Investigating Committee aircraft to make, in the name of the Committee and under its supervision, pacific observation flights over the regions affected by the invasion. Immediately the Governments of Ecuador, Mexico, United States and Uruguay placed at the disposal of the Investigating Committee aircraft to make such pacific observation flights. Even the Nicaraguan, as well as the Costa Rican, Government made similar facilities available. In 1978, a Senior Officer in the Department of Public Security claimed some of the planes made available to Costa Rica (the United States, at the request of the OAS, sold Costa Rica several fighter planes)[41] had been used to drop bombs on the invaders, but this was doubted, and indeed denied, by others. It is quite clear there was no attempt on the part of the Costa Ricans to carry the fight into Nicaragua and the OAS Investigating Committee, which examined the situation in considerable detail, makes no reference to any such bombing. It appears two of the observation planes were apprehended when they crossed into Nicaraguan territory and were interned: it has been said they are still there!

In addition, the Council of the OAS issued a request to all American Governments (no doubt looking hard in the direction of Nicaragua) to take the necessary measures to prevent the use of their territories for any military action against the government of another state. Once again the Investigating Committee acted very promptly and, after many interviews in both Costa Rica and Nicaragua, confirmed there had been foreign intervention in assisting the rebels who had entered Costa Rica from Nicaragua and that bombing and machine-gunning had taken place in San José and various other towns. The Investigating Committee was also able to report that, after the aerial observation system had been established, a land observation system had been set up in strategic zones, as a result of which the attacking forces had abandoned their offensive and retreated into Nicaragua. A year later a formal Agreement was signed between the two countries expressing their willingness to prevent rebels from organising and crossing into each other's territory. Once again it can be said that diplomatic action and endeavours through the Organisation of American States had been successful in bringing hostilities to an end and had prevented the possibility of a serious war – and even the possibility of Costa Rica being induced to restore its disbanded army. Details of the incident extracted from the records of the OAS Library are given in Appendix II.

Hardly had the effects of this second invasion been assimilated than the country suffered disastrous floods. In October 1955 water and wind destroyed property and crops as well as claiming many lives.[42] These two calamities caused Figueres' plans to press ahead with social reforms to be moderated and his subsequent period in office was largely devoted to implementing the programmes already undertaken. Fortunately, during this time coffee prices were high, which assisted the President in his determination to raise the minimum wage. Although his conservative opponents had alleged this would mean a greater sale of liquor, Figueres was able to claim that instead

> the consumption of milk and meat has grown, of rice and beans, bread, eggs . . .[43]

It was further alleged his was the heaviest spending administration the country had ever known, but, although expenditure had risen from 165 million colones in 1952 to 289 million in 1957, receipts in the same period rose from 189 million to 298 million. At the end of his period in office, Figueres was able to say

> The economic level of Costa Rica has risen more than in comparable countries. Meanwhile the prices of articles of popular consumption have risen less . . . We have succeeded in keeping our currency stable.[44]

Sadly for Figueres' intentions to continue with the programme of social reforms, there was a split in the ranks of the National Liberation Party, which had calamitous results. Jorge Rossi Echeverría, Minister for Finance, insisted that time was needed to implement measures already adopted. When he did not receive the nomination for President by the Party, he and a few supporters broke away and formed an Independent Party. Echandi, a bitter opponent of Figueres, who had withdrawn from the contest in 1953 (and had been tried for treason when he supported Calderón Guardia in 1955) was chosen by Ulate's National Union Party and succeeded by 102,851 votes against 94,788 for Orlich, the National Liberation Candidate and 23,910 for Rossi. National Liberation had 20 seats in the Legislative Assembly against 11 Republican (the calderonistas having dropped 'National' from their Party title) and 10 for National Union. Rossi's Independent Party with 3 seats, held the balance of power.

An editorial in *The New York Times* paid tribute to the manner in which Costa Rica had overcome its traumatic experiences of 1948 and 1955 when it noted:

> The elections for President and the Legislative Assembly in Costa Rica were a model of what democratic elections can and should be. This was a splendid example for Latin America as a whole and one that we could expect from such a democracy as Costa Rica and such a confirmed champion of liberty as President José Figueres.'[45]

Somewhat unexpectedly, Echandi did not reverse the social reforms of the previous regimes nor did he denationalise the banking system as had been anticipated. What is even more surprising he embarked upon a policy to continue and consolidate the absence of armed forces in Costa Rica. Soon after the election he announced he would make the country the first in the world to govern itself without armaments. He said:

> We will offer our arms to those who sold them to us, in exchange for ploughs and tractors.[46]

President Echandi also announced his plan that the Civil Guard would confine itself to preserving public order and catching criminals, and that the money saved would be used for public health and improving agriculture. His programme of demilitarisation took definite steps when he announced the abolition of what remained of the Defence Ministry. Towards the end of 1959 the Echandi administration had worked out the details of the 'arms for tractors' plan. It was decided there were about 2,000 small arms which could be exchanged for, it was hoped, about forty tractors. Although the result was to obtain only half a dozen tractors, Echandi was determined to get rid of the surplus arms and declared the only arms needed by Costa Rica were for internal policing. As he said, 'In our small way we are making history by selling arms to the United States'.

In May 1960 Eschandi announced all Civil Guard barracks in the country would be converted into police stations. He felt the barracks had dominated each provincial capital and that his measure would undercut the influence of any military command. The Civil Guard and Police were made more mobile by the enlargement of the radio patrol network and special training in the use of the equipment in the Panama Canal Zone. He endeavoured to encourage disarmament in the Western Hemisphere by proposals placed before the Organisation of American States which included the abstention by all Latin American States from acquiring atomic weapons of any type, and that no conventional weapons should be purchased from outside the Hemisphere. Opposition from the Dominican Republic, Bolivia, Mexico and finally Brazil (whose representative stated his country needed a large military force if for no other reason than for national prestige!) on the ground that it would leave the United States in an even greater dominating rôle finally caused the proposal to be rejected. Subsequently Costa Rica declined to attend meetings of the Inter-American Defence Board. To emphasise his determination, Echandi disposed of the Civil Guard's heavy equipment and, as there were now 14 years of tradition to support the disbanding of the army and the provision in the Constitution banning any permanent army, the future acceptance of the country having no armed forces seems assured, and the people accept the position.[47] In an interview which the author had with ex-President Echandi in 1981, he referred to his proposal to exchange arms for tractors as being a symbolic act and added that 'the best way for peace is to live it'. His object whilst in office was to try to unify the parties and to help resolve the remaining conflict between the groups who had been fighting. It seems inconceivable that, soon after his election, he encouraged Calderón Guardia to return to Costa Rica – not in disgrace nor tried for treason as he himself had been only three years earlier – but to be received and acclaimed by his followers and to live peacefully. Could this possibly have happened anywhere in the world but in Costa Rica? Add to that, two years later Guardia once more engaged in politics and secured a seat in the Legislative Assembly and in 1962 stood as

Presidential Candidate for the Republican Party! Although not elected he received over one-third of the votes against 57% for the National Liberation Candidate, Orlich, whilst Ulate was a very poor third.[48] In February 1960 when a distinguished statesman was visiting Costa Rica, it is recorded that President Echandi sat at dinner with three ex-Presidents, Figueres, Ulate and Calderón Guardia.[49]

Although during Echandi's term as President relations with Nicaragua improved, there was an incident in the summer of 1959 which could have had most serious consequences. A group of about 200 men gathered at Punta Llorona in the isolated and almost deserted area of Osa Peninsula, and were preparing to invade Nicaragua. The Government began to mobilise men to ensure an invasion would not be launched from Costa Rican territory. A Government spokesman met the intending invaders and arranged to return next day to take them prisoners. Next morning only one man remained with a quantity of arms.[50]

Unfortunately for Echandi, coffee prices slumped during his term as President, and large loans had to be obtained from the Export-Import Bank and the United States. As the expensive welfare schemes were continued the national debt was greatly increased.[51] The result has been felt in recent years most dramatically, as the proportion of the country's national funds devoted to service of the National Debt has increased to over 35%, finally overtaking even the amount spent on education.

Finally at the interview referred to, ex-President Echandi observed there is much more moral influence when unarmed

> a referee puts down his arms when making decisions, he does not raise his fists. Even super powers could dispense with arms; hunger is often the cause of conflicts and how much destitution could have been avoided if arms factories had been converted into peaceful uses.

# NOTES TO CHAPTER 10

1. Congress Library, Costa Rica, 16.1.1949
2. Cozean, pp. 68/9, quoting report in New York Times
3. Area Handbook, p. 27
4. British Museum Library
5. Interview with Señor Esquivel, March 1981
6. Gazette, Congress Library, Costa Rica
7. Interview with Señor Esquivel, March 1981
8. Congress Library, Costa Rica
9. Gazette, p. 439, Congress Library, Costa Rica
10. ibid, pp. 534/5
11. Colorado, p. 11
12. Parker, p. 269
13. Area, p. 119
14. Colorado, p. 11
15. British Museum Library
16. Colorado, p. 11
17. Area, p. 119
18. Colorado, p. 11
19. Bell, p. 160
20. ibid, p. 161
22. British Museum Library
23. Parker, p. 271
24. Area, p. 28
25. Cozean, p. 72
26. Area, p. 28
27. Cozean, p. 72/3
28. ibid, p. 73
29. Parker, p. 270 and Area, p. 28
30. Parker, p. 271, from 'Tres años despues' (Three years afterwards) published in La Republica, 11 March, 1959
31. Parker, p. 271
32. British Museum Library
33. ibid
34. Area Handbook, p. 29
35. ibid, p. 29
36. Cozean, pp. 74/5
37. Melendez, p. 147
38. Area Handbook, p. 29
39. Cozean, p. 44
40. ibid, referring to John D. Martz, 'Central America: The Crisis and the Challenge'
41. Area Handbook, p. 29
42. ibid, p. 30
43. Parker, p. 273, quoting from the President's address to Congress on 1 May 1955 p. 293
44. ibid, p. 275/8
45. Parker, p. 276, quoting report New York Times, 5.2.1956
46. Cozean, p. 87, quoting report New York Times, 25.2.1958
47. Cozean, pp. 87/90
48. Area Handbook, p. 31
49. Parker, p. 277
50. Lundberg, p. 152
51. Area Handbook, p. 31

# Chapter Eleven

# PEACEFUL ENDEAVOURS DESPITE PROVOCATION

President Echandi had to contend with a difficulty that all Presidents and leaders of Costa Rica faced for a period of about 30 years. Reference has already been made to the animosity between President Somoza of Nicaragua and President Figueres of Costa Rica which seriously threatened the peaceful relations between the two countries. Indeed at one time, it is reported Somoza challenged Figueres to a duel;[1] the author was told Figueres' response was a typical one, 'Tell him to grow up'. (José Figueres told the author in 1983 it was true he had been challenged by Somoza to a duel. He had replied he would accept if the duel took place on the deck of the Soviet submarine which Somoza had claimed to have captured. Figueres believed there was no such submarine and Somoza had made the claim to impress the USA and secure their continued support. 'He was crazier than a goat in the summer sun' was Figueres' observation about Somoza.) The existence of the Caribbean Legion and its known declared intention to oust all dictators in the Central American and Caribbean area, coupled with the support it had given to, and received from, Figueres, would undoubtedly strain relations between Nicaragua and Costa Rica, whilst the encouragement and support given by Somoza in 1948 and 1955 to the calderonistas ensured the suspicion by Costa Ricans that he still had designs upon the Province of Guanacaste which many years previously had been considered as part of Nicaragua.

Nevertheless, Echandi endeavoured to improve relations between the two countries and bringing back Calderón Guardia, fantastic as that seems, assisted his endeavours in that direction. Whilst he could not prevent all armed forces from entering Nicaragua from Costa Rica, he tried to ensure all such groups were arrested despite the fact that this made him unpopular in his own country.[2] Costa Rican territory became a battleground between the Nicaraguan National Guard and the Sandinista rebels. In November 1959 a group of Nicaraguan guardsmen penetrated

133

two miles inside the Costa Rican border burning several farmsteads and seizing hostages.[3] A month later the Costa Rican government was obliged to call up 100 Civil Guardsmen to track down some of the Nicaraguan exiles. Even small bands of the latter provided a difficult task for the small Civil Guard and a year later the commander of the Costa Rican force was killed in an ambush.[4] All available Guardsmen were sent to the area and it was reported planes from Cuba were being used against them.[5] In December 1960 the remaining guerillas were captured and the emergency was ended.

The difficulties facing Costa Rica in this situation can better be appreciated when budget expenditure is compared as follows:

|  | 1938 | 1958 |
|---|---|---|
| Education, health and social welfare | 20% | 45% |
| Defence | 7% | 4%[6] |

The figure of 4% is even more significant when one takes into account the escalation of costs in those twenty years. Cozean states that expenditure on national security which, in 1948 was a record high at 25% of the national budget, had decreased to 2.2% in 1966.[7]

It is typical of the attitude of the Costa Ricans that ex-President Echandi told the author he had tried to unify the Political parties when he was in office and he related the story of his father who had been a candidate for the office of President in the early 1920s. Despite his success in the election his opponents had manipulated the results and he was declared not elected. His supporters gathered and were prepared to fight to establish him as President. Echandi senior had dissuaded them saying the Presidency was less important than one drop of blood. A few years later he had congratulated the retiring President on his work during his term of office and on his death Echandi had been immediately awarded the greatest honour bestowed in Costa Rica – an award not given during lifetime.

Another serious situation was avoided in 1966 when the National Liberation candidate, Daniel Oduber, during the campaign, warned that two private armies had been organised by Conservative politicans and they would act to prevent him taking office if he were elected; he was, however, defeated, so the threat did not materialise. There were reports that these two 'armies', numbering 500 and 100 men respectively, were the cause of some concern to the administration.[8]

Diego Trejos Fonseca, who was elected President in 1966, was quoted in La República on 22nd August, 1969 as having said 'Costa Rica must now consider the need to set about forming a future army'. The report referred to a meeting the President had had with the Defence Minister of Guatemala and their discussion about the arms race unleashed in Central

America and the rest of the Continent. There were evidently different versions in the press regarding the statement made by Trejos, who very quickly sensed the response which his statement would get in Costa Rica. A reporter from *La Hora* quoted the President very differently:

> in no way do I believe that an army should be formed in Costa Rica. What I said, and I repeat, is that the police system of the country should be reinforced and we should try to find judicial provisions within the international mechanisms in order to defend and protect the sovereignty and integrity of Costa Rica, in the face of an eventual arms race in Central America . . . I want to make it clear in the strongest terms, that I do not support the creation of an army in Costa Rica.

Two years later the Central American Republics met and, against opposition from Costa Rica, agreed on the creation of a Central American army. *La Nación*, in its issue of 17th September 1971, reported that Costa Rica was the only country which opposed the creation of this army and, in its editorial the following day, delivered a scathing attack upon those who proposed the idea. After its sarcastic comment about 'the brilliant idea of creating an army which would repeat the errors made for 150 years' (i.e. since independence) it continued:

> They want to raise above a federation of states which is in its infancy the emblem of arms instead of the banner of education and law . . . It seems to us that our delegation did not go far enough, because we have no business in a community where the first thing that is going to be done is to create an army. This does violence to our tradition as a 'civilianist' and peace-loving people and at the same time it presents a thorny problem, because we are not going to give the slightest contribution to this fortress enterprise, neither men, nor arms, nor equipment, nor generals, since we have not got them even for our own consumption.

The *Diario de Costa Rica* was equally sceptical on 18th September. The writer approved the delegates' opposition and pointed out that this was in accord with Article 12 of the Constitution. He underlined the fact that Costa Rican delegates had constantly resisted pressures to form a dangerous army. The real unity of Central America would come from its artists, writers, teachers, etc. not from its military and he was sure the whole country would support the action. He concluded with the observation that 'Civilianism has deep historical roots and we are not now going to betray this long tradition, so we say NO to a Central American army.'

*La República* on the same day was even more critical in its denunciation and urged that the decision to form such an army demonstrated Central

America's incapacity to the whole world. It reviewed the 'sickness' of the five republics and the accumulation of economic and social problems and added

> A group of countries which, instead of rationally analysing its common problems, and instead of proposing practical solutions, in the first resort leaps into the creation of a Central American army, deserves no respect. A group of parliamentarians who, instead of summoning technicians and intellectuals to collaborate with the politicians in the solution of their problems, has recourse to the prostituted military caste, deserves the repudiation of all civilised people. A Parliament which, instead of fixing new goals and procedures for the solution of our disputes and common social and economic ills, implores help from the military – those who have brought democracy into disrepute in Central America and established odious cliques, hungry for power and wealth – merits, on the part of the Costa Ricans, their contempt . . .

Next day, *La República* reported that writers of the Isthmus condemned the creation of a Central American army and that 'strong epithets such as ignominious and repressive had been used'. The Nicaraguan poet and priest Ernesto Cardenal (who, 18 years later, became a member of the *Junta* Government after the successful Sandinista revolution) with some others drew up a condemnatory motion which all signed and which was sent to all the governments of the isthmus.

José Figueres had been elected President once again in 1970 and he was succeeded by Daniel Oduber, both being candidates of the National Liberation party; the only time since 1948 when a party has succeeded in retaining the office. Despite all difficulties, the abolition of the army seemed now assured.

The escalation of the efforts by the Sandinista revolutionaries to overturn the dictatorship of Somoza in Nicaragua led to a continuation of Costa Rica's dilemma of maintaining friendly diplomatic relations with a regime which was hated by a considerable majority of Costa Ricans. The Sandinistas derived their name from Augusto Sandino, a Nicaraguan revolutionary leader who had fought against United States troops occupying his country in the 1930s and who was assassinated, it was widely believed, at the instigation of the father of Somoza, President in the 1970s. A typical attitude of the Costa Ricans is expressed in a leading article in *The Tico Times* of 21st October 1977. After commenting that the Sandinista Liberation Front was communist-inspired, it continued:

> And curiously enough, the young, passionate Nicaraguans also have the sympathies of a large number of Costa Ricans – and not necessarily leftists, either.

Many Ticos were rooting this week for the Sandinistas – either loudly or quietly – because they share with them an intense dislike for the iron-fisted Somoza regime. They might not agree with the rebels' politics, but they agree wholeheartedly with their objective.

This is, of course, a pretty sad commentary on Nicaragua. That embattled country certainly isn't going to be any better off with a bunch of ragtag Marxists guerillas at the helm than it is under Somoza. But everyone is so fed up with the Nicaraguan strongman that an awful lot of people feel that maybe any change would be for the better.[9]

The same paper, on 23rd February, 1979, a few months before the Somoza regime was ended, carried a report as follows:

Thousands of Costa Rican and Nicaraguan supporters of the Sandinista guerilla group crowded San José's National Park Wednesday night to commemorate the death of Augusto Sandino

In April 1979 *The Tico Times* reported President Carazo, during a trip to other Central American Republics, had been 'bombarded with questions' about Costa Rican aid for the Sandinists and, although the governments of the countries he visited were of military men and feared a Sandinista victory, there was no doubt that public feeling was in support of the rebels.

A senior officer in the US Embassy said, in 1981:

Although the Costa Rican Government denied allowing the Sandinista rebels to group and train on its soil, there is no doubt the population as a whole was implicitly involved; everyone knew the Sandinistas were training in Costa Rica and that arms were being conveyed to them. The Sandinistas also used Costa Rica as a convenient hiding place when pursued by the Nicaraguan army. The Costa Ricans had considerable sympathy for the Sandinistas as they so much disliked Somoza and his oppressive regime.

In the autumn of 1977 there was a most serious incident at a remote part of the frontier between Costa Rica and Nicaragua. The Costa Rican Minister of Public Security and his party had been personally attacked by units of the Nicaraguan Air Force whilst they were investigating a complaint by Nicaragua that rebels had carried out an attack the day before. It appears that a group of the Sandinistas had crossed the frontier and attacked the little town of San Carlos at the southern end of Lake Nicaragua. It was alleged they had killed several people, including some of the Nicaraguan National Guard, before being routed and fleeing back into Costa Rica. This attack had taken place on 13th October and on the following day the Nicaraguan Ambassador to the Organisation of American States called for a special meeting of the Permanent Council of the OAS to inform it of this incident and a similar one close to the Nicaraguan border with Honduras which took place on 12th October.

Complaint having also been made direct by the Nicaraguans to the Costa Rican Minister of Security, he decided to investigate the problem on the spot personally. He had several telephone conversations on 13th October with his counterpart in Nicaragua and says he told the latter he intended to visit Los Chilis (the Costa Rican frontier town) the next day: the Nicaraguan Minister denies he was told this. Whatever the truth of that may be, Minister Charpentier held a Press Conference in San José during the afternoon of 13th October and explained his mission. Details appeared in the Costa Rican press on the following day so that it is difficult to believe the Nicaraguans did not know about the Minister's intentions. *The Tico Times* published in San José a week later carried the following report:

> Three small outboard motorboats left Los Chilis carrying Costa Rica Minister of Public Security, Mario Charpentier, two Civil Guardsmen, three boatmen and fourteen Costa Rican reporters and photographers, on an inspection of Costa Rica's border with Nicaragua on the Rio Frio. It was a routine mission following the attack of Sandinista guerillas against military outposts in San Carlos, Nicaragua, the previous day.
>
> The guardsmen were armed with light rifles. The Minister carried a small two-way radio. The newsmen's arsenal consisted of cameras and tape recorders. Charpenter said he didn't anticipate 'anything unusual' and the twenty men set off at 9.15 a.m. in high spirits, travelling downstream to the border marker in the river, where they turned around and headed back to Los Chilis.
>
> So unaccustomed are Ticos [Costa Ricans] to military activity that when the first bomb fell, everybody thought one of the boat's motors had backfired. A reporter remarked that one of the Nicaraguan Air Force planes the group had seen circling overhead must have cut its engines 'to play games'. It wasn't until a tremendous explosion near the river bank sent water and mud shooting four metres into the air that the Costa Ricans realised what was happening. Those were bombs and they were the targets. 'Get to the shore! Find cover!' shouted Minister Charpentier. The group scrambled for cover in sparse undergrowth on the riverbank, and the Ticos' adventure had begun.
>
> The 250lb bombs continued to fall, along with bursts of machinegun fire from low-flying helicopters. While the reporters tried to shield themselves by burrowing under logs and covering themselves with brush, the Minister tried desperately to stop the attack. 'Listen, tell San José we're being bombed' he shouted into his radio. 'Tell them to call Nicaragua and tell them to cease fire.' Back at Los Chilis, Civil Guardsmen and reporters listened in

disbelief. The message was relayed to Security Officers in San José who contacted Colonel Orlando Zeledon, commander of the Nicaraguan Air Force. Zeledon answered that he could not give the order to cease fire without instructions from Nicaragua's Minister of Defence.

Meanwhile, Charpentier ordered the newsmen to take off all brightly coloured clothes – and to pray. 'Let us put ourselves in the hands of God and let Him decide,' the Minister said. 'This is bad.' The reporters didn't have to be told that. Most were praying out loud, while gunfire whistled through the trees above them. Adolfo Ruiz of *La República* [newspaper] decided the river was safer and jumped in. He became official lookout for the group, shouting whenever he saw a plane or helicopter returning for another attack, then holding his breath and ducking under water. Charpentier was still shouting into the radio. 'What's happening?' he demanded. 'They're going to kill us!'

Finally, almost an hour and a half after the first bombs fell, Ministry Officials told Charpentier over the radio that a ceasefire had been ordered. The group watched the planes moving away, but the helicopters continued to hover. Charpentier told everyone not to move and asked for a white handkerchief. The Minister climbed out of the underbrush, waving the handkerchief at one of the helicopters which landed nearby. Opening the door the pilot greeted the Costa Ricans with a broad grin. 'Well, were you scared?' he asked. 'Very' snapped Charpentier. An unidentified colonel climbed out of the craft and said to the Minister. 'Accept the greetings of General Anastasio Somoza and the respective apologies".

Several Tico newsmen said that at this point a blond man in uniform who could not speak Spanish very well told photographers not to take pictures because 'You're in Nicaragua and we're in charge here'.[10]

(Another report said the Nicaraguan officer offered 'safe conduct' back to Costa Rican territory but Minister Charpentier refused this claiming they were in their own land.)

The Nicaraguans also claimed the canoes were not displaying any identifiable markings. It is especially noteworthy that no shots whatever were fired by any of the Costa Rican Civil Guardsmen nor was any attempt made to arrest the Nicaraguan armed personnel violating Costa Rican territory. A week later the Costa Rican Ambassador to the OAS called a special meeting of the Permanent Council and stated that its (Costa Rica's) air space, perhaps involuntarily, had been penetrated by Nicaraguan Air Force planes and asked that an *ad hoc* Committee be appointed to ascertain the facts of the incident. The *Ad Hoc* Committee duly visited both countries and interviewed many people, Ministers, civil and military authorities, reporters, cameramen, prisoners and others. The Nicaraguans initially said the attack was a mistake but later claimed the Costa Ricans had crossed the border and were on Nicaraguan territory. They appear subsequently to have tried to maintain the attack was not a serious one and when one of the Costa Rican Civil Guardsmen was being interviewed he was asked why he thought they had survived and he had not been killed if the attack were as terrible as had been stated. He did not refer to the poor markmanship of the attackers but said very simply 'Evidently my number wasn't up' but made it very clear he believed every attempt was made to injure or kill them.

The OAS Committee decided it did not have sufficient evidence to state that the Minister of Security and his companions had crossed into Nicaragua but were of the opinion that the attack on them had taken place in Costa Rican territory, about one and a half kilometres from the border. Amongst the photographs in a newspaper office is one showing the members of the Committee examining the metal being dug from a bomb hole in Costa Rica and reference was also made to marks on trees well inside that country's border. The Committee reported the receipt of an assurance from the Nicaraguan Government that instructions had been issued to its officers and troops, as well as air patrols, that Costa Rican territory had not to be entered, and incidents with the Costa Rican authorities were to be avoided. In turn the Costa Rican Government said: it would exchange information with its neighbouring Government to ensure its territory was not used to perpetrate acts of violence aimed against Nicaragua, and would proceed to arrest suspicious persons, to confiscate arms, and to take other measures to safeguard the border: reference being made to the Pacts of Friendship between Costa Rica and Nicaragua entered into in 1949 and 1956.

Perhaps one of the most interesting and significant features of this incident is the satisfaction both parties gained from it. Representatives of both Embassy staffs to whom the author spoke in New York said their Governments were delighted with the result and the report of the Committee to the OAS Council. For their part the Costa Ricans were vindicated in their claim that their Minister and his party had been on Costa Rican territory when they were attacked, and also the Nicaraguans had given assurances they would not encroach into Costa Rica when pursuing any rebel elements. Nicaragua's delight was in securing the further assurance from the Costa Rican Government that measures would be taken to prevent the rebel Sandinistas from organising and preparing to invade Nicaragua whilst they were in Costa Rica.

The people in Los Chilis had obviously been terrified by the bombing. This is a very remote part of Costa Rica so much so that, until comparatively recently, the only way to get from there to the Capital, San José, was to sail down the Rio Frio into Nicaragua, cross the Lake Nicaragua on to the Pan-American Highway and cross the border in the north-west of the country.

One of tbe Civil Guards there related how terrified he had been when the bombs were dropped. The school mistress gave the same story and said all the children had been sent home at once – no doubt they thought dispersal was the better course to take. Others confirmed their stories and one of the journalists who had accompanied the Minister on his inspection admitted 'we were all crying with fear'. Each of these when questioned 'Do you not want an air force or other means to protect you, or to retaliate, if such an incident should occur again?', were quite emphatic they did not; not even the journalist who had had such a terrible experience.

Details of the OAS report are in Appendix III.

It is highly significant of the Costa Rican temperament that the President, Daniel Oduber, before travelling to New York to address the United Nations General Assembly, said his country had been offered military aid by several other countries to defend itself against Nicaragua, but that he had turned these down because of

> his country's permanent struggle against militarism and for national and international peace.[10]

A few days later when inaugurating a gymnasium the President was reported as saying

> Six gymnasiums like this cost a million dollars which is equivalent to the cost of the cheapest warplane of the type being purchased by countries like ours in the Third World. It is more consistent with the Costa Rican tradition to build six gymnasiums than to buy a war plane for Costa Rica.

Stressing Costa Rica's aversion to militarism, he continued

> The wheel of a war plane that has to be changed every three landings costs the same as a house in our housing programme.[10]

After referring to the many border incidents that had occurred between Costa Rica and Nicaragua, the President emphasised that, whilst foreign troops would not be allowed to cross the border, the country would not be used as a refuge for invasions against neighbouring countries.

> because that would mean involving ourselves in the internal affairs of another State, and we would be exposing ourselves to being invaded in the same way, in our internal problems.[10]

141

An editorial comment in the same paper in response to a reader's letter enquiring about the involvement of the USA with the border incident reads

> A spokesman for the US Embassy in San José says that the United States 'does not have a military mission here'. He explained that there is one US Army officer who serves as advisor to the Ambassador and is the Ambassador's point of liaison with the US military authorities in the Canal Zone for search and rescue operations and for disaster relief. Outside the US Marine Guard, whose duty it is to protect the embassy, the extent of the US military presence in Costa Rica is a Lt.-Col. and one non-commissioned officer.[10]

In April 1978 one of the Sandinista leaders, Plutarco Hernández, was apprehended in Costa Rica and related how his guerillas trained for their fight against the hated Somoza regime in Nicaragua. He related how 50 Sandinistas had rented a house in San José's district of Desamparados for a month in order to train with modern weapons but had dispersed when police appeared.[11]

This, and similar information reaching the Nicaraguan Government, coupled with another serious outbreak of Sandinista activity in September 1978 when they gained control of several cities towards the Honduras border and a general strike which virtually paralysed that unhappy country, resulted in repeated violations of Costa Rican territory by Nicaraguan National Guards. In addition to making a protest to the OAS once again, Costa Rica, fearing a threat of invasion from Nicaragua, accepted warplanes and helicopters from Venezuela and Panama.[12] This led to a most serious political battle in the Costa Rican legislature and considerable public disquiet. The Minister of Public Security was criticised for allowing the planes and helicopters to arrive in the country without first enabling the proposal to be discussed in the Legislative Assembly. The incident 'disturbed and was disliked by many people' said one of the University Professors to whom the author spoke in 1981, who added that, despite the general sympathy and support for the Sandinista cause, there was opposition generally to airports and land being used to assist the Sandinistas to obtain arms. In September 1978 there had been many occasions when Costa Rican territory was bombed and citizens injured.[13]

As the *Tico Times* of 20th September 1978 disclosed in its Editorial, President Carazo had a difficult task at the OAS when seeking support for his complaint of incursions by Nicaraguan National Guards and the threat of an invasion. This may well have prompted the action by the Minister of Public Security seeking overt military assistance from Panama and

Venezuela. The Editorial opined

> Costa Rica wasn't optimistic when it demanded action from the OAS. The Organisation, like the Hemisphere itself, is dominated by military dictatorships of the right and left, none of which is terribly eager to mete out punishment to a fellow dictator.

After referring to President Carazo's threat to withdraw Costa Rica from the OAS – and possibly encourage Panama, Venezuela and Colombia to follow suit – the editorial referred to Nicaragua's counter charges that the OAS condemn Costa Rica for permitting Sandinista rebels to launch attacks from their territory. It continued

> While there is no doubt that Ticos generally sympathize with the Sandinistas, Costa Rica has always done exactly what is required of it by international law: it rounds up the guerillas and ships them off to whatever country will accept them (as long as that country does not border Nicaragua). It does not harbour them or support them. Of course it doesn't shoot them on sight, either, and this irks Nicaragua greatly . . .
>
> As Costa Rica has pointed out, it's a lot easier for a country with a powerful and well-trained army to defend its border (and, incidentally, to keep that army from invading its neighbour's territory and shooting at its neighbour's citizens) than it is for a country with no army at all to keep guerillas out of the wilderness near its border.
>
> The fact that the OAS recognized all this is a triumph not only for Costa Rica, but for the entire hemisphere. It means that OAS member nations are capable of putting aside their political differences long enough to acknowledge a violation of international law and to call world attention to it.[14]

A cartoon in *La República* showed a bespectacled Somoza prostrate over the knee of a severe looking OAS and howling as he was whacked with a hefty stick with the caption 'The OAS condemned Somoza'. The same page of *The Tico Times* reproducing the cartoon carried a report of 34 more Sandinistas being deported and 400 Civil Guards being sent to the border to keep guerillas from staging an attack on Nicaragua from Costa Rican territory.

The response of the OAS had been to order the establishment of a team to observe border incidents, two members of which took up positions on the Costa Rican side and two on the Nicaraguan side of the border. The Costa Rican Government decided to expropriate the huge ranch belonging to Somoza which he had in Guanacaste, for which compensation was paid, and also for some weeks, the frontier crossing was closed, despite the serious economic hardship this caused to Costa Rica.

At the beginning of November 1978 the Nicaraguan Government charged the Costa Rican Government with being an accomplice in Sandinista guerilla activities. Foreign Minister Rafael Angel Calderón (son of Calderón Guardia) termed the charges 'false and absurd' and said his country had taken every measure to seek and deport Sandinistas near the northern border and would never allow Costa Rica to become a base of operations for Nicaraguan guerillas.[15] A week later there was an allegation that a Costa Rican ship armed with cannon had been seen in Nicaraguan waters, which President Carazo complained was part of a campaign instigated by Somoza calculated to threaten the long-standing friendship between the people of both countries.[16] The same issue of *The Tico Times* had a report that a group of private Costa Rican citizens intended to stage a symbolic trial of Somoza as a war criminal.

Relations continued to deteriorate and on 17th November, Echevarría, Minister of Public Security, defended Costa Rica's proposing to buy some anti-aircraft weapons when he said the political situation in Nicaragua was becoming intolerable and there would continue to be problems until the situation was defined. (Somoza had just refused to resign as demanded by opposition political groups who threatened to withdraw from peace talks being promoted by the OAS mediation group working to bring hostilities to an end in Nicaragua.)

The situation was indeed becoming intolerable and was made more so by an incident reported in *The Tico Times* of 24th November 1978, a summary being as follows:

> Costa Rica's legendary love of peace is not just picturesque folklore, and at no time in recent history was this so graphically illustrated as during the tragic border incident this week, which left two Costa Rican Guards dead and one seriously wounded.
>
> The Guards, carrying out a routine border patrol to guard against possible infiltration of Sandinista guerillas into Nicaraguan territory, were fired on by Nicaraguan National Guardsmen . . .
>
> Costa Rica's Guards – members of this country's police force, not soldiers – were there helping ensure Costa Rica's neutrality in the continuing struggle between the government of Anastasio Somoza and the guerillas determined to topple it – a struggle which has been nothing but a headache for Costa Rica for years . . . According to one of the Guards who fled after the attack they could have returned the Nicaraguans' fire 'but we were under orders not to shoot under any circumstances'. They probably thought the Ticos would respond to the provocation by shooting back, thereby launching a full-scale conflict. But Costa Ricans aren't made that way. Their tradition is one of peace, and they will do everything they can to maintain it. Yet this same cherished heritage is backed by another, just as strong; a passionate love of freedom and independence.

144

President Carazo's immediate reaction to this week's incident was to break diplomatic relations with Nicaragua, though Costa Rica would rather see the conflict resolved peacefully, Ticos of all ages and walks of life this week repeated a ritual they have carried out whenever Costa Rica's proud and much-loved sovereignty has been threatened. Untrained in warfare and ignorant of weapons, they nevertheless volunteered to defend their country.

No Costa Rican wants this week's incident to develop into war. If there is a civilized way to make Nicaragua see the error of its ways and stop its brutal violations of Costa Rican territory – and now, Costa Rican lives – Ticos would prefer that route.

But in the tradition of courage and pride that has marked this tiny, defenceless nation for decades, no Costa Rican is going to allow anything like this week's tragedy to happen again.[17]

When the coffins of the two dead Costa Ricans were returned by the Nicaraguans, the wreaths sent by Somoza were disgustedly hurled away by one of the men's comrades, a gesture which adequately expressed the feelings of the people. Carazo urged the OAS to expel the Somoza regime as well as to send a team of investigators to the border area where the shooting had taken place. A report emanating from Nicaragua that an army of some 5,000 men was preparing to invade that country from Costa Rica was found to be without foundation but an intensified border patrol of three Civil Guards discovered a Nicaraguan National Guard platoon of 14 men more than two kilometres inside Costa Rican territory. The platoon surrendered without a shot being fired and blamed their presence on an error on the part of a youthful guide who had lost his way.[18]

Later in December, after more fighting which caused the Peñas Blancas border station to be closed once again, Somoza repeated his threat to invade Costa Rica to 'clean out' rebel elements, but a hurried visit by a representative of the OAS avoided this. A significant reflection on and response to arms is contained in a letter written in Spanish and translated by *The Tico Times* staff (who are headed by journalists from the USA). The letter referred to a report of one of the Sandinista leaders attending in Costa Rica the graduation ceremony of his daughter.

> I ask myself, how is it possible that a naturalized Costa Rican can be permitted to carry a weapon at an act of peace like a high school graduation? Applying logic, this would mean that Costa Ricans by birth should be allowed to use revolvers around their waists. An act such as this is more than an insult to Costa Rican democracy.[19]

> Costa Rica will not renew diplomatic relations with Nicaragua as long as General Anastasio Somoza is in power in that country.

declared President Carazo early in February 1979 and added

145

> Costa Rica has proved to the world that it has the right to live in peace and without an army.[20]

Border incidents continued and a little girl, 14 years old, was shot at and killed as she was taking her father's lunch to him whilst he was working in the fields. Nicaraguan army troops were stated to have entered a farmstead some five kilometres from the border, threatened the residents and burned several grass huts. It was also reported that hundreds of residents of the northern zone of Costa Rica had fled for safer ground further south.[21]

The activities of the Sandinistas resulted in another serious attempt to overthrow the Somoza regime when fighting broke out in several of the towns in Nicargua and the Government's position was made the more difficult when the USA Government cut off all military aid and froze all future economic assistance. This was because Somoza had refused to accept proposals advanced by the OAS mediation team and undoubtedly led to greater anxieties on the part of the Costa Ricans as border clashes intensified. When further killings were reported, Echeverría, Minister of Public Security, mounted 'Operation Checkmate' by sending 700 Civil Guards to reinforce patrols and sweep the border area from the Pacific coast to the Atlantic.[22] This resulted in some Sandinista guerillas being apprehended and local farmers who had deserted their crops were reassured and returned to their homes.[23] Operation Checkmate was severely criticized by the Sandinistas, however, who claimed it was part of a scheme promoted by the USA Government to maintain 'Somocismo' without Somoza. Echeverría also was subjected to criticism in the Costa Rican Legislative Assembly where it was said he had illegally accepted arms from Venezuela without Congressional approval; he retorted the arms were borrowed not purchased.

This incident had repercussions in the United States Congress where it was alleged Venezuela had violated foreign aid treaty obligations by shipping the arms to Costa Rica. Public security officials in the latter country, however, maintained the arms were needed to undertake the clean up operations along the northern border.[24] The need for such arms to be supplied does at least indicate that Costa Rica does not have the equipment necessary for an army. The opposition party of National Liberation also criticised Echeverría and accused him of forming an 'army' using Venezuelan loaned rifles but the OAS observers praised the Costa Rican Government for its 'Operation Checkmate' and its efforts to clear the border of Sandinista guerillas.[25] The stance of the National Liberation Party had its sequel when, shortly afterwards, a Unity Party delegate alleged there were some 4,000 government-owned arms in the hands of private citizens – mostly Liberation political figures.[26] In the same issue of *The Tico Times* (20th April) was a special article commenting on the better image of the Immigration Police – being now without their pistols. The Chief Inspector explained the policy was not to round-up and lock-up foreigners but to help them straighten the position out. Also in the same issue appeared an article by Professor Rosenberg of Florida International University, which included the following:

> Costa Rica has two resources which most other Third World and particularly Latin American countries do not: enlightened political leadership and a well-informed cohesive and nationalistic populace. There have been few instances in Costa Rican political history when Costa Rica's decision-making élite has so fundamentally disagreed as to provoke open conflict.
>
> For the most part, Costa Rican élites have shown a willingness to agree on basic issues. While this willingness to agree may have resulted in compromise and a less assertive political programme, the benefits have been reflected in continued political stability with a reasonable distribution of the benefits of economic growth, especially if compared with some of the country's neighbours.

President Carazo completed his first year in office at the beginning of May 1979 and the Tico Times of 4th May had on its front page a picture of the President arriving at the Congress House to give his review to the Legislative Assembly. An 'Honour Guard' presents arms – rifles – but appear to have an armband with the letter 'P' (for Police!) displayed. The President stressed the need for those in power to sacrifice their own political interests so that national debate, criticism and judgement of the government be heard without fear and insisted that on the labour front, as in all national problems, solutions should be found through free and open dialogue. Opposition delegates walked out when Carazo criticised some of their tactics. He referred with considerable pride to the United Nations acceptance of his suggestion for a World University for Peace to be established in Costa Rica as well as an Inter-American Court of Human Rights.[27] To underline the Costa Rican political scene the following appeared on the same page:

> ### CALDERÓN FACTION WINS TOP LEGISLATIVE POST
> The once powerful party of Calderón Guardia 1940-44 showed signs of returning to power this week after more than 30 years of living in limbo. Ramón Aguilar Facio, a Calderonista deputy and member of unity coalition backing Carazo, was elected to the Presidency of the Legislative Assembly. Calderón Guardia's son, Rafael A. Calderón, is the present Foreign Minister.

Later the same month, Carazo was credited with having influenced Mexico to break off diplomatic relations with Nicaragua; this could not do anything but harm to the relations between Costa Rica and Nicaragua.

When Echeverría was questioned about granting political asylum to the Shah of Iran, he replied 'we would even grant asylum to Somoza or Castro if they needed it'.

In June 1979, the Sandinistas commenced their greatest offensive since the previous September and Somoza immediately broadcast to the people of Nicaragua charging Costa Rica with the responsibility for the political and military problems from which his country was suffering; President Carazo maintained these charges had no basis. There were reports of a petition circulating in Managua which was calling for a declaration of war against Costa Rica. Echeverría said Costa Rica might again ask for military aid from friendly countries in case an invasion from Nicaragua seemed likely, and denied reports of 300 Sandinistas invading from Costa Rica, pointing out that OAS observers were present at the border.[28] However, if some hundreds of Civil Guards had been unable to prevent constant incursions into Nicaragua by Sandinistas it is hardly possible that two OAS observers could be fully aware of their movements. At the same time one of National Liberation deputies reported visiting the proposed site for the University for Peace (which is about 40 kilometres from San José in a desolate area very difficult of access) where he discovered about 200 men and two young women carrying out military training. 'I felt afraid' he said 'not for myself but for my country'.[28]

*The Tico Times* of 8th June carried the headline

COSTA RICA MOBILISES DEFENCE FORCES

and related how, in face of continuing threats of invasion, a narrow security zone had been declared resulting in the removal of all civilians, and anti-aircraft batteries had been mounted at the country's only international airport and other strategic points. The announcement continued

> The Costa Rican police forces are composed of the 3,500 member Civil Guard, a Rural Guard of equal strength and a 3,000 man volunteer defence force.[29]

The fighting between the Sandinistas and the Nicaraguan National Guard intensified and the following week *The Tico Times* had on its front page a picture of the Civil Guard on 'Border Watch' with a caption reading

> Costa Rican Civil Guards and a heavy machine gun stand guard on a bluff outside the border town of La Cruz, overlooking the border with Nicaragua and the only road to town from the frontier. Like the residents of the little town, now transformed into a military garrison, the Guards have a clear view of the fighting across the border – and nervously hope it stays there. Costa Rica's policemen-turned-soldiers are new to the war game, but they're

taking their defence duties seriously. For the story of the 'non-existent army' guarding this country's northern border see Page 5.

Page 5 carried the heading

COSTA RICA'S NEW 'ARMY' PATROLS NORTH

and showed a photograph of reporters speaking openly with Civil Guards at a check-point. The report by a USA journalist, who was distinctly sceptical about Costa Rica not having an army when he talked with the author a year earlier, included the following:

Costa Rica's non-existent army was out in force in La Cruz this week. Despite the well-advertised 'fact' that the country has no armed forces, more than 500 Civil Guard troops have turned this town of 3,000 into an armed military garrison.

After relating that the threat of invasion had exploded the myth of an unarmed defenceless Costa Rica, the article continued

the minister of the Presidency, José Rafael Cordero, told *The Tico Times* that the Civil Guard 'is not an institutional army, but an emergency defence force, which naturally operates along military lines'. But the Minister maintained that it is 'neither a traditional nor a permanent army'.

Relations with the press was another area in which Costa Rica's non-army showed itself to be woefully deficient.

and went on to relate how, having been forbidden to go into a restricted area, the journalists had done so without being shot at.

On another page appeared a photograph of a 'Bleak border post' at Peñas Blancas with nothing but a bench, a broken painted chair and 'a nervous Civil Guard'.[30]

We shall examine later the question whether Costa Rica's Civil and Rural Guards are really an army in disguise or a Police Force capable of undertaking the defence of their frontiers.

By the end of June the crisis was deepening; there was intense fighting inside Nicaragua itself: the Sandinistas had moved north from the border, the Nicaraguan National Guards were needed to deal with attacks upon the capital, Managua, and other cities: and accordingly the pressure on Costa Rica and threats of invasion diminished.

The United States was vainly trying through the OAS and diplomatic channels to preserve its interest in Nicaragua and strenuous attempts were being made to reach a settlement between the Somoza government and the Sandinistas. The latter were determined not to agree to Somoza's Liberal Party nor the National Guard having any place in the future government. Attempts by the USA to introduce a peace-keeping force, which the Sandinistas interpreted as designed to protect US interests, and to some extent those of Somoza, were defeated at the OAS. Costa Rica's response can be summed up in the words of a prominent editor and author.

> It's a result of Washington's phobia on Cuba. They feel that any Nicaraguan solution without some Somoza influence would necessarily be controlled by Fidel Castro.
> Washington had to make it as a last gesture to a government they have supported for almost half a century.[31]

Amidst the plans and preparations for the take-over of the government from Somoza which at last seemed inevitable, Gonzalo Facio, a former Foreign Minister of Costa Rica, expressed grave doubts for the future of his country in its relations with Nicaragua. Should Somoza's forces finally succeed there would inevitably be reprisals against Costa Rica for the support and encouragement given to the Sandinistas. He saw the establishment of a totalitarian leftist regime in Nicaragua, should the Sandinistas be victorious, as leading to a social-political upheaval in Costa Rica which would be even more dangerous than the reprisals.[32] The papers were even more full than ever with pitiful stories of refugees, all bitterly condemning Somoza, but appealing for help from their readers and indicating many ways in which this could be given.[33]

The issue of 6th July carried stories of diplomatic and troop manoeuvres – as well as of Somoza packing his bags, but, more importantly, the terrible effect upon the Costa Rican economy the revolutions in Nicaragua had had.

> Not only has Costa Rica lost a major supplier of raw materials and an important market for exports, but also fears of a communist takeover in Managua have put a noticeable crimp into this country's traditional reputation as a safe investment haven.[35]

A banker had assessed the situation in the following words:

> These guys (USA and European financiers) are as conservative as hell, and you can't imagine how scared they get when they hear the word 'communism'; a radical leftist government less than 200 miles away would be enough to keep them out of Costa Rica. The unspoken fear is apparently that a Nicaraguan Marxist government would attempt to export its revolution here, but the chances of this happening are remote. Costa Rica is the only Central American country with a well-entrenched democratic tradition and the communist party is legal here.[33]

Official estimates of between 5,000 and 10,000 people dying during the five weeks war compare vividly with the probable 2,000 killed in about the same period in Costa Rica's revolution of 1948.[33]

A blazing row erupted when two US helicopters and a cargo plane landed in the north of Costa Rica and demonstrations with placards 'Yanks go home' made it clear there was grave suspicion of the purpose. It was said the intention was to be ready to evacuate US personnel from Managua and that permission had been given by the Minister of Public Security, Echeverría, who was almost universally condemned in the Legislative Assembly.

> What's particularly incredible about the whole thing is that it could so easily have been avoided. All the US had to do was make a public request for permission to land the aircraft on Costa Rican soil, explaining to the press and the government well in advance what the whole mission was all about. Assuming the motive really was humanitarian, permission would almost certainly have been granted.
>
> It's simply a matter of courtesy – and common sense. The fact that both these qualities were shockingly lacking from this week's misguided machinations really makes one wonder whether the United States will ever learn how to walk softly – sans the stick – in Latin America.[34]

The paper also reported the bombing by the Nicaraguan Air Force of the area near the border 'but the Civil Guard did not return the fire'.[34]

Amongst the many stories of refugees the following underlines the considerable difference between the two countries:

> Don Octavio, entering Costa Rica for the first time after bombs destroyed his Estelí (Nicaragua) home last September, was immediately struck by the difference.
>
> The people from Nicaragua have war in their veins; it's in the blood. But here, it's different. Shortly after I came here, my truck died in the middle of the road. When two police stopped behind me, I nearly died.
>
> Who would have thought that they came to help me push the truck out of the street? It's those kind of things that make me feel obligated to Costa Rica.[34]

At long, long last the trauma of Nicaragua came to an end; Somoza and his closest associates surreptitiously abandoned Managua on the night of 16th July and told newsmen as he surfaced in Miami 'I was not kicked out by the Nicaraguan people. This is the result of an international conspiracy'.[35] *The Tico Times* editorial, referring to the rebirth of the nation, continued

> Costa Rica has shared its northern neighbour's anguish every step of the way, even risking its own security in the process. Sheltered by a

long and proud tradition of democracy and pacifism, Ticos would only imagine the horrors taking place just a couple of hundred miles from their own capital. They opened their hearts to Nicaragua's suffering, and they did what they could – in some cases identifying so closely with it that they almost plunged Costa Rica into the middle of the war.

The new Nicaragua was conceived in Costa Rica . . . and it was fitting that the new nation should be officially 'reborn' on Costa Rica soil, with the reading of the new government's Statute in San José . . .

But this is one battle that armyless Costa Rica can help fight – openly and proudly. It can help the new nation it helped to create grow into the free, happy, democratic neighbour it has always wanted to have.[35]

The President of the Nicaraguan Congress, Dr Urcuyo, endeavoured to cling to his authority derived from the Somoza régime and caused a last minute hitch when he refused permission for the Archbishop of Nicaragua to fly into the airport at Managua. He even called upon the Sandinistas to lay down their arms saying 'We must forget the past in the name of the present with our eyes fixed on the future'. Some 36 hours later he was taking refuge in Guatemala.[35]

The newspapers were full of photographs of Nicaraguans as well as Costa Ricans celebrating the success of the Sandinistas and an hourly account of the scenes in the early hours of the morning as news came of Somoza's departure. In addition to stories of the Sandinista's campaigns and the *Junta* that was to assume power, there was a catalogue of events between the two countries going back to 1573 when the first boundaries were fixed by King Philip II of Spain. Details were also given of a poll taken in the Central Valley towns from some 470 citizens which showed over 50% considered President Carazo had handled relations with Nicaragua satisfactorily. The poll also stated 70% of Costa Ricans opposed the creation of a permanent army.[35] What an astounding result considering the traumatic experiences they had endured in the past several years.

The following Friday *The Tico Times* had on its front page a photograph of the large crowd marching along one of the main streets of the capital celebrating the Sandinista victory. Prominent was José Figueres, whose thoughts must have gone back to the day thirty one years previously when he had led his victorious Liberation Army down the street at the end of the Revolution in 1948.[36] Casualties were placed at 30,000 dead (which may well be correct, for the three years when the fighting had been intensive) and 300,000 homeless.

Costa Rica could now turn to deal with its own pressing economic problems which had been accentuated by the Nicaraguan situation, but not without first endeavouring to make an important contribution towards its neighbour's acute need for teachers to help overcome the illiteracy. Government sources pointed out there were 2,000 retired teachers in Costa Rica and these were offered, provided the US was willing to meet the costs as Costa Rica couldn't. Sadly the USA refused to pay for any and only some 50 were able to be sent – and were paid for by the European Economic Community!

## NOTES TO CHAPTER 11

1. Parker, p. 310, giving the date as January 1955
2. ibid, p. 311, referring to 'a fairly large scale invasion of Nicaragua from Costa Rica in June 1959'
3. Cozean, p. 124, quoting New York Times, 5th Dec., 1959
4. ibid, p. 125, quoting New York Times, 13th Nov., 1960
5. ibid, p. 125, quoting New York Times, 14th Nov., 1960
6. Parker, p. 279, statistics from U.N. Statutory Year Book 1959, p. 496
7. Cozean, p. 113
8. ibid, p. 126
9. The Tico Times, 21st October, 1977
10. ibid, 21st October, 1977
11. ibid, 21st April, 1978
12. ibid, 12th January, 1979
13. ibid, 26th January, 1979
14. ibid, 20th October, 1978
15. ibid, 3rd November, 1978
16. ibid, 10th November, 1978
17. ibid, 24th November, 1978
18. ibid, 12th January, 1979
19. ibid, 12th January, 1979
20. ibid, 2nd February, 1979
21. ibid, 9th February, 1979
22. ibid, 2nd March, 1979
23. ibid, 9th March, 1979
24. ibid, 30th March, 1979
25. ibid, 10th April, 1979
26. ibid, 20th April, 1979
27. ibid, 4th May, 1979
28. ibid, 1st June, 1979
29. ibid, 8th June, 1979
30. ibid, 15th June, 1979
31. ibid, 22nd June, 1979
32. The Tico Times, 29th June, 1979
33. ibid, 6th July, 1979
34. ibid, 13th July, 1979
35. ibid, 20th July, 1979
36. ibid, 27th July, 1979

# Chapter Twelve

# IS THERE AN ARMY IN COSTA RICA?

When the question is asked 'Is there an Army?' or a similar question 'Is the Civil Guard really an army in disguise?', Costa Ricans answer with an emphatic 'No'. Asked why they don't have an army and why they don't want one, most people give a very simple practical answer 'Any army we could maintain would be too small to defend us, so why have one?' Diplomats and senior authorities, whilst agreeing there is no army and no prospect of having one, are quite clear and say 'We rely upon our treaties and pacts of friendship for our security'. It has often been said that Costa Rica relies upon the USA for its 'defence' but events in the past thirty years do not bear out such an assertion. Even if it did, would it be so very different from Western Europeans? And is any country now 'defended' by its army, or is reliance placed on threats of mutual annihilation?

What is an army? The name is inconsequential; Panama and Nicaragua, as with some other Latin American countries, have a 'National Guard'; is Costa Rica's Civil Guard any different? One University Professor to whom the author spoke in 1981 pointed out the very name 'Civil Guard' was to emphasise the 'civil' character and control of the organisation. Does it have the equipment of a modern army; are there tanks, armoured vehicles, heavy artillery and all the paraphernalia of an armed force? The answer seems to be a resounding 'no' in every respect. There are, however, other opinions which it is as well should be examined.

John Saxe-Fernandez, a teacher at the University of Mexico and California State College at San Diego, California, wrote an article in May 1972 entitled 'The Militarization of Costa Rica'[1] In it he mentioned the persistent pressure from the USA and groups in Central America to secure the incorporation of Costa Rica in North America security, and participation in Condeca (Central American Defence Council). Training in counter insurgency tactics gives the 'civil' corps the same features that characterise Latin American armies, he says. He refers to a campaign in 1966 by the Federation of University Students opposing Costa Rica's participation in a Central American military organisation, a wave of urban terrorism in San José, the right-wing para-military movement to stop communism, 'Free Costa Rica Movement', and the arrest of some of its members being suppressed. He reports an interview with President Figueres by a Mexican journalist, José Reveles.

*Reveles:* The University Students claim Costa Rica is being militarised and the police are, in fact, an army.

*Figueres:* In Costa Rica I am the foremost supporter of the idea of civilian rule and the first to be opposed to any militarisation of the police.

*Reveles:* There is no army, but are the police becoming something of that sort?

*Figueres:* The Legislature and I are very carefully studying reforms which may have to be made within the police force. We are very carefully avoiding its becoming militarised.

*Reveles:* But the Costa Rican police receive advice from the North American military.

*Figueres:* Yes, for years we have sent officers for training in Panama. The US military mission there helped us form our own police academy. But we must always separate the military from the police . . . we cannot leave police tasks to be determined by a convent of nuns. The restlessness of the University students is all right; it seems to me to be proper and beneficial: but there is no militarisation.

(This interview was apparently in Figueres' third period as President 1970-1974). Fernandez argues that the distinction between police and military is purely formal and of no importance and that Figueres' would have to give way to AID (USA assistance programme) advisers. He supports his contention by reference to the latter's stressing the need for a 'Project Target and Course of Action' plan to improve the training and calibre of the police and refers to Costa Rica being second only to Nicaragua in the number of students sent to USA counter insurgency courses by the countries of the isthmus. He quotes Charles Meyer, a US Assistant Secretary of State for Inter-American Affairs as saying

> The US is anxious to maintain counter insurgency capabilities of Latin American forces in order that an internal atmosphere conducive to social and economic progress can prevail.

Fernandez relates an episode from a US Congressional enquiry:

*Senator Church:* I would like to examine for a moment the cost of these military groups we maintain in Latin America; e.g. in Costa Rica our figures show that the administration costs, based upon the minimum figure of $25,000 per man per year, came to $300,000, while the military assistance programme administered came to only $100,000. Your comments?

*Nutter:* Yes sir, I am advised Mr Chairman, that the main purpose of the mission in Costa Rica is not to administer the military assistance programme but to advise the security forces in Costa Rica.

*Church:* Well, why can't the security forces of Costa Rica, if they need to be advised by anybody, be advised by our military attachés? Why do you need a dozen officers and men in a military mission in Costa Rica?

Fernandez does not place a date upon this episode but in 1978 the author was told by one of the senior officials in the US Embassy in San José, 'Yes, there was a military mission but it consisted only of two men and confined itself to arranging the supply of uniforms, small arms, etc.' He said they had given up since 1966 trying to sell other arms to that country. This was confirmed by an article in *The Tico Times* on 21st October, 1977, mentioned in the last chapter.

Fernandez continues that the programmes train officers in theories and methods on how to reorder the political structure of their respective countries. This policy-orientated training improves the possibility for the administrators of North American national security to maintain a high degree of influence once students enter key positions; students are the future leaders of the people. He concludes

> The fact is, in Costa Rica, these tasks (police tasks) are being determined from the lofty Olympian heights of the Department of Defence and AID

Was Saxe-Fernandez' purpose to establish that Costa Rica was being 'militarised' or to attack the USA Government and administration? Had he been to Costa Rica and how much did he know of the local scene?

Condeca, to which reference has been made, was formed in 1964 by the Ministers of Defence of Guatemala, Honduras, El Salvador and Nicaragua largely at the instigation of the USA. Costa Rica did not sign the pact but was encouraged to participate in the status of 'observer'. Two years later the charter was amended to include security officers, in order to facilitate the inclusion of Costa Rica. There has undoubtedly been some pressure upon Costa Rica to form a 'proper' army and become a full member of Condeca, which it appears not to have done.

José Marín Cañas, in an article on 20th December, 1978, in *La Nación*, made some interesting observations, amongst them were the following:

> The backbone of a nation is the Army; this must be true since all the countries of the civilised world have an army except us.

After referring to the tense situation between Costa Rica and Nicaragua and the way young men had rushed to enlist patriotically 'as if war were a punch-up' he continued

> War is not, essentially and fundamentaly, firing shots. It is not a series of skirmishes, like that of 1948 when scarcely 32 people were killed (sic). On the contrary, it is, when the die is cast and the match is lost, the total destruction of a nationality, with its monuments, and its way of life; with mourning spread throughout the whole country, with homes sacrificed, trade destroyed, railways without bridges or rails, the nation paralysed and pulverised, like France after the 1914 war, like Moscow flattened after 1940, like Spain after ending in 1939 the war which began in 1936.
>
> One needs an army, apolitical, well prepared, with professional leaders.

After pointing out the high degree of training required, Cañas says:

> It's not for nothing that there are armies in every country except Costa Rica. Part of our youth amuses itself with vices, with drugs, with vagrancy and the sport of crime, robbery and degradation. This is because they have not been through the barracks where rigour – the rigour which the country needs to make its men complete – has brought them back from the barracks, grumbling about the time spent there, but turned into men not only ready and patriotic enough to enlist but also trained to form an army which can resist the attacks of the enemy.

Evidently no-one had told him Costa Rica has one of the lowest crime rates in Latin America, nor that the countries with armies suffer the same problems with their youth as those to which he refers.

*The Tico Times* had an article on 7th December, 1979, with the headline

### IS 'NON-EXISTENT ARMY' REARING ITS UGLY HEAD?

> High on the list of casualties of the Nicaraguan Revolution was the myth of an unarmed defenceless Costa Rica

it said, and went on to state that a growing number of Costa Ricans were voicing their concern over the military trappings the Nicaraguan conflict had left behind. It quoted the newspaper *La Nación*, printed in Spanish, which had published a four-part series claiming, amongst other things, that all security forces (formerly under separate command) had been brought under the authority of the Minister of Public Security. This was believed to add up to some 8,000 'troops', with a modicum of military training. It had engaged the attention of the legislators and an Investigating Committee had been appointed to examine 'the recent charges of a possible militarisation of public security forces' but its efforts had been slow and ineffectual. The Minister admitted that 500 automatic rifles lent by Venezuela, and two helicopters lent by Panama, during the Nicaraguan crisis had been retained because the 2,000 rifles forming the backbone of the country's arsenal were obsolete. Although the Minister, defending the training of civilian reserve forces and the formation of rural neighbourhood associations into paramilitary groups, claimed this was perfectly legal, the report had the following paragraph:

> The training of reservists and volunteers is harshly viewed by those who fear creeping militarisation in a country that supposedly has no army.

Reference was made to arms trafficking that had taken place because of the involvement of Costa Ricans in the Nicaraguan struggle, about which Echeverría said 'it has got to stop'. Not long afterwards he found it necessary to resign when it was alleged he had been personally involved in such arms violations. He admitted his concern that 'truly extremist right and left wing groups are arming themselves'.[2]

Any fears of interference in the democratic processes of the election in 1982 were not justified, and this again saw a peaceful changeover from a party in power to the opposition. In 1978 when the author interviewed Echeverría and asked pointedly if there were any likelihood of the Civil Guard becoming an army the reply was 'No, the people wouldn't stand for it'.

It has already been made clear that the problem for Costa Rica during the Sandinistas' struggle was not to allow their sympathies for that cause to prevent their complying with their duties under the treaties of friendship negotiated by the Organisation of American States after the invasions of 1948 and 1955. The Civil Guard had to deal not only with armed guerilla bands of Sandinistas operating in the wild and desolate country forming the border between Nicaragua and Costa Rica but also with the many incursions by Nicaraguan National Guards, violating the territory of Costa Rica when pursuing the marauding Sandinistas. With most countries the actions of the Nicaraguans would have led to an outright state of war between the parties – but not so with Costa Rica.

Cozean argued that a literate highly trained voluntary mobile Civil Guard was an efficient army, and that, in spite of Article 12 of the Constitution, there definitely was an army – or something suspiciously like an army in Costa Rica at that time (1966). He quoted several writers and politicians to support this view, including Somoza saying the Costa Rica army was never disbanded.[3] He conceded the Civil Guard was not an army in the traditional sense but maintains that it was considerably more than a mere police force.[4]

In fact it can be argued that Costa Rica may well be the most military non-military country in the world.

He compared Costa Rica with several other countries which spend little on armed forces and have been cautious about building up their armed forces – as he included both Uganda and Tanzania in this category, recent events would seem to cast grave doubt on this comparision. He saw a difference in that only Costa Rica had followed through with a concerted policy of demilitarisation.

From almost any point of view, it must be concluded that Costa Rica is one of the most anti-militaristic countries in the world.[5]

Cozean mentioned the alteration of the Constitution in 1951 to permit nationals to volunteer for service in Korea; but none did.

In 1965 Costa Rica sent 21 policemen, rather than soldiers, to the Dominican Republic as part of the five nation OAS occupation force. A US Department of State pamphlet says the Costa Rican force was dressed in typical Latin American policemen's uniform with 'National Police' shoulder patches. The other OAS contingents wore UN style combat uniforms.[6]

He maintains there was, and would always be, some type of a military organisation in Costa Rica. The reason was the same as that which has justified standing armies since the dawn of civilisation: 'The world as yet knows no higher law than force'.[7]

Incidents involving Nicaraguan National Guards' activities in 1959 and 1960 (his observations on the vastly increased provocation of 1977-79 would have been most illuminating) are referred to, along with the use of Civil Guards to maintain order during strikes, to support his contention that an armed force, large enough to take care of incidents that could break out simultaneously in various parts of the country, was needed.[8] He quoted José Santos Delcore, director of the Civil Guard, who, following a conference of American armies which dealt largely with the Cuban threat, declared

When I leave this Conference I will do all within my power so that the theme of our public forces shall not be 'business as usual'; we will make a maximum effort to raise the operational level of our modest security force in all its facets, so as to be better prepared to answer the constant challenge of our common enemy: Communism.[8]

At this point Cozean concluded:

The present Costa Rican Civil Guard cannot be classified as a national army in the traditional sense of the word – it is too small,

159

too lightly armed and too lacking in normal military values.[8]

At the same time the Civil Guard is more than a police force – for it is charged with preserving the sovereignty of the nation. In order to perform this unique role, the Civil Guard has been altered and realtered through the years until today it has become stabilised at what may be its equilibrium position; an effective security force small enough to be neither a drain on the budget nor an important political factor.

That was the goal of José Figueres on 1st December, 1948.[9]

His conclusions are most valuable and deserve careful study, but can be briefly summarised as follows:

> The abolition of the Costa Rican army is one of the most significant events in Latin American history.
>
> Figueres knew that a large standing army would be a challenge to his own authority and, idealistically, he wanted to banish force and military influence from the Second Republic. He was looking beyond the borders of Costa Rica and wanted to challenge the traditional order in Latin America – an order that all too often allocates their small resources to building armies rather than to fighting poverty, disease and illiteracy.[10]

After referring to the plight of the developing nations which represent two-thirds of the world's population and where the 'military is little more than a parasite', Cozean quotes Major Robert L. Burke of the US Army writing in the Military Review, Oct. 1964, as saying military forces have always constituted a drain upon the human and material resources of a nation, even in peacetime.

> They produce nothing, consume much, and – except for the jobs they produce as consumers – they make no direct contribution to the progress of the national community.

Burke also noted that the problem in under-developed countries was particularly grave, because the military diverts into the armed forces many of the skills which are needed so badly among the civilian population.[11]

Cozean thought most other countries cannot automatically follow the example of Costa Rica as it was uncommonly fortunate. It has no population antagonisms, little internal turmoil, a high educational level, and a long tradition of constitutional government with little military influence; and has always been isolated from external troubles. (This was altered in 1977-9 as we have seen). He went on to observe that, in case of external aggression, Costa Rica could always count on the protection of the United States and in support of this quoted John N. Plank in Foreign Affairs, October 1965:

under no circumstances would the United States tolerate a Communist regime in the Caribbean region.[12]

He had ignored Cuba, and, of course, in recent years there are other conundrums for the USA, which is often quoted as referring to the 'Marxist-dominated Nicaraguan government'. Cozean quoted Costa Rica's proximity to the Panama Canal as making her security of vital interest to the United States, but that is an element that has now disappeared.

In addition, there is the proven peace-keeping machinery of the OAS in cases of emergency.[12]

This undoubtedly proved to be the case in 1948, 1955 and in the stormy years of the Sandinistas' revolutions. To quote Cozean again:

Costa Rica has aptly demonstrated that international organisations can preserve the peace – more than most people care to admit – Such international protection may be even more likely when a country renounces her arms in favour of such protection.[13]

He still maintained, however, that Costa Rica has a small professional army, having developed the Civil Guard into a well-trained and highly mobile force. By improving the pay and living conditions, he says, Costa Rica has gained a better soldier and better security but, at the same time, has maintained civilian control over an army which is now largely without traditional military values.

Even more importantly, scarce funds have been diverted away from the military and into the nation's infrastructure such as roads, hospitals and schools. This, according to the Costa Rican theory, is the best way to fight poverty and international communism.[14]

Cozean's final conclusion reads:

In short, Costa Rica has proved the value of a demilitarised military. She has set an example for developing nations to follow. The fact that most of the rest of the world is not even aware of this example is one of the real tragedies of our time.[15]

When the author interviewed José Echeverría in 1978 and asked about the police being armed with revolvers, the response was 'Tell me a country where the police are not armed'. Before one could say 'England', Echeverría was saying 'Northern Ireland', where, although governed along with Britain, the police have been armed for some time. In recent years there have been more and more occasions in England when police have been armed for specific tasks. In 1981 in Costa Rica there was only one (apparently) automatic rifle visible; with the guard outside the local gaol in San José.

161

Perhaps the most pungent observation came in an interview with a Civil Guard by one of the USA journalists on *The Tico Times*.

'Sure we've got an army', one sergeant admitted. 'You'd better not say who you talked to, 'cause they'd fry me if they knew'. He went on to admit that he was of many Guardsmen who have been sent to US Army bases in Panama for special military training, primarily in anti-guerilla warfare. 'It's frustrating when they say all we do is keep order in the cities' he continued, clearly warming to a subject he had never talked about publicly, 'I hope now that it's obvious, we can admit that we really do have a double function, half of which is definitely military.' The young soldier's comments were partially confirmed by Minister of the Presidency, José Rafael Cordero, who told *The Tico Times* that the Civil Guard 'is not an institutional army, but an emergency defence force, which naturally operates along military lines'. But the Minister maintained that it is 'neither a traditional nor a permanent army'.[16]

Set against all this there is the constant reiteration by people, officials – and even Presidents – that Costa Rica does not have an army. Would they be anxious to assert this if it were otherwise? Could it be said at such events as the United Nations Special Session on Disarmament if it were not correct? Reference has already been made to statements by different Presidents since 1948 drawing attention to the absence of armed forces and claiming as is often said, 'We used to say we had more teachers than soldiers; now we have more schools than soldiers'. Ex-President Echandi, in the interview referred to, made a comparison between Costa Rica's Civil Guard and the Spanish Guardia Civil and pointed out the former was not to become an army because there was a minimum training in arms and only small arms were provided. Fernando Volio, a Professor of Law at San José University categorically asserted 'There is no army nor any military police'.

This was at an interview at the University, when he went on to relate the results of a survey of High School students in 1979; 2% were in favour of an army and 20% in favour of a stronger police force. This, he pointed out, was from young people some of whom had been exposed for the first time for very many years to guns in the hands of young Sandinistas. At the Headquarters of Angel Calderón's Unity Party, a spokesman was sceptical of the claim that the plane and helicopters from Venezuela and Panama were for the protection of Costa Ricans and considered they had become too involved with the Sandinistas. He maintained they felt better because they had no army. Several people expressed grave doubts about the bringing of the aircraft just referred to and it was clearly not considered in keeping with their tradition and background. A University Professor said when the officer in charge of the guard around the aircraft was asked why there was such a substantial guard, he had replied 'because they were terrified something might happen to damage them and Costa Rica couldn't afford to pay for them'.

One of the most telling comments came from a senior official at the US Embassy when asked if the Civil Guard were really an army. 'No', he replied, 'it is not an army under another name, it is an ill-equipped police force'. The point was also made that the name Military Mission had been changed to 'Office of Defence Co-operation' and that the USA had given up trying to sell armaments to Costa Rica and was only concerned with the sale of uniforms and small arms for their police duties. He was sure Costa Rica had realised it could not defend itself and relied on the Rio de Janeiro treaty of 1947. An intelligent and very politically minded young lawyer said

> Costa Rica is better without an army. It is more dangerous to have an army than there are benefits. There are three threats or disadvantages to having an army:
> 1. The cost.
> 2. The threat to our democracy
> 3. The threat to our other liberties.

He also confirmed there had been a real threat of invasion by troops from Nicaragua or of San José being bombed; people had laid in a stock of food. This was because Costa Rica had become too involved with the Sandinista cause and accordingly it could be expected that Somoza would take steps to nullify this.

Amongst the many public statements made by President Carazo referring to Costa Rica's reliance on treaties and absence of arms, is one quoted in *The Washington Post* of 4th April, 1979:

> 'Driving through the countryside, one looks in vain for squatter cities, barefoot children, soldiers with machine guns, so characteristic of many other Central American countries.
> 'The explanation is very simple' Rodrigo Carazo said. 'We don't waste money on weapons, so we have resources for other things. The needs of our people come first.'

The sentiments and beliefs of Costa Ricans are illustrated by words of Luis Alberto Monge, elected President in February 1982:

> Significantly, in one of his earliest statements after the election, he expressed the hope that the United States would not concentrate on providing military aid to El Salvador and ignore the economical and social problems afflicting the nations of Central America.[17]

An official of the Canadian Embassy considered José Echeverría, when Minister of Public Security, had been trying to militarise the police; he had to resign when some arms were discovered in his house and a Committee of Investigation was set up. This speaker pointed out there is not only division of control of the Civil Guard, the Rural Guard and other branches of the police force but also, after the four yearly elections when there have been changes in respect of the political party in office, substantial changes have also been made in the Civil Guard. Although this has tended to make it less efficient because of lack of training and experience, it prevents there being any domination by any individuals or groups. Control of the Civil Guard is taken out of political hands during the period before and during the elections and placed under the authority of the Supreme Electoral Tribunal. No opportunity to influence the result of the elections by manipulating the use of the force as was believed to have happened in the 1944 and 1948 elections. There is considerable opposition to any idea of militarising the National Guard, was the opinion from this Embassy official.

'Costa Rica has not enough money to buy sophisticated modern weapons and would therefore have to do with second rate ones' said one of the University Professors to the author in 1981 and asserted 'some may want arms but certainly not the majority'. This view was borne out by the report in the *Disarmament Times* during the United Nations Special Session on Disarmament in 1978 of an interview with the Costa Rican delegate. He maintained very strongly there was no army in Costa Rica and that 'We Rely on our Weakness'.[18] The official report of the contribution made by the Costa Rican delegate at that Special Session on Disarmament appears in Appendix IV and the official report of Costa Rica's contribution at the Second Special Session in 1982 is in Appendix V.

The author's visit to Los Chilis, the town near the border with Nicaragua that had been the scene of the attack in 1977, disclosed that although people had been terrified not a single one interviewed expressed any wish to have an air force or armed forces to 'defend' them, much less to retaliate. It is noteworthy that even in 1955 when San José and other cities in the Central Valley were bombed by the calderonistas with assistance from Nicaragua, there was no question of retaliation from Costa Rica by using planes loaned by sympathetic countries. Nor after the invasion in 1955 was there any proposal to revive the army.

Commenting on aid given by the United States to Costa Rica, Parker states:

> (In 1946-60) $27 millions were for highways, chiefly the Inter-American. Another $11 millions were for economic and technical assistance, and only $9 THOUSAND for the military.[19]

Lundberg says:

Costa Rica's Army is probably the most democratic in the world. Really, there is no army and the country is rightfully proud that it has more school houses than Civil Guards.[20]

In an article headed 'Crocodile Tears' in *La República*, Ricardo Blanco Segura in commenting on those who were criticising the Government for its attitude towards the Sandinistas said:

> nobody in his right mind could believe that in present world circumstances an army could be any use to Costa Rica: however many arms we bought, or were lent, they would be no good against the might of the great powers. And not even in a regional Central American war because others would come and sort it out in a few hours with the consequent useless shedding of blood.
>
> Costa Rica does not need nor should it at present have an army. Our unarmed pacifist and civilian condition is a better defence against the world because it involves a moral force of incalculable value.[21]

This was, of course, at a time when the Sandinistas had been especially active in their struggle against the Somoza regime and border incursions by the Nicaraguan National Guard had intensified.

The same newspaper carried an article by Luis Fernando Moya Mata, Legal Adviser to UNA, which commented on the fact that the recent affair (the bringing in of the plane and helicopters etc. from Panama and Venezuela) had cost 30 million colones and continues:

> This was a necessary expenditure but it reminds one of the enormous cost of maintaining an army. Recent events in Nicaragua have shown that not all that vast expenditure on arms and military could stop the people winning their freedom from Somoza. Once again it has been shown that ideas are stronger than bullets, that thinkers are more convincing than generals and that books are more powerful than tanks. It is important to spend money on education and not waste it on arms.[22]

On 7th December, 1979, *The Tico Times* displayed a photograph with its article 'Is "non-existent army" rearing its ugly head?', to which reference has already been made, which showed two of the Costa Rican Civil Guard with rifles and the caption reads:

> Military trappings for Costa Rican police are upsetting many citizens of 'armyless' Costa Rica. Photo above was taken during Nicaraguan conflict, when Tico Civil Guards were sent to guard the northern border.

The same newspaper on 6th July 1979, quoted a meeting of Costa Rican officials with the United States Human Rights representative, when a

165

plea was made for special treatment by the Minister of the Presidency, José Rafael Cordero:

> It isn't fair that a country like Costa Rica, which doesn't have an army, gets no favourable treatment[23]

And on 5th December 1980, *The Tico Times* had an Editorial pleading for less encouragement to be given to hunters coming to the country from the United States and said:

> Costa Rica has established itself as an enlightened, humanistic peace-loving world leader in the areas of human rights – and conservation . . . The simple fact that foreign hunters can afford the luxury of shotgun shells when most Ticos can't is a type of discrimination Costa Rica doesn't need to underscore.[24]

In an Editorial a few weeks earlier, there had been a comparison between war and smoking which is almost worthwhile reproducing in its entirety but some extracts can be made:

> Smoking calms your nerves, keeps you going, helps you cope. A mighty military is your guarantee of freedom and democracy, your bulwark against communism and fascism.

After referring to the lack of rationalizing in Iran and Iraq and the self-deceptive double-talk in the USA and that no-one seemed to be questioning this, it continues:

> People are becoming dangerously, frighteningly fatalistic. The trigger-happy war addicts are getting encouragement – like the smoker in a smoke-filled room. Perhaps it's because there are so many problems and they all seem so overwhelming and so insoluble. Economic crises, ecological disasters, leadership wastelands, corruption cynicism . . .
>
> A war would give us all a common scapegoat, consolidating all our worries, focussing all our fears in one direction. We wouldn't have to think any more (or even pretend to be reasonable). It would clear the air.
>
> And like the tobacco addict, we could watch all our dreams of human progress go up in smoke.[25]

The danger of relying upon reports issued in another country is underlined by a Commentary by Fernando E. Naranjo V in *La Nación*. He had recently been in Mexico meeting with economists, educators, politicans and others and noted the news items about Costa Rica which were appearing in the main Mexican newspapers.

> It was really alarming to read abroad, news items, comments and declarations by officials of our government about the necessity for

166

Costa Rica to acquire military equipment of various kinds, to train and prepare the Civil Guard and to enlist volunteers for the purpose of defending Costa Rican sovereignty.

Rightly or wrongly we were constantly asked in Mexico if it were true that Costa Rica was forming an army, how far the arms race was going to go in our country, if power was passing into the hands of the military, what would be the function of the groups of armed civilians and many other questions and comments.

We prudently tried to convince many friends that assertions of this kind were not correct and were partly due to the news distribution of the media which was not always exactly consistent with the truth.

This brief experience in Mexico a few days ago filled us with sorrow and worry. From outside our own frontiers we were able to observe that the image which Costa Rica has had as a democratic and 'civilianist' country, where there are more teachers than policemen, has begun to change.

This image, for which Costa Rica is respected in international forums, is fading away. We must all contribute to maintaining our 'civilianist' tradition; otherwise we shall have many years of lamentation in the future.[26]

This confirms the doubts raised by the contributions quoted from Saxe-Fernandez and, to some extent, Cozean, whose sources seem to be mainly newspaper reports in the United States.

An interesting comment is made by Lt. Col. Theodore Wyckoff, US Army in a thoughtful article on military elements in Latin American politics, that

where democracy flourishes – and even where it flourishes with occasional military intervention – there is also to be found the condition of powerful countervailing forces.

Such a system of countervailing forces, he finds

could serve as a framework for a democratic party system. This, in fact, is what seems to have happened in Costa Rica.

Lt.-Col. Wyckoff is primarily concerned with classes and political parties. The countervailing forces in Costa Rica have arisen in large measure out of the system of land distribution, of numerous proprietors. In this sense, Lt.-Col. Wyckoff's allusion to Costa Rica is entirely correct.[27]

It may be considered the most authoritative comment on the question whether or not the Costa Rican Civil Guard is an army comes from an interview given to *The Tico Times* by Mario Charpentier, Minister for Public Security in 1976. It will be recalled it was Charpentier who was attacked by the Nicaraguans when inspecting a border incident in October a year later. Said *The Tico Times*:

167

Charpentier must use his 3,500 member public security force to maintain order and guard the safety of a country of almost two million people. And he has to do it without an army.

'As you know, Costa Rica's political constitution of 1948 prohibits formation of a standing army' explains Charpentier. But, strangely enough, the Minister believes this is one of the reasons why Costa Rica has little to worry about in protecting itself.

'We could never think of arming ourselves to the extent of our neighbours (Panama and Nicaragua). Our budget is not even $10 million a year. After paying salaries, what would be left for purchasing fighter planes, tanks etc? Maybe we could afford a few spare parts, but spare parts for what?

'When you think about it, we're just a little defenceless country, and it would probably be a simple matter to invade us. But this, believe it or not, is where I believe our strength lies.

'Could you imagine what the international reaction would be if a purposely defenceless nation were attacked by a heavily-armed one? It would be a shame that would be hard to live down. I think this is the key. Our vulnerability makes us strong.'

The interview continued by indicating the division of command of the separate forces, the Civil Guard being responsible for maintaining law and order in San José and the six provincial capitals and the Rural Guard responsible for security elsewhere. The Radio Patrol and Military Police are recruited from the Civil Guard, the functions of the former being to guard the city streets and maintain order on the highways. The Military Force, the report continues, has nothing to do with what their name implies. Before January 1st 1976, its members' primary function was to watch over the President's offices, but that has now been turned over to the newly-formed Presidential Guard. The Military Police now confines itself to policing the 2 p.m. Guard and performing ceremonial functions, which include patrols at the National Theatre and appearances at official functions.

'In Costa Rica, there exists a great fear of any one person gaining too much power' says Charpentier. 'This is why we keep the police forces separated. A person would think twice before trying anything, because that other force would still be there. We sacrifice efficiency to safeguard this principle.'

'The base pay is colones 1,100 a month, which is very low', admits Charpentier, 'But we're trying to raise it.' One difficulty is that Public Security receives only 2.5% of the National Budget whilst Education gets more than 30%.[28]

Could any sort of army be maintained with that minimum of expenditure? An Editorial from *The Tico Times* shall have the last word; this was on

15th June 1979 just before the final efforts of the Sandinistas toppled the Somoza régime and pressure on Costa Rica's northern boundary was intense. The headline ran

IN DEFENCE OF STAYING DEFENCELESS

and referred to Costa Rica's proudest tradition – and greatest strength – its defencelessness in a world of military might.

> But the current conflict in Nicaragua has changed all that. Suddenly Costa Rica has an army, through subtle but steady transformation of a crack police force into an inexperienced, but carefully-trained, defence force. The Civil Guard, which most of the time concerns itself with maintaining order in Costa Rica's towns and cities, is now wearing helmets and carrying machine guns, and is patrolling the nation's northern border in undeniably military fashion.

> It's disconcerting, if only because most Ticos have accepted the metamorphosis without a murmur. National security is at stake; invasion has been threatened; viva the Civil Guard! This is understandable, but it does raise a disturbing question. Will Costa Rica wake up one morning and find that it has somehow acquired a full-time, permanent army?

> No, says the government. The soldiers at the border are not an 'institutionalised' military force. They are there to protect Costa Rica against attack, not to wage war. Though they may have all the trappings of an army, they're policemen, and the business of war is foreign to them.

> The Civil Guards themselves agree. While they admit they're an army now, they admit it in whispers. Officially Costa Rica is still an armyless nation.

> The distinction is delicate, but important. As long as Costa Rica believes it has no army – as long as it can perpetuate the 'soldiers – schoolteachers' cliché, even while it mobilises real troops – it is safe from the insidious mentality of 'defence' that has created armies (and caused wars) in countless countries throughout history. As long as Costa Rica believes it has no army, it won't feel the need to equip or maintain it: it won't feel pressure to buy a tank here, a bomber there, or a couple of dozen machine guns, 'just in case'. It won't be caught up in the mindless, paranoid one-upmanship which is a way of life in military nations, and which gave birth to the Cold War.

> Ticos must remain alert to the difference between a 'temporary defence force' composed of policemen and the monster that could grow out of it. They must not let the current emergency become the status quo, or accept without question the Costa Rican soldiers on the northern border.

> They must cling to the 'no army' myth, and when things calm down, they must insist that the myth becomes reality again.[29]

# NOTES TO CHAPTER 12

1. Saxe-Fernandez, p. 195
2. Tico Times, 12 Dec., 1979
3. Cozean, p. 92
4. ibid, p. 93
5. ibid, p. 114
6. ibid, p. 114
7. ibid, p. 123
8. ibid, p. 126
9. ibid, p. 127
10. ibid, p. 128
11. ibid, p. 129
12. ibid, p. 131
13. ibid, p. 132
14. ibid, p. 133
15. ibid, p. 134
16. Tico Times, 15th June, 1979
17. (London) Times, 11th Feb., 1982
18. Disarmament Times, 23rd June, 1978
19. Parker, p. 278 (quoting Foreign Grants and Credits by US Government)
20 Lundberg, p. 153
21. La República, 28th March, 1979
22. ibid, 26th July, 1979
23. Tico Times, 6th July, 1979
24. ibid, 5th Dec., 1980
25. ibid, 10th Oct., 1980
26. La Nación, 21st Dec., 1978
27. Colorado, p. 72
28. Tico Times, 16th Jan., 1976
29. ibid, 15th June, 1979

# Chapter Thirteen

# UNIVERSITY FOR PEACE

On the 27th September, 1978, Rodrigo Carazo, President of Costa Rica from 1978 to 1982, addressed the General Assembly of the United Nations. He laid before the Assembly the idea he had of creating the University for Peace to be located in Costa Rica. He said, among other things, while stressing Costa Rica's proposition:

> Peace is a right of the human species, but it is also a duty. It follows that every man, and mankind as a whole, must be not only the object, but also the subject of peace. Men may enjoy this right, but they must, at the same time, keep it in being! Peace is the work of justice and the fruit of love, but it must also be the product of education, or, better said, education must be one of its most effective instruments of action.
>
> If you desire peace, prepare for peace.
>
> The University for Peace must be the laboratory of the spirit of peace, the crucible in which we must form the new mentality of peace over the decades to come. For the Twenty-first Century shall be peaceful, or it shall not be.[1]

President Rodrigo Carazo continued:

> Peace is not the end of a conflict or an interlude between wars; it is a constantly renewed challenge. It must be our supreme objective and, as such, we must provide concrete means for affirming it, recalling that the present generation reserves its trusts for words that are accompanied by deeds.
>
> Peace is not merely a matter of noble sentiments. It requires, by its very nature, some measure of precise and diversified knowledge, both theoretical and practical. That is why it is urgent that man's intelligence and culture should be directed towards peace. What is involved, as has been proposed by one eminent voice, is marshalling all man's intellectual faculties, all of the cultural and scientific heritage of mankind, in order that they become instruments of peace. What this implies, finally, is preparing and training man's

171

will and intelligence for peace. Peace is made, not found. Peace is not rest. It is not another word for fear. It is the pulse of life.

In order to reach peace, we must put to use one of the greatest and most effective means of ennobling and transforming man: EDUCATION. In this way we may forge in man the thoughts and habits of peace, bringing peace first into the minds and hearts of men, and then into world politics.[2]

Costa Rica's proposal was for the creation of a new international institution within the framework of the United Nations University System.

As this was only shortly after the first Special Session on Disarmament of the United Nations, it might have been expected that unqualified support and encouragement would be given to this generous proposal by a small nation. It was, however, resolved by the Second Commission of the General Assembly:

'To take note with satisfaction of the proposal submitted by the President of Costa Rica for the establishment of a University for Peace . . .' and the Secretary General was asked to consult with the member States, with UNESCO, with the Rector and Council of the United Nations University as well as with all other organisms that he considers convenient.[3]

The 87th plenary session of the General Assembly accepted the proposal and asked that a report regarding the project be presented by the Economic and Social Council to the General Assembly during its next 34th period of sessions.

Costa Rica's enthusiastic and energetic President then undertook the production of a detailed exposé of the proposal. On 20th December, 1978 a Presidential Commission was designated through an Executive Decree of Costa Rica with the purpose of co-ordinating all the decisions and activities necessary to ensure the University for Peace was established in Costa Rica. A booklet was produced in Spanish and translated into English which, after setting forth a brief chronological introduction and expressing the need to strive for the establishment of a permanently peaceful world, expounded the academic structure of the proposed University for Peace. It is especially noteworthy that, in explaining why the University should be situated in Costa Rica, one paragraph reads:

Costa Rica has been successful in creating a mentality of civil tradition deeply rooted in its national reality. It has had to pass through difficult times in the process of its internal organisation and in the confirmation of its international unity. It has appealed frequently to competent international organisations in order to solve definite conflicts within the framework determined by international treaties and agreements. It has done this because it considers that only by respecting the established legal frameworks will it be possible to continue advancing as a nation, along the road that it has freely chosen.[4]

Undoubtedly the invasions of 1948 and 1955 and the many provocations from Nicaragua during the Sandinista revolutions in 1977, 1978 and 1979 would be prominently in the minds of those who wrote these words. The succeeding paragraph in the booklet reads:

> Its (Costa Rica's) fully peaceful life, its evident social, political and economic advances, as well as the respect for the human dignity of every citizen of the Republic, constitute the historical letter of presentation behind the proposal for the creation of a University for Peace at the international level. An effective democratic system and the constitutional derogation of the ARMY as an institution in 1949 (the year the Constition was amended it will be recalled) contribute to the comprehension of its historical singularity.[5]

After setting forth Article 12 of the Constitution prohibiting a permanent army, the paragraph continues:

> Thus, after one hundred and fifty eight years of independent life dedicated to educational and cultural improvement, there comes forth the great initiative of creating a new educational experience, this time with a global projection in the permanent search for an active peace, sole guarantee of survival for the human race.[6]

It was observed that the proposal was envisaged as a short, medium and long-range international effort. A period of fifteen years is contemplated for the construction and definite integration of the plans.

The intention is not to be solely an academic exercise:

> Costa Rica considers that, once the University for Peace is established, it will effectively contribute to the strengthening of world peace. Its research and teachings, within the concept of 'EDUCATE FOR PEACE', will produce models for society as well as concrete instruments in the reduction of tensions. Men and women, the principal subjects of its action, will have a propitious and creative environment, coupled with the direct interchange of different cultures, in which to produce the answers necessary for the attainment of that distant and ardently desired goal.[7]

Very wisely the booklet observes:

> Peace is not one man's task . . . The task of peace should be the obligation of all men, of all societies, of all nations; only by inculcating that idea, expanding it and spreading it can integral peace be truly attained: peace of the person, of society and that of nations.[8]

173

The Council of the United Nations University gave 'careful considera- tion to the General Assembly resolution' relating to the establishment of a University for Peace within the system of the United Nations University and, at its twelfth session, examined the proposal and welcomed the initiative taken by the President of the Republic of Costa Rica. Doubts were, however, expressed as to whether the proposed University for Peace could be included within the United Nations University system. It was emphasised that the financing of the proposed new University should be organised in such a manner that it involved no diversion of financial resources from the United Nations University. Further consideration was promised if the University for Peace established programmes contribut- ing to the effective operation of the network of collaborating institutions within the UN University system, which, it was pointed out, included 23 associated institutions and more than 80 research and training units.[9]

President Carazo persevered and on 14th December, 1979 the General Assembly of the United Nations approved the idea of establishing a University for Peace, and on 5th December 1980

> approved the establishment of the University for Peace in conformity with the International Agreement for the Establishment of the University for Peace and with the Charter of the University for Peace, whereby the University headquarters is to be located in Costa Rica.[10]

On that date Costa Rica and Venezuela were the first nations to sign the International Agreement, which came into force on 7th April, 1981 when ten States from more than one continent had signed it. By that date, in addition to Costa Rica and Venezuela, Chile, Colombia, Ecuador, Panama, Pakistan, Senegal, Nicaragua and El Salvador had signed the International Agreement. When India signed the International Agree- ment on 10th December, 1981, twenty two nations had signed and included Italy, Peru, Spain and Mexico.[11]

Although the University Council held its first meeting in San José from 15th to 19th December, 1981, it was not formally inaugurated until 6th March, 1982 at a meeting held in the Costa Rican National Theatre. At that date agreement was reached as to the structure, organisation and relations with the host country and President Rodrigo Carazo was appointed president, of the Executive committee. A visit was paid to the planned site of the University located in what was described as a 'wild' area about 25 kilometres from San José. From personal experience of a hazardous journey to the site, the author can confirm the description is an accurate one!

The campus, situated about four miles west of the nearest little town of Ciudad Colon, commands a superb view over the Meseta Central to the

174

distant volcanoes, Poás, Barba and Irazú. The late Costa Rican philanthropist, Cruz Rojas Bennet, whose family had owned the land for almost a hundred years, donated it to the Costa Rican Government, which has made about 700 acres available for the University for Peace.[12] Of this area, 500 acres are to be preserved as virgin forest, which, conserved by the original donor, is considered priceless and unique in Central America. The University buildings will be erected on the remaining 200 acres and on 15th November, 1982, the main building was completed, which is on three levels and, in addition to the administrative offices, and some seminar rooms, has the Chamber where the University Council meets. This is equipped with booths for instantaneous translation of speeches and contributions. An inner courtyard planted out as a garden and with a beautifully designed fountain provides a splendid vista for those not enjoying the distant view to the volcanoes. The next stage is the construction of a 250 seat auditorium and other buildings will be added as the University develops. Three years earlier when the site was found with difficulty in the forest, it seemed inconceivable that so much progress could possibly be made so quickly and this is a measure of the importance attached to the proposal.

In February 1982, Costa Rica held its four-yearly elections for President and National Assembly. Señor Rodrigo Carazo was prevented by the country's Constitution from standing for a second term but his close interest in the University for Peace was continued when in March of that year he was appointed President of the University Council. Although there was a change of the party constituting the Government as well as the office of President as a result of the elections in February 1982 it was confidently expected the University for Peace would continue as all opposition parties had indicated support. It is constantly emphasised this is a United Nations development and not one restricted to Costa Rica itself.

The problem of securing the necessary finance is made the more difficult because of the severe stress to which Costa Rica, like many of the under-developed countries though not as badly as most, has been subjected in recent years. The considerable increase in oil prices, coupled with the decrease in the prices realised for her staple exports of coffee, sugar and bananas, has occasioned a terrific reduction in the value of the colon as against the US dollar and other foreign currencies. It can be well understood, therefore, why the succeeding President, Luis Alberto Monge, and his National Liberation Party which took office early in 1982, felt obliged to indicate that Costa Rica would be incapable of financing the project in the absence of funds being forthcoming from international sources.[13] It is certain there have already been very substantial contributions from abroad and the administration building and the

175

auditorium, together estimated to cost about eight and a half million colones, are expected to be paid for by contributions from Taiwan and Korea.[14] In the grounds of the University is a statue to a Japanese philanthropist, Mr Ryoichi Sasakawa, reputed to have donated more than a million colones for the University.

Perhaps the most encouraging development was the establishment of a 'Mexico-Venezuela' Foundation by five oil-importing countries of the Central American and Caribbean region. This was signed early in 1982 by Costa Rica, the Dominican Republic, El Salvador, Nicaragua and Panama. This Foundation proposes to levy a surcharge of 20 cents on each barrel of crude oil imported from Mexico or Venezuela. The funds will be invested and the resulting income made available to the University. Señor Carazo estimated that fifteen million US dollars would be raised during the next three years by the Foundation. By agreements made in 1980 with Mexico and Venezuela some countries in that region were to pay only 70 per cent of the OPEC base price in US dollars, the balance being credited to the exporters in local currencies, and made available for development loans within those countries.[15]

Doubts were expressed by the special representative of the UN Secretary-General, Robert Müller, when referring to the Mexico-Venezuela Foundation. He said 'there is no precedent for such a sacrifice being made by a group of countries which are not, in themselves, well off'. No doubt had the proposal awaited the support of the relatively well-off nations, it would have made little, if any, progress. None of the larger nations, with the exceptions already noted, have signed the Agreement to establish the University for Peace, nor offered any financial or other support. With the inauguration of a University Foundation, an international body whose function is to receive and invest funds, then supply proceeds to the University to be used towards capital and recurrent costs,[16] and the subsequent issue of an invitation to individuals, as well as governments and other sources of funding, the problem of finance is receiving attention.

Meanwhile the work of organising the University for Peace continues to gain impetus as its existence becomes more and more widely known. The Second International Council Session held at the University site from 16th to 19th January 1983 recommended the publication of a newsletter intended to facilitate communication between all those wishing to collaborate with the implementation and strengthening of the new worldwide organisation. The University for Peace, together with the University for Life of the Philippines, sponsored a Seminar on 7th and 8th April, 1983, in Manila on the 'New International Human Order; Moral Aspects of Development'.

In July 1983, the University for Peace held an International Conference at the Palace of Nations, Geneva on the theme 'Peace now – what can be done?' at which four Nobel Laureates and three former heads of state were present. Another International Conference on 'Terrorism and Violence in Democratic Countries' is proposed to be held in Spain and a work programme is being designed to permit academic activities to be initiated by 1985. Perhaps the University's most important assignment has been the first research programme on a regional theme. 'The social, political and economic impact of refugees in Central America, Mexico and Panama from 1978 to 1983: lessons for the future' is the basis of the research programme commenced in August 1983 and intended to be completed a year later. Towards the cost of this the University was awarded US \$25,000 by the United Nations High Commission for Refugees.[17] Having regard to the many thousands of refugees from Nicaragua, Guatemala and El Salvador in recent years, the University should be well placed to undertake such an important task.

At United Nations Headquarters in New York on September 20th and 21st, 1983, the University for Peace sponsored an International Colloquium on the renowned philosopher Pierre Teilhard de Chardin. This is intended to be the first of a series entitled 'Visionaries of World Peace', which will include, amongst others, universal giants like Mahatma Gandhi, Martin Luther King, Jose Marti and Bertrand Russell. At this Colloquium the Secretary General of the United Nations, Javier Pérez de Cuéllar said:

> This is the first activity at the United Nations headquarters by the new University for Peace which was created under the auspices of the United Nations Organisation. The University has my complete support since I consider it most timely and I might also say, prophetic, that this institution was created at a moment when the desire for peace is manifesting itself with an unprecedented intensity. In order to support this movement and to encourage the realisation of concrete actions, it was necessary that the International Community possess a University dedicated to the study, teaching and formation for peace. It couldn't be more appropriate that this University originate in Costa Rica, a country which had the courage to eliminate its army by constitutional means and has had the sense to demonstrate that a disarmed nation can live in peace, secure, as has been the case since 1948.[18]

# NOTES TO CHAPTER 13

1. Booklet, 'University for Peace',; Costa Rica Government, 1979, page 1
2. ibid, page 1
3. ibid, page 2
4. ibid, pages 4 and 5
5. ibid, page 5
6. ibid, page 5
7. ibid, page 6
8. ibid, page 15
9. Document A/34/496, Annex 11, issued by the Council of United Nations University, pages 1 and 2
10. University for Peace Council First Session, Agenda item 7
11. ibid, Agenda item 6
12. Tico Times, 23rd April, 1982, page 11
13. ibid, 12th March, 1982, page 15
14. ibid, 12th March, 1982, page 15
15. ibid, 12th March, 1982, page 15
16. ibid, 12th March, 1982, page 15
17. University Peace Newsletter, Vol. 2, October, 1983, page 5.
18. ibid, page 3

# Chapter Fourteen

# THE QUAKERS OF MONTEVERDE

At the time of the Korean War several Quakers in the USA were imprisoned for refusing to be drafted into the army. As with many pacifists, they were asked why they should live in the country if they were not willing to fight for it. After pondering on this, they decided not only did they not want to fight for the USA but also they were not prepared to pay taxes to be used to support a military economy and enable others to fight. After searching several areas in Central America, they embarked on the difficult journey to the mountainous area to the north-west of San José in Costa Rica. Their journey had to be made by horseback along a difficult and dangerous trail into an area where few people lived. They decided to settle there with their families, purchased the land and left the United States.

Comparison has been drawn between their emigrating because of their conscientious objection to military service and the earlier experience of William Penn and many other Quakers who emigrated to the USA from England because of religious persecution. The adventurous journey of some of these families on their way to Costa Rica makes a story in itself. At one point where the Pan-American highway now runs, it took them a month to hack their way ten miles through the forest. Finally as they climbed from the Pacific coastal plain up the mountain side, their vehicles bogged down in the muddy track and often they needed the friendly help of the Costa Rican farmers to bring their teams of oxen and pull the jeeps upwards.

In addition to buying the land the Quakers had to buy out the squatters as in Costa Rica the latter gain rights more quickly than in most other countries. A few shacks could be used as houses, storehouse and Meeting House but most of the other settlers pitched tents. A saw mill was soon built and provided boards for walls and floors as well as doors and windows. The clearing of sufficient land to enable grass to be planted and support cattle for the dairy farms intended was a herculean task. The forest trees towered 150 feet or more and were six to eight feet thick. In addition the web of lianas and bush rope, strong as steel cable, with the dense undergrowth, had to be cut and removed. At first the clearings were planted in vegetables to provide subsistence until larger areas could be put down to grass, when milk and butter became available.

The condition of the track down to the coastal plain and towns was such that it was impossible to get milk there in a saleable condition. Their decision to make it into cheese was handicapped by two things. First, they hadn't a cheese factory and secondly, no-one knew how to make cheese commercially. A Friend in the States was persuaded to go to Switzerland and learn the rudiments of cheese making whilst the settlers built a small factory. This has been so successful it has revolutionised the economy of the neighbourhood to the benefit of the Costa Rican farmers and the factory has been enlarged three times. Now they cannot produce as much cheese as they can sell: 'Los Quakeros' are well known in Costa Rica for 'los deliciosos quesos'.

The Meeting House also serves as a School and a Library and a Workshop were recently built in the grounds. Meetings for Worship are held on Sunday and Wednesday mornings. Visitors are speedily persuaded to speak upon whatever subjects interest them most. The households have an ingenious telephone system with a code of rings to tell who is wanted. In addition, there is a short wave radio connecting with an agent in San José, on which a long chat was enjoyed when circumstances did not permit undertaking the rough journey up to Monteverde. Two pensions and an hotel provide accommodation for visitors but these, together with the increasing demands for 'country homes' by San José citizens, have caused sharp differences of opinion and some of the original settler families have left. Others, however, have taken their places and in recent years provision has been made for Friends when they become too old or infirm to provide for themselves. A large building provides accommodation for up to eleven residents together with rooms for a visiting doctor and a resident nurse. As there is no medical care readily available in the settlement and the oldest inhabitant is now over 90, the importance of this provision is apparent.

At the outset it was agreed that about one-third of the land purchased would be left as virgin forest not only to safeguard their water supply but also to serve as a refuge for the wild life. This has now been supplemented by a much larger area designated as a 'Nature Reserve' by the Government. Large tracts of this are still quite unexplored and four days there with Wolf Gwindon, one of the Quakers who acts as Director of the Cloud Forest, was both an exciting and shattering experience.

Monteverde is translated as 'Green Mountain', the name chosen by the early settlers and lying as it does at 4,600 feet above sea level it has a temperate and beautiful climate. A Statement of Monteverde's Aims and Ideals will be of interest:

Monteverde was started by families from the United States whose desire was to leave behind the constant worry of war and free ourselves from our increasing involvement in militarism and government control in all phases of our lives. In contrast, we hope to discover through Divine guidance, a way of life which would seek the good of each member of the community and live in a way that will naturally lead to peace in the world rather than war. We do not believe Monteverde is a place in which to become wealthy but we do expect to make an adequate living which is all that we desire.

Our community is made up of privately owned homes and businesses. We cooperate in work of mutual interest such as road maintenance. The success of the community depends on the members understanding one another, sharing common interests and need, and seeking solutions together. For this reason we feel it is important that anyone considering moving to Monteverde should, for the sake of their own happiness as well as the good of the community, share our ideals and desire to work toward their realization.

This is a religiously-motivated community, founded on the belief that every person must seek to carry out in everyday life Jesus' teachings of the way of love and non violence. We do not feel that anyone would be happy here who does not share our conscientious objections to war or to being a part of a military system.

The only non-Catholic church here is a Friends Meeting which is the centre of the community. It is an unprogrammed meeting based on the silent personal communion with God, and each individual has the responsibility and privilege to speak if he has been given a message for others. However, it seems necessary to us that all community members respect the sincere religious beliefs of other people.

Anyone coming to Monteverde should truly enjoy nature and rural living. We are in a remote mountain district with an unbelievably poor road, so that it is often a year or more between visits to towns or cities for those of us who do not have urgent business there. At present farming is done by hand and anyone who holds any feelings that manual labour is inferior or insignificant, and is not willing to identify himself with the working people of the community, should look elsewhere for a location. Similarly, any feeling of race or national superiority would be a drawback. We hope, as speedily as possible, to fit ourselves into the life of Costa Rica so that we will no longer be 'foreigners'.

Although Monteverde is in the tropics, we are at a high altitude which keeps the weather cool. We are above the malaria and yellow fever zone. At present there is no doctor in the district, though first aid treatment and some drugs are available.

Farming is the basic means of livelihood here. A new dairy plant, cooperatively operated, is receiving milk from the farmers in the community, which includes our Costa Rican neighbours, and making a high quality cheese which sells readily in San José and Puntarenas. A privately owned sugar mill has been built, making brown sugar from the cane growing on our farms. A furniture factory was built. Besides furniture they make doors, window sash and cabinets for new houses. A saw mill, 25 Kw. generator, guest house, drug store and general store are also owned and operated by other members of the community.

We believe all business should be conducted honestly and generously, being careful not to exploit or take advantage of anyone. There should be an attitude of cooperation for the common good of the large community of Costa Ricans. This includes conservation rather than exploitation of land, timber and other natural resources.

We believe that our bodies are the temple of God's spirit and that they should be kept healthy without hindrance from tobacco or other narcotics or alcoholic drinks.

We believe we should try to create an atmosphere for our children in which real values, as we see them, are given first place. As part of this a school is maintained in which we try to help our children grow strong spiritually and physically as well as mentally. We know we have a long way to go to attain these goals and we welcome those who wish to help in this undertaking.

# EPILOGUE

Since the Somoza dictatorship in Nicaragua was finally overthrown in July 1979, the situation in Costa Rica has not reverted to normal as was hoped. This is to a large extent due to the U.S.A. which has sought to encourage and assist the *somocistas'* endeavours to stage a counter-revolution and to dislodge the Sandinista government.

Although the *somocistas* have almost entirely been based in Honduras, and made sporadic invasions of Nicaragua's northern territory, Costa Rica has been to some degree involved because Eden Pastora, one of the leaders of the successful Sandinista revolution, subsequently disagreed with his colleagues and fled to Costa Rica, and in accordance with that country's policy of providing sanctuary for all refugees, was allowed at first to remain there.

However, Pastora not only resided in San José, but set up a headquarters there and rallied others who had fought with him against the Somoza dictatorship from 1977 to 1979. He repeated the tactics he had employed then, basing his group in the south of Nicaragua, attacking villages and remote settlements there and, when pursued by its armed forces, fleeting across the frontier into Costa Rica. Nevertheless he resolutely refused to co-operate with the 'official' *somocista* faction and undoubtedly received less support from the U.S.A. in consequence.

During the early part of 1984 three events occurred which reduced the pressure on Costa Rica. Firstly, Pastora had a most serious disagreement with some of his most ardent supporters, possibly about his refusal to join the *somocistas*; secondly there was an attempt to assassinate him when a bomb exploded at a press conference, seriously injuring him and a British journalist and killing a representative of the *Tico Times*. While he was in hospital in San Jose, President Monge of Costa Rica said he would no longer be allowed to stay in the country; thirdly, there was an agreement with the Nicaraguan government to improve border security.

Pressure continued from the U.S.A. to adopt a more hard line attitude towards the *sandinistas*. Costa Rica found it extremely difficult to resist the demands because of her economic plight. Increases in the price of oil, which she must import, the depreciation in the value of her staple exports, and austerity measures demanded by the International Monetary Fund promoted internal discord and the refusal of further loans made the financial position desperate.

An announcement in January 1984, by the U.S.A., that one thousand engineers were to be sent to Costa Rica to help in constructing roads in the region adjacent to Nicaragua led to that country accusing Costa Rica of actively assisting the U.S.A.'s anti-Sandinista campaign. The proposal was at first postponed and then refused by the Costa Rican government. Subsequently it was revived under the guise that the engineers from an army combat unit would construct roads in the south of the country and improve an airfield to enable planes diverted from San Jose in bad weather to land there instead of having to fly on to Panama.

It has been pointed out that, with a press openly anti-communist and pro-U.S.A. it is increasingly difficult for a centre-left government to pursue an independent foreign policy. Nevertheless, a high pressure invitation to send observers to a meeting of defence ministers of El Salvador, Honduras and Guatemala on board the U.S.A. aircraft carrier Ranger, was refused. President Monge also refused an invitation to tour a U.S. ship along with several other Latin-American leaders, and rejected a request for a 'goodwill' visit by another U.S. warship. The requests from the U.S.A. were persistent and unending, and had to be treated with diplomatic delicacy. Pressure from U.S.A. on one hand and hostility from Nicaragua on the other imposed severe strains on the Costa Rican government, and President Monge trying to maintain a neutral position between the two, followed up a formal declaration of neutrality he had made the previous November by running a series of newspaper advertisements featuring messages of support sent by, among others, President Mitterand of France and Señor Gonzalez, Prime Minister of Spain.

In June 1984 the President embarked on a tour of twelve European countries, not only to seek economic aid but also support for his effort to maintain neutrality and resist being drawn into an anti-Nicaraguan campaign. He was embarrassed when U.S.A. officials in Washington announced that Costa Rica was joining in U.S. military manoeuvres: this was angrily denied. In London he was asked about a report from New York that it was 'when' not 'how' Costa Rica was to be militarised. He replied this was part of a campaign carried on against Costa Rica over a period of two years, and repeatedly emphasised that his country would maintain its everlasting unarmed neutrality, saying:

> "We are irrevocably opposed to war: our neutrality is unarmed neutrality as Costa Rica has no army and does not wish to have one. We are not a military power and have no wish to be one.

"We are not ideologically neutral; we support democracy and oppose all dictatorships. Costa Rican neutrality reflects the special circumstances of our history.

"Neutrality must be unarmed; we disarmed unilaterally. There is no such thing as a military solution. We have no wish to create an army; we have no money to buy weapons. We remain convinced – as we have been over thirty-five years since we disbanded our armed forces – that poor countries do not have resources for education and an army. We choose education, health and the welfare of our people. There is no alternative, we do not have resources for both these and an army. We intend to maintain our position."

# APPENDIX I

*Extract from the archives of the Organisation of American States, December 1948:*

The conclusions of the Committee, which were presented to the Provisional Organ of Consultation at the meeting of 24 December, 1948 were as follows:

1. There is no doubt on the part of the members of the Committee that the revolutionary movement that erupted in Costa Rica was organized mainly in Nicaraguan territory. It was in Nicaragua that a large group of Costa Rican political exiles, led by Calderón Guardia, prepared the expedition that subsequently crossed the frontier between Nicaragua and Costa Rica. There is not the slightest doubt of the failure of the Nicaraguan Government to take adequate measures to prevent revolutionary activities directed against a neighbouring and friendly country from being carried out.

2. It appears that after 10 December the Government of Nicaragua did begin to take the necessary measures to prevent the rebels who had crossed the frontier from continuing to receive aid emanating from Nicaragua. The most important group of revolutionaries, composed of Costa Ricans and Nicaraguans, had, however, already entered Costa Rican territory when the measures mentioned were taken.

3. The Committee found no proof whatsoever that armed forces of the Nicaraguan Government had taken part, on Costa Rican territory, in this revolutionary movement against the Government of Costa Rica. As a result of its investigations, however, it does have the impression that some members of the Nicaraguan military forces might perhaps, on their own initiative, have given technical aid to the groups that later crossed the border.

4. The Committee had no actual knowledge of contact between the armed forces of Nicaragua and the armed forces of Costa Rica.

5. According to certain Costa Ricans, the failure to carry out the amnesty measure that had been formally adopted explains in great measure why the great majority of the exiles felt constrained to resort to desperate and violent measures, which had serious international repercussions.

6. On the other hand, it cannot be denied that for many months before the invasion the so-called Legion of the Caribbean, or Caribbean Legion, with material and moral help from the Costa Rican Government, enjoyed official sympathy and facilities for carrying out its programmes and activities, both of which, according to general opinion in the Caribbean area, were designed to overthrow certain governments, among them the present regime in Nicaragua.

7. The existence of active military centres of international ferment is, as can naturally be supposed, a justifiable cause of concern on the part of the governments affected.

8. This situation, which is abnormal and dangerous to inter-American peace,

explains why the majority of the Central American and Caribbean Republics have, for some time, been living in an atmosphere of mutual distrust, constant anxiety, and open hostility.

9. The situation is all the more lamentable inasmuch as, because of the features we have pointed out, international relations between the republics involved must inevitably grow worse each day, since a country that is fearful of a neighbouring country feels compelled to take whatever precautions it feels are absolutely necessary, and thus it seriously damages its own economy and gravely endangers the life of its institutions.

(s) Luis Quintanilla
Ambassador of Mexico, Chairman

(s) José María Bello
Representative of Brazil

(s) Silvio Villegas
Representative of Colombia

(s) Paul C. Daniels
Representative of the United States

**Resolution of 24 December, 1948**
The Committee submitted the following resolution, which was approved by the Provisional Organ of Consultation:

THE COUNCIL OF THE ORGANIZATION OF AMERICAN STATES,
ACTING PROVISIONALLY AS ORGAN OF CONSULTATION,
after studying the detailed report of the Committee that was in Costa Rica and Nicaragua for the purpose of investigating the facts and antecedents of the situation created between those sister Republics,
RESOLVES:

I. To request the Governments of Costa Rica and Nicaragua, in compliance with the Inter-American Treaty of Reciprocal Assistance, to give full assurances to the Provisional Organ of Consultation that they will immediately abstain from any hostile act toward each other.

II. To make known, with due respect to the Government of NIcaragua, that, in the light of data gathered by the Committee of Information especially appointed for the purpose, that Government could and should have taken adequate measures at the proper time for the purpose of preventing: (a) the development, in Nicaraguan territory, of activities intended to overthrow the present regime in Costa Rica, and (b) the departure from Nicaraguan territory of revolutionary elements who crossed the frontier and today are prisoners or are still fighting against the Government of Costa Rica.

III. To make known, with due respect to the Government of Costa Rica, that it can and should take adequate measures to rid its territory of groups of nationals or foreigners, organized on a military basis with the deliberate purpose of conspiring against the security of Nicaragua and other sister republics, and of preparing to fight against their governments.

IV. To request very respectfully that both governments, by every available means, faithfully observe the principles and rules of non-intervention and solidarity contained in the various inter-American instruments signed by them.

187

V. To continue in consultation until positive assurances have been received from the Governments of Costa Rica and Nicaragua, that, as they are assuredly disposed to do, they will adhere strictly to the lofty principles and rules that constitute the juridical basis of American international life.

VI. To recommend that all American Governments actively cooperate toward the best observance of all the principles which inspire this resolution.

VII. To inform all States Members of the Organization of the steps taken in this case.

**General Conclusions**

1. Each Government appeared to be sympathetic toward the political enemies of the other. This sympathy has been translated into a mutual distrust with respect to maintenance and effectiveness of the neutral position that the two States are to take with respect to each other.

2. This mutual distrust and the revolutinary outbreaks in the vicinity of the Costa Rican-Nicaraguan border could give rise to border incidents between the armed forces of the two countries. Such incidents could be avoided if the forces of the two countries were kept at a distance from each other to prevent any contact between them. This cannot, however, be done because:

(a) The Costa Rican forces must, in their own territory, reestablish order, which was disturbed as a result of the aforesaid revolutionary outbreaks;

(b) The Nicaraguan forces are responsible for making certain that any armed persons who cross the frontier are disarmed and interned.

Therefore, the problem and its solution are basically within the political, and not the military field. Once the present mutual distrust is eliminated, not only will there be no border incidents, but real cooperation by the armed forces of both countries, in carrying out the specific missions entrusted to them, will also be possible.

3. The fact that Costa Rica does not have an organized army presents another difficulty in this particular case. Lack of knowledge as to the technical nature of arms and the way in which they should be used could lead, involuntarily, to the adoption of measures that might be considered provocative in view of the distrust prevailing at present.

4. The Commission noted, upon its arrival in Costa Rica, that there was a feeling of anxiety over the danger of an armed conflict with Nicaragua. The unmistakable fact that this anxiety diminished, visibly and gradually, and that confidence was restored by the presence of the Commission and its activities, was a source of real satisfaction to the Commission. This attests to the wisdom of the measures that were taken by the Council.

5. Given the integrity of the Governments of Costa Rica and Nicaragua, the Military Commission was guided by official documents in its reports to the Council and in the carrying out of its work. In our opinion, if the measures taken to carry out the resolution of 24 December, had been more opportune and better executed, the questions under discussion would have been settled with greater rapidity.

6. Inasmuch as the Council is much better acquainted with the political situation in Central America than is this Commission, the Commission does not believe it necessary to outline the whole picture, of which the Costa Rican-Nicaraguan problem is but a part. Moreover, the Commission feels that the question, being basically political, does not in any way come within the scope of its power or its duties.

(s) Colonel Decio de Escobar
Brazil

(s) General Francisco Tamayo
Colombia

(s) Colonel T. Alfonso Sapia-Bosch
United States

(s) Colonel Manuel Robledo Rojas
Mexico

(s) Colonel Carlos M. Bóbeda
Paraguay

## Settlement of the Incident and Final Action of the Council

Finally, the Organ approved the following Resolutions:
WHEREAS:

By resolution of 14 December, 1948, the Council of the Organization of American States at the request of the Government of Costa Rica, convoked a Meeting of Consultation of Ministers of Foreign Affairs to study the situation created between Costa Rica and Nicaragua, and at the same time constituted itself provisionally as Organ of Consultation, in accordance with Article 12 of the Inter-American Treaty of Reciprocal Assistance;

On 24 December, 1948, the Council of the Organization of American States, acting provisionally as Organ of Consultation, after hearing the report of the Committee that conducted an on-the-scene enquiry into the facts presented by Costa Rica and their antecedents, requested the Governments of Costa Rica and Nicaragua to take all necessary measures for the solution of the difficulties that had arisen between them;

In accordance with the report of the Inter-American Commission of Military Experts, appointed by the Council of the Organization of American States acting provisionally as Organ of Consultation, the Government of Nicaragua took the suggested measures to guard its frontier border with Costa Rica effectively and to fulfill its obligations as a Party to the Convention on the Duties and Rights of States in the Event of Civil Strife, signed at the Havana Conference of 1928; and the Government of Costa Rica took all measures necessary to provide that no organization should exist on its territory whose purpose it was to conspire against the security of the Government of Nicaragua or other American States;

The Governments of Costa Rica and Nicaragua, displaying a noble example of continental solidarity and of respect for the fulfilment of the Treaties, have signed a Pact of Amity which puts an end to the differences that gave rise to the provisional action of the Council of the Organization of American States as Organ of Consultation, recognizing the obligation that exists between them to submit all disputes that may arise to methods for the peaceful settlement of international conflict, and reaffirming the traditional ties of friendship that bind the two peoples together,

THE COUNCIL OF THE ORGANIZATION OF AMERICAN STATES,
ACTING PROVISIONALLY AS ORGAN OF CONSULTATION,
RESOLVES:

1. To express its gratitude to the Governments of Costa Rica and Nicaragua for the cooperation they have given the Council of the Organization of American States, acting provisionally as Organ of Consultation, in the solution of the difficulties that existed between the two Governments.

2. To present this noble act of American solidarity and of respect for peaceful solution as a new and lofty example for all the peoples of the continent.

3. To terminate, as of this date, the functions of the Inter-American Commission of Military Experts, and to express its gratitude to the Commission for the intelligent and effective manner in which it fulfilled its duties.

4. To inform the American Governments of the happy solution of the incident that arose between Costa Rica and Nicaragua, and that consequently there no longer exist the reasons that prompted the convocation of the Meeting of Consultation of Ministers of Foreign Affairs effected by the Resolution of December 14, 1948.

5. To terminate the provisional role of the Council of the Organisation of American States as Organ of Consultation.

# APPENDIX II

*Extract from the archives of the Organisation of American States:*

## APPLICATIONS OF THE INTER-AMERICAN TREATY OF RECIPROCAL ASSISTANCE 1948-1956

### CONCLUSIONS OF THE COMMITTEE

As a result of its work, of the exhaustive investigations carried out in Costa Rica and Nicaragua, and of an objective examination of various material elements, the Committee wishes to point out the following facts:

1. There was foreign intervention in the preparation, financing, furnishing of arms and ammunition, and transportation facilities to the persons who entered Costa Rica by force.

2. A substantial number of the rebel forces and the war materials used by them, whatever their origin, entered by way of the Costa Rican-Nicaraguan frontier.

3. One or more clandestine radio stations, apparently operating outside Costa Rica, incited the people of that country to support the rebel government.

4. Aircraft proceeding from abroad dropped arms and ammunition for the rebels at predetermined points in Costa Rican territory.

5. Transport and combat planes, proceeding from abroad and without identification marks, landed clandestinely on Costa Rican territory and made flights in which they bombed and machine-gunned various towns of that country, including San José, the capital of the Republic.

6. There was violation of the territorial integrity, sovereignty, and political independence of Costa Rica.

7. After the Investigating Committee had established a system of pacific aerial observation over Costa Rican and Nicaraguan territory, had also, through its military advisers, established a system of land observation in strategic zones of both countries, and had set up Security Zones in areas of Costa Rica and Nicaragua contiguous to the frontier, the attacking forces abandoned their offensive, and fell back toward the northwestern frontier, a large number of them being ultimately interned in Nicaragua.

8. Even after the rebels who had been fighting in the western part of Costa Rican territory were interned in Nicaragua, a considerable number of them reappeared and fought again on Costa Rican territory, this time in the central region of the frontier with Nicaragua.

A large majority of the members of the attacking forces and the political leaders of the movement were of Costa Rican nationality. This circumstance does not, however, in any way alter what has been pointed out in the preceding numbered paragraphs.

It was possible for these basic facts to be impartially established by the

191

Investigating Committee and they further justify the decisions taken by the Council of the OAS, and later by the Council acting provisionally as Organ of Consultation, including its approval on 14 January, 1955, of a Resolution 'to condemn the acts of intervention of which Costa Rica is victim'.

## THE RECOMMENDATIONS WHICH THE COMMITTEE SUBMITS TO THE COUNCIL

The territorial integrity, sovereignty, and political independence of Costa Rica has now been re-established with the action of the OAS. Since this is so, and in view of the co-operation given to the Investigating Committee from the very start by the governments of both Costa Rica and Nicaragua, it is reasonable to think that Costa Rica and Nicaragua, assured of their internal peace and without foreign intervention of any kind, will soon be able to resume peaceful relations that will enable both countries to develop freely their basic institutions on the foundation of mutual respect which characterizes the relations between American states.

Finally, in view of the foregoing, and inspired by the spirit of Article 7 of the Inter-American Treaty of Reciprocal Assistance and by the principles of American solidarity, the Committee would like respectfully to suggest that it is desirable:

1. That the 'Pact of Amity' signed on 21 February, 1949, by the Governments of Costa Rica and Nicaragua, under the auspices of the Council, acting provisionally as Organ of Consultation, for the purpose of preventing a repetition of acts such as those that have in the past seriously disturbed the relations between the two countries, be perfected and strengthened.

2. That the Governments of Costa Rica and Nicaragua prepare and sign the Bilateral Agreement mentioned in Article IV of the aforesaid Pact 'as to the best manner of putting into practice the provisions of the Convention on the Duties and Rights of States in the Event of Civil Strife, in cases contemplated by that Convention, so that it may be applied immediately whenever a situation of this kind arises, in the manner provided for in the said agreement, especially with respect to measures for the control and supervision of frontiers, as well as with respect to any other measure intended to prevent the organization or existence of any revolutionary movement against the Government of either of the two Parties in the territory of the other.'

3. That when the aforesaid Pact is revised an additional article be included for the purpose of preventing the preparation of terroristic acts in the territory of either Party against the Government of the other.

4. That the Governments of Costa Rica and Nicaragua, for the purposes set forth in the aforesaid 'Pact of Amity' in force between them, proceed at once, without prejudice to any other procedure they may agree upon, to appoint the members of a Commission of Investigation and Conciliation in accordance with Chapter Three of the American Treaty on Pacific Settlement (Pact of Bogotá) that would constitute a permanent guarantee, for both, of the friendly and satisfactory settlement of any difficulty that might arise as a result of situations such as those envisaged in the aforementioned 'Pact of Amity'.

5. That, as a general measure, desirable for all the American States, consideration be given to the improvement of the systems for controlling the traffic in arms and ammunition and also to the effective application of the recommendation contained in Resolution XI of the Inter-American Conference for the Maintenance of Continental Peace and Security that 'no stipulation of the

Treaty nor any of the obligations created under it should be interpreted as justifying excessive armaments or may be invoked as a reason for the creation or maintenance of armaments or armed forces beyond those required for common defence in the interest of peace and security'.

6. That the Council of the Organization of American States, acting provisionally as Organ of Consultation, offer its collaboration to the two governments concerned for the purpose of perfecting the 'Pact of Amity' to which the preceding paragraphs refer.

7. That, taking into consideration the gradual re-establishment of a normal international relationship between Costa Rica and Nicaragua, the provisional action of the Council as Organ of Consultation be duly terminated and the American Governments consulted with respect to the cancellation of the Meeting of Ministers of Foreign Affairs as Organ of Consultation.

Finally, it is the sincere hope of the Committee that, as soon as circumstances permit, the Governments of Costa Rica and Nicaragua and the Chief Executives of those sister nations will be able not only to take steps to reestablish their peaceful relations but will also take steps to aid one another mutually in the realization of their common purposes and aspirations.

Luis Quintanilla
Ambassador, Representative of Mexico
Chairman

John C. Dreir
Ambassador, Representative of United States

Fernando Lobo
Ambassador, Representative of Brazil

José R. Chiriboga
Ambassador, Representative of Ecuador
(With Reservation)

Guillermo Enciso Velloso
Ambassador, Representative of Paraguay

Pan American Union
Washington, DC
February 11, 1955

## ADDRESS DELIVERED BY DR LUIS QUINTANILLA, AMBASSADOR OF MEXICO AND CHAIRMAN OF THE INVESTIGATING COMMITTEE

The pacific settlement of controversies and conflicts between the American governments is always a source of satisfaction because the most constructive feature of our regional system is precisely its repudiation of force as an instrument of foreign policy. From the dawn of Pan Americanism in 1826, the republics of the New World have proclaimed the goodness of international peace and the need of developing procedures of pacific settlement so as to establish firmly in our nations a system of life based on law, which is the best protection for the weak and, at the same time, ensures to weak and strong alike the kind of stability without which neither can prosper.

The happy solution of a controversial situation between Costa Rica and

Nicaragua, our two loved sister republics, should thus stimulate our faith in achieving peace within the framework of law and liberty. We have received useful instruction from Europe and other parts of the world in many phases of civilization and culture. In the field of international relations, however, it is Pan Americanism that has been the outstanding leader. What, in 1826, was considered to be a romantic ideal has, today, become an impressive reality. In our era no conflict should arise among the 21 States of the American community of nations that would justify the use of violence. War is something inconceivable in this corner of the globe. That is to say, we Americans have achieved what the peoples and governments of other parts of the world have as a remote goal which they are hoping to achieve.

Such fundamental principles as those of non-intervention, the pacific settlement of differences between governments, international cooperation, and collective security, were originally proclaimed at inter-American meetings. These are principles of transcendental importance. Without them any international organization, including the United Nations, would lose its reason for being. Our having discovered and put into practice these basic rules is a legitimate reason for pride on the part of the American family, especially since we have unequivocally shown, as in the situation between Costa Rica and Nicaragua, that these rules are not a mere aspiration but, on the contrary, effective and practical methods of procedure.

We have not completed our struggle to build a strong and true Pan American movement. We do not, however, have much more ground to cover as what are perhaps the most difficult obstacles have already been overcome. We can therefore face the future more optimistically than ever before. The world needs the contribution that America can make. We are a force not only because of the extent of our territory and the growth in our population but because of the fact that ever since America first gained its own liberty, its young and determined voice has spoken out in favour of independence, peace, law, and brotherly relations among all peoples. This voice must ever be heard more clearly and more strongly. This voice cannot be silent because it is the voice of history. It vibrates in this room as though it were a new ratification of our purposes.

Since it was my honour to have presided over the Investigating Committee that operated in Costa Rica and Nicaragua at the request of the Council, I should like to congratulate the governments of both those splendid countries on the successful completion of their negotiations. The document signed here is solely the product of the sovereign will of the governments concerned. We, however, hope that it will be translated into a final rapprochement between the two States that geography has made neighbours and that history has united in the accomplishment of unforgettable undertakings. In the name of the members of what was the Investigating Committee, and in my own, I should like to express gratitude for the timely and decisive cooperation that the governments of both countries and their Chief Executives, Dr José Figueres and General Anastasio Somoza, in particular, extended to the Organization of American States so as to enable our Committee to carry out its high mission. Thanks to that cooperation, the regional system was able to prove its excellence once again and to demonstrate to the entire world the vigour of its principles.

Our solidarity is so closely knit that for us there can be no isolated cases. A failure of our ideals in any part of the hemisphere is a collective failure. Likewise, the triumph of our ideals in any part of the hemisphere gladdens all equally. I say, therefore, to the Representatives of Costa Rica and Nicaragua – we are all happy, and we all share with you the joy of this historic moment.

## ADDRESS DELIVERED BY DR. JOSE A. MORA
## AMBASSADOR OF URUGUAY AND CHAIRMAN OF THE SPECIAL
## COMMITTEE

The act of the signing of agreements between the Governments of Costa Rica and Nicaragua, which we have the pleasure of witnessing here today, is highly important because it is proof of the ability and effectiveness of the Organization of American States as an organ for the strengthening in America of a juridical system of peace.

At the same time we see here today an official demonstration of the firm determination of Costa Rica and Nicaragua to carry out to the fullest the recommendations made by the Organ of Consultation when the Council of the Organization resorted to the application of the Rio de Janeiro Treaty of Reciprocal Assistance to take care of a situation with which we were all deeply concerned.

It wil be recalled that, when on 8 September, 1955, the Council cancelled the call for a Meeting of Consultation of Ministers of Foreign Affairs, it provided that the signing of the bilateral agrement provided for in the Pact of Amity to which both governments are parties were in course. The purpose of the Council was for the Special Committee to continue to cooperate with both parties whenever they might require such cooperation, to the end that a final agreement might be obtained. At that time the Council also stated that it was pleased that Costa Rica and Nicaragua had established the Commission of Investigation and Conciliation and repeated that it was confident the two Parties would utilize the services of the aforesaid Commission, in accordance with the treaties in force between them and, very particularly, the Pact of Bogota.

In my opinion, what the Council did in cancelling the Meeting of Consultation was to pay a tribute to Costa Rica and Nicaragua by placing in both governments the full confidence that they would very shortly establish their good relations with the signing of these two Agreements. Today we see the happy result of that foresight. The very terms of these documents is an inspiration. Costa Rica and Nicaragua, in the desire to prevent a recurrence of differences and difficulties between them, are establishing specific rules for the functioning of the Commission of Investigation and Conciliation. They recall their common destiny as members of the American community of nations, and also recognise that their relations have special characteristics because these States share a common boundary and in the past have been, together with the other sister republics of Central America, members of a single nation.

While signing the Agreement that supplements the Pact of Amity they jointly proclaim their desire to prevent any difference that might interfere with their fraternal relations from arising in the future. We should congratulate ourselves therefore on these constructive measures that are being taken by Costa Rica and Nicaragua. Their two governments thus provide a splendid example that will strengthen the juridical procedures of our regional Organization that seek not only the peace and security of the hemisphere but also the development of friendship and cooperation among our peoples. The pacts that were signed today are the product of the free will of Costa Rica and Nicaragua. Both governments pledge themselves with complete freedom of will to correct a bilateral situation that in itself has very special characteristics.

In the name of the Special Committee of the Council, I warmly congratulate the Representatives of Costa Rica and Nicaragua. I should like to repeat what I said at the time the convocation of the Meeting of Consultation was cancelled. No matter the difficulties that may arise in America, no matter the alternatives we may have to face in our history, which are frequently the product of the vigorous youth of the peoples of this hemisphere, international peace is a tradition that has already been achieved and which is sustained by our Organization of American States.

We are today celebrating the noble contribution that Costa Rica and Nicaragua have made toward the enrichment of that tradition and we applaud that contribution as a new victory in our regional system of peace.

## ADDRESS DELIVERED BY AMBASSADOR CESAR TULIO DELGADO CHAIRMAN OF THE COUNCIL OF THE ORGANIZATION OF AMERICAN STATES

Representatives of Costa Rica and Nicaragua,

Messrs. Ambassadors:

There is very little left to add at this time to the words of the Plenipotentiaries of Costa Rica and Nicaragua and to what has also already been said by the Ambassadors of Mexico and Uruguay. We are witnessing one of the most important events in the life of the Organization of American States. We are holding a festival of peace. This point has been reached because of the good will and intelligence demonstrated by two remarkable men who have most perfectly and completely interpreted the sentiments of their respective countries. This ceremony is, therefore, first of all, a triumph for the Ambassadors of Nicaragua and Costa Rica, for their respective governments, and, of course, for the eminent Chief Executives who are the heads of those two sister republics. It is also, however, a triumph for the Council of the Organization acting provisionally as Organ of Consultation, which was then guided and directed with sureness of hand and purpose by Dr José Antonio Mora, the Ambassador of Uruguay, whose spirit, so devoted to the cause of American peace and brotherhood, should surely rejoice on this memorable occasion. Yet, it is a triumph for the Provisional Organ of Consultation that acted with such great effectiveness through the Investigating Committee whose chairman, the eminent Luis Quintanilla, presided over it with is fine intelligence and warm heart. For the Committee has won a notable victory for both Parties by its advancing of solutions upon which the two countries were able to agree without damaging the relations between them. On the contrary, it sought to bring them closer together on the fraternal path that has been theirs in the past and that should be theirs in the future. And, without doubt, this is an unforgettable occasion in the life of each of us who is a member of this illustrious body that holds such an important position in the hemisphere today because it has shown itself worthy of the confidence that America has placed in it. I remember particularly those historic meetings, held at midnight and at dawn, that were religiously attended by each and every one of the Members of the Council and by the officials of the General Secretariat, all of whom overcame their weariness and fatigue to work with passion and enthusiasm for the peace and solidarity of the hemisphere. And, finally, this ceremony is a triumph for all America.

While the spirit of man is disintegrating and dying in the Old World and in other places, we here today are providing a magnificent example of unity. We are offering a superb spectacle of peace; we are showing how two countries that only yesterday were at odds are today embracing in a conclusive gesture of affection and brotherhood that should be imitated by all peoples of the earth.

Permit me to say that I consider my presiding at this formal meeting one of the greatest privileges of my life. We here are joyfully about to embrace Nicaragua and Costa Rica, two countries that, although they have certainly not reached their goal as yet, have, however, become today better qualified to continue along their common pathway, for the Pacts they have signed mark the beginning of a greater union, of more understanding cooperation, and of closer and richer relations that will ennoble them both. Thus, these two beloved lands will make their contributions towards the security and the progress of all America.

# APPENDIX III

*Extract from the archives of the Organisation of American States:*

## VERIFICATION OF THE EVENTS BROUGHT TO THE ATTENTION OF THE PERMANENT COUNCIL BY THE GOVERNMENTS OF COSTA RICA AND NICARAGUA WITH REGARD TO THE BORDER INCIDENTS AND THE MEASURES TAKEN BY THOSE GOVERNMENTS

The Ad Hoc Committee of the Permanent Council, established to verify the events brought to the Council's attention by the Governments of Costa Rica and Venezuela, after having visited those countries, having received information from their civil and military authorities, having inspected the border zones where the events took place, having taken statements from witnesses to the events, and having gathered material to serve as a basis for clarification of the events, wishes to report the following to the Permanent Council:

1. That in the early morning hours of Thursday, 13 October, 1977, the Police Barracks of the locality of San Carlos, in Nicaragua, was attacked by armed persons belonging to the *Frente Sandinista de Liberación Nacional* (FSLN) (Sandinista National Liberation Front);

2. That, in light of the events that took place during the early morning hours of 13 October in the town of San Carlos, both the Nicaraguan and Costa Rican authorities took measures to ensure tranquility and to maintain security in their respective border sectors;

3. That on the morning of 14 October, 1977, the Minister of Public Security of Costa Rica, Mr Mario Charpentier Gamboa, accompanied by civilian and military authorities and a group of journalists and photographers, travelled to the border zone between Nicaragua and Costa Rica in three small boats that bore no visible marks of identification. They left from the town of Los Chiles and followed the course of Río Frío northward.

4. That on that same morning, October 14, 1977, aircraft and helicopters of the Nicaraguan Air Force bombarded and machine-gunned the three boats bearing the Minister of Public Security and his group in the waters of the Río Frío. On this particular point, the Nicaraguan authorities stated that what was involved were warning shots so that the boats would stop and identify themselves, while the Costa Rican authorities affirm that at no time was identification requested of them, and that the shots were not warning shots.

5. That, according to the information and statements provided by the authorities of the Government of Nicaragua, the Minister of Public Security of Costa Rica, Mario Charpentier Gamboa, and the group that accompanied him crossed the border line identified by boundary marker XII-A on the Río Frío and entered Nicaraguan territory to a distance of approximately 800 metres;

6. That, according to the information and statements provided by the authorities of the Government of Costa Rica, the Minister of Public Security and the group that accompanied him went only as far as boundary marker XII-A which marks the border between the two countries, and from where they returned southward;

7. That the authorities of the Government of Nicaragua presented a video tape filmed by Costa Ricans that, according to them, is proof of the fact that the group that accompanied Minister Mario Charpentier entered Nicaraguan territory; that the authorities of the Government of Costa Rica presented another version of that same video tape that, according to them, is proof that Minister Mario Charpentier turned around and went south when he reached boundary XII-A. That this Committee, in accordance with the information provided to it in the above-mentioned projections of video tapes and during the inspection tours it made in the two territories, does not have sufficient evidence to state that the Minister of Security and his companions had crossed the border limit marked by boundary marker XII-A.

8. That, on the basis of the following: (a) on-site inspection tours, both in the Nicaraguan and Costa Rican sectors; (b) information provided by officials of both governments; (c) statements by individuals who took part in the events, who include civil and military authorites and private citizens; (d) verification of the locations through photographs showing the presence of aircraft and helicopters, as well as Nicaraguan military personnel along with the Minister of Security and his group at the site indicated by the Costa Rican Government as the site of the bombardment, the Committee is of the opinion that the incident took place in Costa Rican territory, approximately one and one half kilometres from boundary marker XII-A, which marks the border between the two countries.

9. That the Committee has been unable to determine whether the Nicaraguan authorities were aware that Minister Charpentier and his group were the persons travelling aboard the boats. The versions differ on this point, as the Minister of Defence of Nicaragua, General Heberto Sánchez, stated that Minister Charpentier did not inform him of his plans to tour the zone, while the latter stated that he did advise General Sanchéz to that effect during the numerous telephone conversations he had with him on 13 October.

What can be stated is that the trip made by Minister Charpentier was a matter of public knowledge in Costa Rica, as the news of the tour appeared in the press on the morning of the 14th, before the trip began. Furthermore, according to witnesses present, a Nicaraguan helicopter flew over the locality of Los Chiles just as the Costa Rican Minister of Public Security was arriving there.

10. That the Government of Nicaragua, in response to the Ad Hoc Committee's request, reported that it took the following measures in an effort to avoid border problems with Costa Rica:

(a) The standing instructions to the military posts situated along the border with Costa Rica, to the effect that proper vigilance be maintained without provoking problems of any kind or entering Costa Rican territory, have been reaffirmed;

(b) Officers and troops that cruise the Río San Juan, the Río Frío, or any other tributary of the Gran Lago or along the border with Costa Rica on patrol are not to cross the border and are to avoid incidents with the Costa Rican authorities;

(c) These same instructions have been issued to the air and land patrols in the border zone.

199

11. That, with regard to the request from the Government of Nicaragua to the effect that Costa Rica take the necessary measures to see to it that Costa Rican territory is not used to perpetrate acts of violence aimed at subverting the institutional order of Nicaragua, the Committee has verified that the Government of Costa Rica is exchanging information with the Government of Nicaragua in that regard. It has proceeded to arrest suspicious persons, to confiscate arms, and to take measures to safeguard the border, in accordance with the provisions of the 'Convention on Duties and Rights of States in the Event of Civil Strife', of 1928, the Pact of Friendship between Nicaragua and Costa Rica of 1949 and the 'Agreement to carry out the terms of Article IV of the Pact of Friendship' of 1956.

Escobar, Ambassador, Representative of Paraguay, Chairman of Ad Hoc Committee
White, Ambassador, Representative of USA, Member of Ad Hoc Committee
Listre, Representative of Argentina, Member of Ad Hoc Committee.

# APPENDIX IV

*Address delivered to the United Nations Tenth Special Session of the General Assembly, 1978, by Mr Piza-Escalante, of Costa Rica (translation from Spanish):*

Costa Rica is attending this tenth special session of the General Assembly barely one month after a change of Government which occurred under the strictest democratic procedures; a change not only of its leaders but, more profound, a new emphasis on achievement of the common good in the ideas, aims and, above all, the modes of action which will govern the country's advancement, as long as the people desire it.

It is natural, then, that there should be some curiosity within and outside our world Organization as to what the consequences of this change will be with regard to our foreign policy both on the specific subject of disarmament and on the other fundamental international problems which are discussed at their highest level in the United Nations. As I have the honour of representing my nation and its President in this world forum, I shall try to satisfy this curiosity at least in general terms.

First and foremost, I represent, as representatives must know, a very special nation and people which, rising above their national limitations and their internal ideological or political differences, have achieved a high level of stability, peace and freedom and justice which cannot be altered simply as the result of incidental changes of Government. I represent a very special nation and people which have created an advanced and genuinely democratic system of Government in which all citizens and parties freely participate, with complete mutual respect based on the common conviction that only the sovereign people has the right to choose its leaders and decide its own future. I represent a very special nation and people which have achieved a balanced and steady rate of economic and social development, which far exceeded its apparent potential, through the rational use of their resources to promote production and, above all, through the constant improvement of education, health, social security and justice, within an effective legal system that fully respects the universally recognized human rights and freedoms. These efforts are reflected, *inter alia*, in the fact that the Government spends 34 per cent of the national budget on education, 30 per cent on health and social security, and over 50 per cent on social development in general.

I represent a very special nation and people that 30 years ago decided to entrust its internal security to a constitutional régime and its external defence to international order and solidarity, totally eliminating their small military forces by a constitutional prohibition and leaving in place, with no attempt at subterfuge, a small Civil Guard for the protection of the citizens. That Civil Guard today consists of less than one policeman for each 1,000 inhabitants – which may not really be enough – and its total cost, including men, equipment and materials, for a country of almost 2.5 million people represents less than 1 per cent of the public budget or less than 1.5 thousandth of the national product and less than $2 annually per person. Compare that to what is occurring in many parts of the under-developed world, where military budgets absorb up to six times the total for all the other public services.

If figures mean anything at all, I should like to add that Costa Rica earmarks more than 40 times more for education, 35 times more for health and 60 times more for social development in general than for the forces of public order, that is to say, police to maintain order and security only, since military expenditures are literally zero.

I believe that it was important for me to mention these facts concerning my country, not to weary you with boasting but because I wish to assure you that the great principles of our international policy, based on the same principles which underlie our democratic achievements, are not the legacy of any particular political party in power but the mature and well-considered result of our national tradition and conscience which already forms an inseparable part of our way of life. Some of the representatives here, or the representatives of their Governments who may have heard the statement made by our President Mr Rodrigo Carazon on 8 May last, may have had personal experience of this living reality of a country that is truly disarmed, which works in peace, and at the end of the working day can rest with an easy conscience.

Although the change in the Government that I now represent here, is far-reaching and decisive in terms of standards, procedures, and the emphasis and pattern of our activities both domestic and international, yet we remain firmly devoted to our great traditions of peace, freedom, dignity and justice in both domestic and international policies.

We shall therefore continue to strengthen our full support for the major principles of international law; we shall also continue to support and place our faith in this world Organization and, closer to home, in the Organization of American States and the Central American Community. We shall continue our efforts to see that the outworn idea of unlimited national sovereignty, born of different historical circumstances, eventually yields to effective international jurisdiction, represented by the United Nations in general, and in particular by the International Court of Justice and other similar bodies. We shall continue to strive to ensure that, in conjunction with respect for the legal equality of States, pluralism and détente, self-determination of peoples, and non-intervention by any State in the internal affairs of other States, we hope that there will be steady progress towards international solidarity, respect for the dignity and freedom of the human person, the sovereignty of the people, which can be brought about only as the result of representative democracy, and the institutional need for effective international collective action to guarantee peace and security between States, together with human rights within States.

In this latter connection we shall never cease to make efforts which our country has made at every level for many years to ensure the full application of the Conventions on human rights; the establishment of international courts of justice with binding jurisdiction in special fields, modelled on the Strasbourg example; recognition of man as the direct subject of international law, with access to jurisdiction, which is the only way effectively to guarantee his fundamental rights; the establishment of a High Commissioner's Office or similar authority for human rights at the world level. Similarly, we shall continue to fight tenaciously within our continent to see to it that the Inter-American Declaration is implemented immediately and that the Regional Court for Human Rights begins to function without delay – and President Carazo in his inaugural statement formally offered our country once again as the permanent headquarters, as it was for the Central American Court of Justice, which was the first international court in history.

In these connections the change we envisage will be reflected principally in a greater decisiveness and aggressiveness as we defend our basic principles, and the direct participation we shall give, or seek, in various international programmes and organizations likely to promote those ends.

Furthermore, the change will chiefly stress the independence of our foreign policy that is non-aligned and without any preconceived notions of any kind, and of course without prejudice to the special feelings of solidarity which binds us to those communities to which we naturally belong. Specifically, I refer to the Latin American Group, the Iberian American union, the Western hemisphere, the Western world and all the poor nations of the world. We shall stress the defence of our legitimate resources and sovereign rights on the earth, in the air and on the sea demanding the same respect for those rights as we ourselves pay to the legitimate sovereign rights of other nations.

The convening of this session and the statements that we have heard here show that there is a striking convergence of views on six fundamental points.

First, disarmament is the crucial problem of today's world. We must put an end to the arms race once and for all and bring about total disarmament, on which the survival of mankind depends.

Secondly, all civilized peoples and their Governments say that they want total disarmament.

Thirdly, in spite of the fine words and good intentions and many pacts and declarations that have been issued, especially since the Second World War, the arms race has escalated to an inexplicable level. Existing nuclear arsenals are enough to destroy mankind four times over and the two nuclear Powers alone have quadrupled those arsenals in the 10 years that the Treaty on the Non-Proliferation of Nuclear Weapons has been in existence.

Fourthly, while two thirds of mankind are lacking what is needed for a decent life and many are impoverished, the world spends $400 billion a year on arms – more than the developing countries spend on health and education together and 14 times more than all the assistance they receive from the developed countries.

Fifthly, in spite of this frightening situation and the growing risks of nuclear armaments, it is the poor countries of the world which are spearheading the conventional arms race. Their military expenditure absorbs more than 60 per cent of their public budgets and is more than six times greater than their total expenditure for services provided to their peoples.

Sixthly, it also seems that there is agreement to the effect that the problem of disarmament is not something to be resolved exclusively by the Powers concerned, because it is a problem that affects all mankind and for that reason this Organization should tackle it at the highest level.

I respectfully invite Members to reflect on the series of contradictions implicit in the outline I have just given you, and particularly on the seriousness of the reservations and the reluctance which are frequently concealed and sometimes actually apparent in the very words in which these fine intentions are proclaimed.

Here we have come precisely to speak about these things and at least to raise the possibility of viable and concrete solutions. It is little but it is enough. We believe in the value of words as a driving force, slow perhaps but sure, in history. It is with words that we have built and we continue to build the United Nations; it is with words that we are forging international law.

However, words are of value only when they strengthen the spirit and the

203

impulse to action, and that only when they are sincere, generous and effective – sincere because inspired by good intentions, generous because offering more than it is hoped to receive, effective because they lead to appropriate and effective action.

There is a proverb which says, 'the words of the wise man reflect what he has in his heart', and another which says, 'the road to hell is paved with good intentions'. If we truly want the thousands of words which have been uttered at this session and the millions more which have been lavished before on the subject of disarmament and peace really to be valuable driving forces for a better world, that world that we all want to bequeath to our children, let us be really sincere and generous and let us really proceed to appropriate and effective action.

We are not unaware that the problem of disarmament is difficult and complex, even from the theoretical standpoint, and all the more in its practical implications.

We recognize that the immediate achievement of total nuclear disarmament, which is something that impatient people call for, is not possible in the present state of the world, and even if it were, until we have at our disposal the means of effective international control and other complementary means such as a genuine, recognized international authority and a genuine established international executive power, it would be Utopian. Indeed it might even turn into a kind of two-edged sword and become a danger in its turn, because, on the one hand, even if nuclear arsenals disappeared as if by magic, the fact is that the technology for constructing them would still be in existence, while, on the other hand, pure and simple denuclearization might dispel the fear of a holocaust, a fear that from day to day is the only guarantee, albeit precarious, of world peace.

Let us recognize also the impracticability of total conventional disarmament until we achieve an international order which will guarantee to States their external security and internal tranquility, and the complications which arise if we consider, on the one hand, the legitimate right of peoples to resist oppression and even to have recourse to violence when there is no other institutional way available for them to impose their will and, on the other hand, the fact which is wrong but inevitable, that oppressors in their turn always repress by force any threat to their power. To whom then if not to an international authority, even one that has the right to err, could we confer the power of judging and resolving those twilight-zone, borderline, ambiguous cases, that are the kind that occur most frequently?

Let us also admit that there has been a great lack of sincerity, generosity and effectiveness in the approaches to this very problem and the search for a solution to it. There is no sincerity in making proposals for disarmament and peace, in lavishing praise on the United Nations and in making reference to the majesty of international law by way of throwing up a smokescreen to conceal clear examples of aggression, penetration or domination, be they politcal, economic, ideological or mere matters of prestige. There are many such cases.

There is no sincerity in making reference to domestic or international security or to the great principles such as that of non-intervention in order to conceal the repression of freedom and the rights of citizens, whatever the political or ideological justification that is invoked.

There is no sincerity in referring to the rights and principles of one side alone – rights and principles which are recalled only to censure and blame régimes which do not share our views or do not serve our ends, and which are carefully shelved when it is a matter of applying them to ourselves.

In this sense, it seems to us that there is a fundamental problem of sincerity and good faith which has even succeeded in contaminating some of the resolutions of the United Nations and of other international organizations solely because of the irrationality of mechanical made-to-measure majorities. We must demand sincerity, objectivity and impartiality from States, whether Members or non-members of our Organization, but we must also insist on these qualities in our Organization and in ourselves, because we are the people who embody its will. Those who are on our side politically and ideologically are not all good or always good; those against us are not all bad or always bad.

And there is no generosity in making high-sounding declarations of principles and attractive promises and offers of negotiation, if they are full of reservations or hesitations, and above all in calling upon others to be the first to commit themselves, to be the first to submit, to be the first to disarm. Disarmament, like all major problems of mankind, is fundamentally a question of political will, generosity and good faith.

In all this, the major, though not the exclusive, responsibility falls on the nuclear Powers and, among them, on the two greatest.

It would be wrong to fail to recognize that so far these major Powers have also laid claim to the relative merit of having achieved a balance which, although based on negative considerations, such as mutual distrust and fear, has succeeded at least in removing the 'subjective' danger of a nuclear war.

However, these same negative considerations are to blame for keeping mankind in a state of anguish and of stimulating the arms race, of increasing the eagerness of other States to enter or to form part of the so-called atomic club and thus to turn themselves into insuperable obstacles to the affirmation of peace and the elimination of the objective danger of universal disaster.

In a fundamental paragraph of his statement, Mr Mondale, Vice-President of the United States of America, said:

'. . . the United States will not use nuclear weapons except in self-defence; that is, in circumstances of an actual nuclear or conventional attack on the United States, our territories or armed forces, or of such an attack on our allies.'

For his part, Mr Gromyko, Foreign Minister of the Soviet Union, stated:

'. . . the Soviet Union will never use nuclear weapons against those States which renounce the production and acquisition of such weapons and do not have them on their territories.'

To sum up, both, speaking on behalf of the two most powerful States on earth, have joined forces to tell us in different voices that they do not renounce recourse to their nuclear arsenals – one, in case of legitimate self-defence, but with such a scope that it practically cancels that limitation; the other, against another nuclear Power, as if only that Power and not the whole of mankind would suffer the consequences of such an act.

We, of course, would hope that both, in a complete response to the vast concern of this Assembly, would make a solemn undertaking purely and simply to renounce nuclear war and the arms race once and for all until the other necessary instruments for total disarmament under effective international control are established.

We know that from day to day this answer is impossible. But we shall always continue to ask for what it is possible to offer: an absolute and unconditional renunciation of nuclear war except in the case of proven legitimate self-defence, and then subject to the prompt intervention of the United Nations. But this, certainly, applying to legitimate self-defence the juridical principle of proportionality of the means employed, which would be equivalent to undertaking not to use nuclear arsenals except in legitimate self-defence against a nuclear attack.*

*The President returned to the Chair.

Nor would it be exaggerating to ask the nuclear Powers to comply with international undertakings already enterd into by them such as the Treaty on non-proliferation of nuclear arms, already mentioned, which unfortunately events have proved to be ineffective, precisely because of the undertakings they have already entered into, that they once and for all suspend the nuclear arms race and the race in weapons of mass destruction, especially bearing in mind that they can never use all those they have. Use of a quarter of those weapons would leave no one in the world to use the other three quarters.

However, nothing has been done. And something must be done now to reduce or at least to limit the production and distribution of conventional weapons, which show the highest index of growth in the arms race. It has been said that conventional weapons absorb 80 per cent of expenditures on arms and that the consumption of such weapons by developing countries is highest and getting higher every day in a kind of competition that would be ridiculous if it were not tragic, so tragic that in the international field it is those developing countries that have been the protagonists in more than 100 wars which, in the 30 years since the end of the Second World War, have caused more deaths than did that war. And, internally speaking, today in the world there is a desolate picture of despotic military régimes in which repression and violation of the most elementary human rights go hand in hand with poverty, disease and ignorance.

If the consumption of conventional weapons is justified for reasons of security, internal or international, it should at least be possible to limit it to what is strictly necessary for such purposes. In this sense, the nations which manufacture arms, particularly the developed countries, bear major responsibility but not exclusive responsibility. We consider this to be one of the fundamental fields in which it is urgent and would be advantageous to have the active participation and intervention of the United Nations.

Finally, the vast disproportion we have indicated between what the world is spending on the arms race and military expenditures in general and what it is spending on economic and social development, particularly in the poorest countries, compels us to stress the need to begin to reduce these expenditures and to allocate a substantial part of the resultant savings to reducing what is in our view the most important cause of international tension, which is the ever widening gap between the developed and the under-developed countries, which we now call 'developing' countries because with that euphemism we paint the distressing reality of their poverty in a rosy colour. We say a proportion of these savings but not all of them because we believe that, along with assistance to development, it would also be right and highly fruitful for peace for another important proportion to be devoted directly to recompensing the countries which agree to disarm and in fact do disarm and thus give incentive to others to follow suit.

In this last context we announce the presentation of a concrete proposal, which would complement those already approved by the General Assembly, to call upon the States of the world at once to reduce their military expenditures by at least 10 per cent and to constitute with the resultant savings a fund part of which would go to economic and social development assistance and part to recompensing nations that reduced military expenditures by at least 1.5 per cent of the public budget and by at least 0.5 per cent of their national product concurrently, without taking into account their level of development.

Costa Rica presents to the Assembly as a contribution to the task of disarmament these specific proposals for immediate action, and above all the example of its own reality, as a demonstration that it is possible, without any loss of dignity or independence, to do this and even much more. We are aware that

206

these proposals do not remove the danger we can see hanging over the human race, but we do believe that they constitute firm steps towards disarmament that would do a great deal to contribute to creating an international climate of diminished fear and distrust and that they would be positive signs of good faith and readiness to make new advances in the future.

This depends, of course, on many other things, and above all on the sincerity and generosity with which we are ready to create an effective international jurisdiction and provide it with the necessary juridical instruments and the human and international resources necessary for it to perform its tasks of imposing and guaranteeing peace, with all its consequences. It also depends upon the capacity we demonstrate to ensure that disarmament shall be effective.

Mr President, before I conclude permit me to congratulate you upon your election as President of this session of the Assembly. The fact that we have you conducting these proceedings means not only recognition of your efforts and those of your country in bringing about, along with other countries and with the enthusiastic acceptance of all, the holding of this fundamentally important meeting on disarmament; it is also a guarantee of the success we are already beginning to glimpse.

I should like to extend my congratulations and those of my country to the Secretary-General, whose untiring efforts for disarmament, peace and international security are too well known for me to limit them by enumerating them.

Permit me also to greet and express my gratitude at the honour of the presence of the first lady of my country, Madame Estrella de Carazo, who has headed the delegation accompanying the Youth Symphony Orchestra of Costa Rica, and the presence of these young Costa Ricans who, having shown their mastery and skill at the Kennedy Centre in the District of Columbia and at the White House, upon the special invitation of Her Excellency the wife of the President of the United States, as well as in other parts of the United States, are going to end their tour with a concert that will be given here.

In fact, way beyond the words I have uttered here, limited as they have been, Costa Rica wants these young people, our 'army', with our 'weapons', which are their musical instruments, to speak to you of disarmament in the unlimited language of music and to show you a little of the much that can be done with good faith, through which the Lord will grant us peace.

# APPENDIX V

*Address delivered to the United Nations Twelfth Special Session of the General Assembly, 1982, by Mr Zumbado of Costa Rica:*

The decision to disarm unilaterally also requires deep respect for and almost boundless confidence in the rule of law and in the international machinery established to preserve peace and security. For that very reason, Costa Rica, which is among the 51 original signatory countries of the United Nations Charter, is committed to the strengthening of this Organization and is determined to see it play an increasingly useful and active role in responding to the numerous challenges we face today.

Costa Rica, a nation without arms, lives in a region which has today become a major focus of conflict and which would seem to have institutionalized resort to arms as a means of acquiring or maintaining power. This is aggravated by the fact that the region's geopolitical importance has made internal struggles spill over national borders, with the world's great Powers involved in those struggles in one way or another. This has set off an arms race which has obvious adverse effects upon the peace and security of our region. Costa Rica maintains that arms are in themselves a cause of internal and external tension. Accordingly, if we are to give peace and tranquility a chance to prevail in our own lands, it is imperative that we initiate a process of demilitarization in Central America.

It is ironic that we should be meeting here at a time when the world is passing through a period of great belligerence, with serious conflicts in the Middle East and the South Atlantic, where our Argentine brothers in particular have been seriously affected, and with grave tensions apparent in other parts of the developing world, where the precarious conditions that prevail could lead to war.

Unfortunately, the history of mankind shows us that arms races follow such conflicts in a chain reaction, affecting not only the countries that were parties to the confrontation but also countries which had no direct part in it. The harm that such arms races do our countries' development opportunities is sometimes as devastating as war itself.

So-called conventional wars are proliferating today so readily that world opinion appears to have been numbed to them. This tendency goes so far as to present such situations as victories so long as they remain within the confines of the developing world and do not unleash a nuclear war.

Perhaps the well-documented horrors of the possible consequences of nuclear war have made the international community insensitive to the effects of so-called conventional wars. It is cause for indignation that the mass media nowadays sometimes focus greater attention on the performance of certain machinery of destruction or the efficiency of an army than on the suffering, death, deprivation and humiliation wreaked upon the vanquished.

The last few weeks have even shown how the military establishments in the market can turn conflicts themselves into advertising campaigns. Even as we debate here about how to achieve disarmaments, thousands of scientists the world over are drawing object-lessons from the latest conflicts with a view to improving and refining their capacity for destruction, backed by the mounting billions of dollars in appropriations set aside for this purpose.

One can foresee that, unless we can marshal the necessary political will to turn the tide, technological developments and investments in the war industry will rule out any chance of overcoming the problems of under-development and poverty. It will, moreover, become increasingly difficult, in view of the growing strength of certain interest groups, to create the minimum political conditions for the achievement of significant agreements on disarmament and development in the future.

It is time that we ask ourselves the following: when will the developed world begin to adopt the same treatment for countries beset by economic difficulties that it adopts for its clients when they are at war?

As the representative of Ecuador indicated in his recent statement, we are living at a time when the leading industrialized Powers, paradoxically, are reducing their contributions to programmes designed to promote the transfer of resources through multilateral channels, while at the same time increasing their military budgets. At the same time, little headway is being made in the North-South dialogue towards the achievement of a more just and equitable order, an elementary condition for laying the foundations of lasting peace.

Costa Rica unreservedly supports the recommendations contained in the report of the Secretary-General in document A/36/356, which examines the relationship between disarmament and development. We feel that there is a need for a more broad-ranging debate on disarmament, including considerations relating to the need for structural changes necessary to put an end to violence in all its forms. It is obvious that the sluggishness of our economies, the exhaustion of physical resources available for world growth, as well as the tensions generated by the skewed distribution of income and wealth nationally and internationally, are factors adversely affecting world security. This is also pointed out in the report of the Brandt Commission, which states that world security is linked to the enormous gap separating rich and poor countries, with grave injustices and the neglect of the most elementary needs in poor countries acting as a further cause of insecurity. If military expenditure could by some means be kept within bounds and part of the savings channelled towards development, world security would be strengthened. To that end, we feel that serious consideration should be given to the proposal for the creation of an international fund to be replenished by resources emanating from the efforts which countries made towards disarmament.

In addition to these recommendations, we further suggest that consideration be given to the following proposals.

Firstly, that arms-producing countries limit their production of conventional weapons. Let there be an end to the cynical excuse that 'what we do not sell others will'. We should likewise do away with the immoral perception of the war industry as merely one industry among others, trade in weapons being considered as legitimate as trade in tractors. We must bear in mind that the right to life is the first and most essential of all human rights. War is the antithesis of all human rights. The war industry has a cause-and-effect relationship with violence, and it must be perceived accordingly.

Secondly, since it has been pointed out that each instance of strife brings in its wake an acceleration of the arms race, it would seem highly desirable for every armed confrontation to be followed by some kind of conference in the United Nations, including all the parties involved in the conflict – together with those who supplied the arms – in order to forestall the expected arms race.

Finally, Costa Rica has for many years argued that, in the allocation of resources through international cooperation programmes, special attention be given not only to the comparative poverty of countries but also to the efforts their peoples make towards disarmament.

Our nation, with barely more than 2 million inhabitants, has a deep sense of mankind's concern for survival. We are not given to rhetoric, but we have lived according to the words of a great Latin American Benito Juarez. Those words are inscribed at the entrance to this hall and they sum up the spirit of our Organization: 'Respect for the rights of others is peace'. We hope that that spirit shall some day guide the conduct of all the world's Governments.

# AUTHORITIES CONSULTED

Costa Rican Newspapers: *La Nación, La Hora, La Prensa Libre, La República, Diário de Costa Rica* and *Tico Times*
Professor Carlos Meléndez: *Historia de Costa Rica*
Professor John P. Bell: *Crisis in Costa Rica*
Professor F. D. Parker: *The Central American Republics*
Professor Donald E. Lundberg: *Costa Rica*
John and Mavis Biesanz: *Costa Rican Life*
John D. Cozean (US Congress Library): *The Abolition of the Costa Rican Army*
Saxe Fernandez: *The Militarisation of Costa Rica, Monthly Review, May 1972*
Foreign Relations of the United States 1948, Vol. IX: *The Western Hemisphere*
University of Colorado Studies: *Notes on Costa Rican Democracy*
Foreign Area Studies of the American University, Washington DC: *Area Handbook for Costa Rica*
Costa Rican Congress Library
Organisation of American States Library, Washington DC
British Museum Library: *Constitution of Costa Rica 1949 (as amended)*
*New York Times*
London *Times*
University for Peace Booklet and Newsletters
United Nations University Papers

# INDEX

ACCIÓN DEMÓCRATA Party: formation of, 38; newspaper issued by, 50; merger with Centro, 51.
AGREEMENT: 1948, Junta's functions defined, 82.
ALLAJUELA: founded 1782, 23.
ARCHBISHOP SANÁBRIA: Vanguardia Popular (Communist) Party recommended, 46; attempts to intercede in post-election 1948 by, 69; some success of, 68.
ARÉVALO: (President of Guatemala): arms agreement with Figueres, 58.
ARMY: more professional in war years, 41; small, with non-professional officers, 52; 300 in 1948, 71; new army of Figueres, 84; Dissolved, Chapter 8, et seq.; if necessary to be re-formed, 91; no protest at abolition of, 97; 1848 abolition, 98; crimes of, 100; economic factors influencing abolition of, 102; Presidential address omits reference to abolition of, 118; coup d'etat would be aided by increased numbers, 120; Junta supported by, 120; new Constitution proscribes, 121; President Ulate and, 125; President Figueres and, 126; President Echandi and, 129 et seq.; acceptance of absence of, 130; reforming of, 134; proposals for Central American, 135; assurance of abolition, 136; control of guerillas difficult in absence of, 143; emphasis on absence of, 146; activities of 'non-existent', 149; emergency defence force not an army, 149; 70% opposition to, 152; Cañas article about, 156 et seq.; existence of, 157; financial effects of, 160; authorities against existence of, 162; only 2% students in favour of, 162; disadvantages of, 163; after 1955 invasion no revival of, 164; costs of, 164; reality of myth of absence of, 169; equipment needed for, 168.
ARROYO: Senator: prohibition of army proposals questioned by, 123.
AUDIENCE OF THE BOUNDARIES: established 1542, 22; terminated, 23.
AUDIENCE OF GUATEMALA: established and replaces Audience of the Boundaries 1570, 23; President of, aids move to independence, 29.
BANKERS: closure of Banks 1948, 67; attempts at mediation by Association of, 69.
BLOQUE DE LA VICTORIA: formation of, 48.
BOGOTÁ: Meeting of American countries in, 73.
BUENA VISTA BARRACKS: Conversion to Museum of, 89.
CARDENAL: (Ernesto) Central American Army and, 136.
CALDERÓN (RAFAEL ANGEL) GUARDIA: President 1940-44, objective of, 36 et seq.; Cortés breaks with, 38; war involvement with U.S.A. weakens program of, 40; criticism of, 41; communist support gained by, 41; advance of social legislation of, 42; Figueres attacks social provisions of, 42; Social Security System first in Central America, 43; Constitution amended to include social provisions, 43; Labour Code, 43; allegations of corruption by Cortés against, 44; budget deficit, 44; not considered corrupt by U.S. Minister, 45; amnesty for supporters declared unconstitutional, 45; pledge to tax incomes not attempted by, 45; workers' supported continued to be attracted by, 46; unable to stand for Presidency, 1944, 48; Picado's supporters prohibited from rallies, 49; goes to U.S.A., 50; élite and Centro join to oppose, 50; opposition concentrates attack

212

215

# NORTHERN FRIENDS PEACE BOARD

The Northern Friends Peace Board, which has sponsored the research for and publication of this book, is a Quaker body which exists to express the historic testimony of the Society of Friends against all war. It was founded in 1913 by Friends in the north of Britain to maintain and promote the Peace Testimony. From its inception it has had a full-time paid secretary and an appointed and representative membership.

Its work falls into three main areas:

strengthening and upholding the Peace Testimony of the Society of Friends;

education for peace and disarmament in the widest sense;

traditional Quaker work of reconciliation and bridge building.

It has been active over the troubles in Northern Ireland, and produced a classic analysis of the problems there called "Orange and Green". More recently it has published "Northern Ireland – a Problem to Every Solution", jointly with Quaker Peace and Service.

The major area of its work in recent years has been in E-W reconciliation, through an increasing and continuing dialogue with the Soviet Peace Committee and regional peace committees in the USSR. Leonard Bird, a member of the Northern Friends Peace Board, initiated this co-operation when he visited the Soviet Peace Committee during the Olympic Games in 1980. A delegation from the SPC visited this country the following year at the invitation of the Board. In 1982 two return delegations to the Soviet Union were organised by the Board Secretary: one from representatives of the British peace movement, and the second from the Board itself.

A list of the Board's publications can be obtained from the Secretary at 1 The Grange, Hall Lane, Horsforth, Leeds, LS18 5EH, England.